# Soft Living Architecture

# Soft Living Architecture

## An Alternative View of Bio-informed Practice

**RACHEL ARMSTRONG**

BLOOMSBURY VISUAL ARTS
LONDON • NEW YORK • OXFORD • NEW DELHI • SYDNEY

BLOOMSBURY VISUAL ARTS
Bloomsbury Publishing Plc
50 Bedford Square, London, WC1B 3DP, UK
1385 Broadway, New York, NY 10018, USA

BLOOMSBURY, BLOOMSBURY VISUAL ARTS and the Diana logo are trademarks of
Bloomsbury Publishing Plc

First published in Great Britain 2018
Paperback edition published 2020

Copyright © Rachel Armstrong, 2018

Rachel Armstrong has asserted her right under the Copyright, Designs and Patents Act, 1988, to be identified as Author of this work.

Cover design by Eleanor Rose
Cover image © Imogen Holden and Assia Stefanova, 2016

All rights reserved. No part of this publication may be reproduced or transmitted in any form or by any means, electronic or mechanical, including photocopying, recording, or any information storage or retrieval system, without prior permission in writing from the publishers.

Bloomsbury Publishing Plc does not have any control over, or responsibility for, any third-party websites referred to or in this book. All internet addresses given in this book were correct at the time of going to press. The author and publisher regret any inconvenience caused if addresses have changed or sites have ceased to exist, but can accept no responsibility for any such changes.

Every effort has been made to trace copyright holders of images and to obtain their permission for the use of copyright material. The publisher apologizes for any errors or omissions in copyright acknowledgement and would be grateful if notified of any corrections that should be incorporated in future reprints or editions of this book.

A catalogue record for this book is available from the British Library.

A catalog record for this book is available from the Library of Congress.

ISBN: HB: 978-1-3500-1135-9
PB: 978-1-3501-5450-6
ePDF: 978-1-3500-1133-5
eBook: 978-1-3500-1134-2

Typeset by Integra Software Services Pvt. Ltd.

To find out more about our authors and books visit www.bloomsbury.com and sign up for our newsletters.

# Contents

List of figures  ix

Preface  xii

**1  Life as You Don't Know It**  1
   1.1  Prototyping life  1
   1.2  Beyond the bête machine  2
   1.3  Replaying the tape of life  2
   1.4  Parallel worlds  4
   1.5  Nature of matter  5
   1.6  Mineral sensibilities  7
   1.7  Origin of life  8
   1.8  Biogenesis and vivogenesis  11
   1.9  Dissipative life  12
   1.10  Dissipative adaptation  14
   1.11  Phantasmagoria of life  14
   1.12  Life as material subversion  16
   1.13  Subnatures  17
   1.14  Chicken and egg: The paradox of lively matter  17
   1.15  Worlding  18

**2  Experimental and Soft Living Architecture**  21
   2.1  Experimental architecture  21
      2.1.1  Twenty-first-century experimental architecture  22
   2.2  Soft living architecture  24
      2.2.1  The character of 'life' in soft living architecture  25
      2.2.2  Soft living architecture: Examples  26
      2.2.3  Soft living architecture: Body  29
   2.3  Storytelling  31
   2.4  Ambient poetics  32

**3  World in Meltdown** 35
    3.1 End of Utopia 35
    3.2 The Tower of Babel 36
    3.3 Babelsphere 37
    3.4 The changing character of nature 38
    3.5 Nature of nature 39
    3.6 Venetian nature 41
    3.7 The gluttony of death 43
    3.8 Breaking up 46
    3.9 Design and death 46
    3.10 Urban (Terra)toma 48
    3.11 Insurrection and death 49
    3.12 Sewage 50

**4  Synthesis: Entangled Materials, Tools and Methods** 53
    4.1 Nature as technology 53
    4.2 Modes of computation 55
        4.2.1 Computing with humans 57
        4.2.2 Natural computing 59
        4.2.3 Dissipative structures 59
        4.2.4 Consciousness and living materials 61
    4.3 Softness 64
    4.4 Making soils 67
    4.5 Liquid soils 71
    4.6 Ice computer 72
    4.7 Aeroso(i)ls 73

**5  Embracing Change** 75
    5.1 Choreography 75
    5.2 Evaluation 76
    5.3 Alternative impacts 78
    5.4 Alternative methodologies 79
    5.5 Alternative experiments 81
    5.6 Fertility as value 82
    5.7 Alternative architectures 83
    5.8 Parallel apparatuses 85
    5.9 Alternative roles for architects 88

## 6 Laboratories and Convergences 91
- 6.1 Babel fish 91
- 6.2 The soft city of Venice 92
- 6.3 Living stones of Venice 93
- 6.4 Automatic Venetian chess 94
- 6.5 Invisibility 96
- 6.6 The invisible laboratory: An alternative synthetic platform 99
- 6.7 Ectoplasms 99
- 6.8 Jellyfish 101
- 6.9 Sensible apparatuses 101
- 6.10 Lost music: Antonio Vivaldi 104
- 6.11 Channelling and knotting 106
- 6.12 Phantasmagorical laboratory 107
- 6.13 Immersive sensible kaleidoscope 109

## 7 Prototyping Practices 111
- 7.1 Parallel beauty 111
- 7.2 Parallel soils 113
- 7.3 Golem 116
- 7.4 Weeki Wachee maids 117
- 7.5 Witch bottles 119
- 7.6 Gog and Magog 121
- 7.7 Sound walk 123
- 7.8 Land and community 125
- 7.9 Mirror puddle 128
- 7.10 Doggerland: Uncertainty, prophecy and the near-shore experience 130
- 7.11 Babel chandelier 133
- 7.12 Corresponding with the cosmos 134

## 8 Projects 137
- 8.1 Living Architecture 137
  - 8.1.1 Microbial fuel cell 138
  - 8.1.2 Photobioreactor 138
  - 8.1.3 Synthetic bioreactor 138
  - 8.1.4 Integration and uses 140

    8.2  Diversifying bricks  140
        8.2.1  Soft brick  142
        8.2.2  Embryological brick  143
        8.2.3  Lamprey shoe: Blood bank  143
    8.3  Programmable bricks  143
        8.3.1  Living brick for Venice  145
        8.3.2  Titrating tensions: Hips and teeth  147
    8.4  Transfiguring Venice  151
        8.4.1  City of soft living architecture  151
    8.5  Future Venice  155
        8.5.1  Protocell city  156
        8.5.2  Future Venice II  157
        8.5.3  Melma Verde: Island of useless things  159
    8.6  Living walls  160

**9**    **Performances**  163
    9.1  Persephone: Constructing the Babelsphere  163
    9.2  Persephone: Worlding instrument  164
    9.3  Persephone: *The Temptations of the Non-linear Ladder*  165
    9.4  Persephone: *The Capsule of Crossed Destinies (the Hanged Man)*  168
        9.4.1  Introduction  168
        9.4.2  Biospherical bottle  168
        9.4.3  The Hanged Man  169
        9.4.4  Knitted fetish  169
        9.4.5  Fibonacci  170
    9.5  Babelsphere: Inhabiting a world in meltdown (Radical Circus)  170
    Epilogue  177

Glossary  179

References  189

Index  203

# List of figures

**1.1** Protocell Phantasmagoria: Portrait of an origin of alternative life. Drawing by Simone Ferracina, from a movie of dynamic droplets courtesy of Rachel Armstrong, 2016. 15

**3.1** A beach composed from masonry entering the system of currents in the lagoon is mixed together with garbage, conjuring strange and uninhabited land. Drawing courtesy of Rachel Armstrong and Simone Ferracina, S. Alvise, Venice, Italy, September 2015. 44

**4.1** Plaster of Paris droplets pass through three sets of liquid interfaces: olive oil, diethyl phthalate (DEP), glycerine (from upper to lower layers), recording their surface deformations as they fall. The final forms visualize the resilience and remodelling, which underpins the dynamic frameworks of soft living architectures. The softness is counterbalanced in this experiment with 'hard' crystalline structures, in this case table salt. This can be seen as particles producing a storm of liquid trails where food colourings reveal water molecules that travel alongside the crystals in their clear oil medium and have not been modified by their descent through the liquid interfaces. Photograph courtesy of Rachel Armstrong, Newcastle University, February 2016. 66

**4.2** The Silk Road discusses an architectural fabric that regenerates lands and societies in an ecological flourishing made possible through joining the webs of life and death. Digital drawing by Imogen Holden and Assia Stefanova, 2016. 70

**6.1** Activated gels act as a landscape of chemical potentiality. As salt gradients diffuse through these terrains, they become embryonic bodies whose rolls and folds establish new spaces for material expression. Photograph courtesy of Rachel Armstrong, Newcastle University Chemistry Outreach Laboratory, February 2015. 103

**6.2** This phantom light notation that dances on canal water is written upon dark biofilms that capture the lost music of Vivaldi, in metabolic blooms that detail physical changes in Venice's 'living' stones. Photograph courtesy of Rachel Armstrong, Venice, Italy, November 2016. 105

# LIST OF FIGURES

**6.3** Notation of chemical fields producing complex structures that perform at interfaces between liquid layer, which may be read as radical 'circus' bodies that transit active chemical fields to produce surprising traces and transformations. Photograph courtesy of the Experimental Architecture Group (EAG: Rachel Armstrong, Simone Ferracina & Rolf Hughes), Newcastle University, May 2017. 108

**7.1** Petrified African mask, tennis racket, boot and soft toys suspended in the petrifying waters of the Mother Shipton well. Photograph courtesy of Rachel Armstrong, Knaresborough, Yorkshire, 2012. 115

**7.2** Male and female golem figurines invite flows of matter within their bodies, which become sites of fertility that promote the colonization of life forms that can transition between land and water and so enable the site to respond to encroaching tides. (Artwork by Rachel Armstrong: 'golem', April 2016, ceramics, 50 × 20 × 15 cm, site-specific installation at Robert Rauschenberg Foundation, Captiva, Florida.) Photograph courtesy of Rachel Armstrong: Robert Rauschenberg Foundation, Captiva, Florida, May 2016. 117

**7.3** A series of witch bottles themed on the elements of air, water and fire draw from symbolic and local practices, aim to establish a site-specific protective charm over the Rauschenberg property and provoke conversations about tactical responses to the damaging consequences of climate change. (Artwork by Rachel Armstrong: Glass bottles, sand, shells, nails, glass, miscellaneous found objects, April 2016, 75 × 50 × 50 cm, Robert Rauschenberg Foundation grounds, Captiva, Florida.) Photograph courtesy of Rachel Armstrong: Robert Rauschenberg Foundation, Captiva, Florida, May 2016. 120

**7.4** Moon writing: A waning half-moon writes on the surface of the bay around the Fish House. Photograph courtesy of Rachel Armstrong, digital editing by April Rodmyre: Robert Rauschenberg Foundation, Captiva, Florida, May 2016. 135

**8.1** Multispecies bioreactor designs or 'bricks' for the construction of 'living architecture'. Drawing courtesy of Simone Ferracina, January 2017. 139

**8.2** Living brick technological prototypes: Venetian bricks (as a single unit and in array) have been machined to form microbial fuel chambers within the structure, which can produce sufficient power to operate digital thermometer displays. Photograph courtesy of the Bristol BioEnergy Centre, University of the West of England, Living Architecture Consortium, 2016. 146

## LIST OF FIGURES

xi

**8.3** Living bricks in a Venice rio adjacent to the Campo San Stefano. Responding to a natural computing 'punch card' based upon the first forty courses of brickwork, a system of cabling and struts selectively facilitates growth of native marine wildlife. Drawing courtesy of Matthew Sharman-Hayles, 2017. 148

**8.4** A mosaic of spatial experiences is observed through the lens of a Murano glass chandelier bead during a psychogeographic walk about the city, which reveals previously hidden dynamic building elements and parallel terrains. Graphic design by Simone Ferracina; photograph courtesy of Rachel Armstrong, Venice, Italy, December 2016. 150

**8.5** Scryed through waterways reflections, a fragment of Future Venice is observed through its transformed window frame details. Photograph courtesy of Rachel Armstrong: Venice, Italy, July 2015. 155

**8.6** Background: bank of eight aquariums installed for the IDEA Laboratory at the Vita Vitale exhibition, fifty-sixth Venice Biennale; cultures of plastics with local biofilms to produce 'living' bioplastic composites. Foreground: 'intelligent' briccole with algae 'brains' and sensors by EcoLogicStudio. Photograph courtesy of Rachel Armstrong, with Artwise Curators and IDEA Laboratory, Venice, May 2015. 158

**8.7** Concept of a living wall developed in response to the call for prospective contractors to build Donald Trump's wall. Drawing courtesy of Simone Ferracina, 2017. 161

**9.1** Dark scrying circus: Methinee Wongtrakoon and Alexander Dam encounter the experimental performance space centred on a dark mirror and reflective silvered surface, with a rubbed underbelly that can be moved up and down using a pulley system. Photograph courtesy of Rachel Armstrong, Palais de Tokyo, 8–10 April 2016. 167

**9.2** Two cockroaches survive under extreme environmental conditions as the heating element in their capsules fails and temperatures plummet to around −40°C – the surface temperature of Mars. Movie still from stratospheric balloon flight – a collaboration between Rachel Armstrong and Nebula Sciences, August 2015. 169

# Preface

*Our starting points and destinations were not logically composed. We had begun to discover a natural world that simply wasn't rationally designed. Our nature was rich with material entanglements, synchronicity, spooky events, quantum tunnelling, aberrations in space-time, baroque spectacles, wonder and enchantment.*

**B**iology stirs us in many ways. Sometimes it invites a scientific reading, while at other times it is bizarre or mysterious and calls for wonder and incompleteness. Biodesign, which is inspired by biological phenomena and their narratives, adopts a modern, scientific understanding of living systems, where life is regarded as a soft component within a broader framework of industrial machines. Consequently, biology-inspired designs are rational, efficient, functional and beautifully designed, so they neatly fill particular needs, or solve specific problems. They do not however, propose alternative modes of embodiment or offer a unique philosophy of life.

Biological thinking is important to architectural design, as throughout the ages buildings have been conferred with anthropomorphic and biomorphic qualities (Cairns and Jacobs, 2014, p. 12). Indeed, there is no single image, body or story that accounts for a universal notion of living things. The concepts that shape our conventions of biology, or 'life' itself, reflect our cultural preferences for certain attributes or behaviours and are not absolute indicators of the phenomenon.

> When we speak the word 'life', it must be understood we are not referring to life as we know it from its surface of fact, but that fragile, fluctuating centre which forms never reach. And if there is still one hellish, truly accursed thing in our time, it is our artistic dallying with forms, instead of being like victims burnt at the stake, signalling through the flames. (Artaud, 1958, p. 13)

Changing the protocols for life therefore alters our expectations of architecture through its associated ideas, design possibilities and ethical concerns. *Soft Living Architecture: An Alternative View of Bio-informed Design Practice* is an experimental work in terms of its philosophy and methods. By including *lively matter* and *parallel biology* as part of the design portfolio of the living realm, it seeks to expand current notions of the living world beyond established frameworks and definitions that shape modern biology and the associated tools of *modern synthesis*. It seeks to diversify the protocols of life to enable a more agile understanding of the relationship between creature and niche, physics and reality or building and site – by embracing the fundamental strangeness of the living world. This does not mean that anything is possible, but that life's continuum can be considered through an augmented materiality, rather than being bounded by the extremes of an existing spectrum of biological possibility, interpreted through a mechanistic relationship with 'brute' matter (Newton, 2007). It also embraces a concept of time as encountered in the natural realm. Here time is not a geometric abstraction of reality but a material process that operates at small scales in highly localized situations and produces its effects on only a few molecules. In this fertile space, lively matter has the capacity to retain or increase its order. Tim Maudlin observes that standard geometry, which is algebraic and designed for making directionless spaces, considers time to be an artefact of space (Musser, 2017). In this case, either nothing alters or events can be reversed. Accordingly, soft living architecture engages with Ilya Prigogine's concept of 'third time', where qualitative local changes melt into and permeate one another without precise outlines and are characterized by irreversibility, which provides a source of creativity for the living realm, which exists in spacetime rather than standard geometric space (Armstrong, In press).

> Standard geometry just wasn't developed for the purpose of doing spacetime. It was developed for the purpose of just doing spaces, and spaces have no directedness in them … if all we've got are spatial dimensions, then it seems to me nothing's happening in the universe … Physics has discovered some really strange things about the world, but it has not discovered that change is an illusion … things are derivative from, produced by, explained by, derived from the laws operating. And there, the word 'operating' has this temporal characteristic. (Musser, 2017)

Soft living architecture is an ecological project that aims to fully explore the possibilities of designing with lively matter, which actively participates in our engagement with the natural realm and renders life possible (see Section 2.2). *Soft Living Architecture* therefore considers the starting point for biodesign as vivogenesis – the spectrum of events that made possible the transition from inert to lively matter. This (parallel) methodology is informed by iterations of a thought experiment, which was first proposed by Stephen Jay Gould, who asked how different biology would be if the tape of life was replayed from any point since life's origin. His starting point was in the fossil evidence amassed in the geological formation, the Burgess Shale in the Canadian Rockies that revealed previously unknown types of animals. This archive of the Cambrian explosion raised the question of how many different kinds of creatures could have existed on earth if they lived in alternative circumstances.

> I call this experiment 'replaying life's tape.' You press the rewind button and, making sure you thoroughly erase everything that actually happened, go back to any time and place in the past – say, to the seas of the Burgess Shale. Then let the tape run again and see if the repetition looks at all like the original. If each replay resembles life's actual pathway, then we must conclude that what really happened pretty much had to occur. But suppose that the experimental versions all yield sensible results strikingly different from the actual history of life? (Gould, 1989, p. 48)

*Replaying the tape of life* seeks to establish how far biology is determined by its genetics. If the nature of a creature is centrally determined by its genes, then no matter what circumstances occur, organisms will always evolve in more or less the same way. Conversely, if the tape is replayed where the protocols of life are distributed throughout the environment, then changes in context play a significant role in biological development, where even small alterations in circumstances may significantly alter the way creatures evolve, to a point where they are unrecognizable to us today. Soft living architecture holds that while certain characteristics of living things are highly conserved in genetic codes like *homeobox* genes, environmental factors also significantly shape evolutionary processes and therefore invoke the forces of chance, or unexplained phenomena. This raises the possibility of parallel modes of development which embrace the unpredictable aspects of the living realm and may suggest alternative ways of constructing and inhabiting buildings, which deviate from recognized biological pathways or architectural typologies. Examples of parallel biodesign narratives appear in a unique font throughout the text, without being followed with a formal citation, as follows:

> This embryonic island, our proto-city, makes sense of the world by sampling the lagoon's rich mixology of chemical trails, biomolecule standing waves, water memory channels and complex bouquets of solutes. It does not need our permission to evolve but spontaneously actualises events through the movement of sands, the flow of currents and the precipitation of minerals.

Such accounts often exceed current assumptions about organisms, material performance, infrastructures and networks of exchange. Design practice can respond to permutations of these variables through the process of *worlding*, where parallel worlds are prototyped so that they may be interrogated – a technique that has been used by Lebbeus Woods, Leonardo da Vinci and Albrecht Durer.

> In their art, they had the great ambition to project an entire living world, in which the human and the natural were co-dependent and unified not through mere symbolism but by a richness of differences and diversity … For Da Vinci, drawing was his prime means of analyzing the phenomena of the living world. Painting was the synthesis. Analyzing in the way I use it here, however, is not 'taking apart' something observed or experienced, nor is synthesis 'putting parts back together.' Da Vinci's method of analysis was by analogy. Rather than pick apart a phenomenon, separating what he perceived as its components, he created in a drawing a parallel world, an analog to reality … Da Vinci, in this way as in others, anticipated future developments – he created hypothetical worlds that revealed the hidden structures of nature. These, in turn, helped him create paintings of great originality that are imbued with a lasting aura of conceptual power … inadvertently imagining an architecture of radical transformation, close to the spirit of our own times. (Woods, 2010a)

Parallel approaches to biodesign therefore draw on biology's capacity for novelty, disobedience, monstrosity (an entity that defies categorization by formal classification systems) and radical creativity, which constrained by the laws of chemistry, may result in surprising protocols of matter and spacetime, an example of which is Leo Lionni's *Parallel Botany* (Lionni, 1977).

> The discovery of the first parallel plants, of an unknown vegetal kingdom, which, being by nature arbitrary and unforeseeable, appeared and still appears to challenge not only the most recently acquired biological knowledge but also the traditional structures of logic. 'These organisms,' writes Franco Russoli, 'whose physical being is sometimes flabby and sometimes porous, at other times osseous but fragile, breaking open to display huge colonies of seeds or bulbs which grow and ferment in the blind hope of some vital metamorphosis, that seem to struggle against a soft but impenetrable skin – these abnormal creatures with pointed or horny protuberances, or petticoats, skirts and fringes of fibrils and pistils, articulations that are sometimes mucous and sometimes cartilaginous, might well belong to one of the great families of jungle flora, ambiguous, savage, and fascinating in their monstrous way. But they do not belong to any species in nature, nor would the most expert grafting ever succeed in bringing them into existence.' (Lionni, 1977, pp. 4–5)

Soft living architecture adopts the practice of worlding to explore the specific thought experiment that if the fundamental building blocks of life should alter, even just a little at any point since life's origin, then in a parallel world, substrates that are not considered alive today may become lively. A parallel view of biodesign therefore raises the architectural possibility of constructing buildings with lifelike properties through the application of lively materials and *living technology*, which are associated with origins of life sciences.

The city of Venice – *La Serinissma*, the most serene Republic – provides the main experimental setting in this book for prototyping parallel worldviews. In keeping with Aristotle's notion of a city as organism (Mayhew, 1997), the constant flow of matter, people and dreams are integrated with the city's lagoon infrastructures, which – like a circulatory system, or amniotic sac – are a platform for growth, development and transformation. Concepts, tools, materials and methods that link design with the living world are explored using experimental architecture techniques and, as in *Invisible Cities* (Calvino, 1997), the reader encounters alternative portraits of Venice, as if they are experiencing a new city each time. This re-evolution of the city is not limited to the nature of organisms but extends into its fabric – such as the ornate architectural 'stones' described by John Ruskin (Ruskin, 1989). Consequently, Parallel Venice is increasingly lifelike and sur/real being capable of mysterious acts of transformation that exceed our current expectations of nature. Mythologically, the city acquires the status of a forest – a liminal environment that possesses innate agency, is teeming with life and is never fully rationalized.

These parallel portraits of Venice embody uncertainty, continual unfolding and flux, and are expressed through a range of experimental media such as living technologies, narrative portraits, prototypes and installations. They generate juxtapositions between actualities, possibilities and expectations of the living realm. Such provocations to not attempt to sanitize the site raise further questions that create frisson, confuse, seduce, repulse and delight audiences. They also foreshadow the advent of an emerging technology of *living bricks*, which not only possess specific lifelike material qualities but also alter the nature of living spaces and habitats. Indeed, inhabitation is critical to the development of soft living architecture, as the presence of beings influences the way its materials respond and spaces are shaped. Such agility and responsiveness raise ethical questions that can be explored through design protocols and by prototyping parallel spaces.

Programmatically, soft living cities are compatible with Babel – an ancient city described in the book of Genesis that grew prosperous through the advent of new technology that challenged the power of God. It was therefore cursed with the evolution of multiple languages, through which many misunderstandings arose, and the city fell apart. In these changeable times of climate change and the complexities of a globalized world, the problematic condition of Babel represents more than a city, but embodies the ecological character of our world. This *Babelsphere* seeks alternative forms of diplomacy than obedience to fixed laws to maintain the coherence of communities, so different cultures can live alongside each other and even become united through their differences. Agile spatial protocols are needed to realize the inclusive spaces that can bring the Babelsphere to functionality. This may be achieved through an architectural practice of *worlding*, which aims to transform our current modes of inhabitation into an ongoing process of mutual synthesis that enhances the living realm through many expressions of nature.

A range of experimental approaches are needed to realize the potential of worlding as a portfolio of design protocols. Alternative methods for choreographing and inhabiting space that exceed what Richard Lewontin calls the 'just-so' stories of scientific (biological) doctrines can be explored by developing experimental prototypes that embody aspects of the ecological principles at stake.

> We take the side of science in spite of the patent absurdity of some of its constructs, in spite of its failure to fulfil many of its extravagant promises of health and life, in spite of the tolerance of the scientific community for unsubstantiated just-so stories, because we have a prior commitment, a commitment to materialism. It is not that the methods and institutions of science somehow compel us to accept a material explanation of the phenomenal world, but, on the contrary, that we are forced by our a priori adherence to material causes to create an apparatus of investigation and a set of concepts that produce material explanations, no matter how counter-intuitive, no matter how mystifying to the uninitiated. (Lewontin, 1997)

Soft living architectures, 'parallel' Venice and the *Babelsphere* go beyond organic aestheticisms or genetic algorithms and connect biology to the worlding process. They probe the nature of living things, identity and environment, further than is possible through the study of biology or genetics alone, to produce alternative narratives about the living world, which are receptive to the principles of *new materialism*. However, the source of material liveliness is not the cell but 'dissipative systems'. These 'paradoxical' objects arise spontaneously in nature as an expression of continual material and energetic flow and are recognizable as vortices like whirlpools. They express the radical, generative, fluid and highly situated character of life itself and suggest architectures that exceed the classical worldview. This is a necessary discourse for the built environment, which ethically engages with the living world from a first principles approach by dealing with the situatedness of living things, as well as the specificity of particular sites.

Casting its reach widely, this book immerses the reader in short portraits and prototypes of parallel worlds that constitute alternative manifestations of nature. Drawing together the threads for an ambitious alternative practice of biodesign, an expanded view of matter is presented through biotechnology, ecology, spandrels, planetary systems, computing, the prebiotic realm, compost and environmental influences. These are founded on alternative notions of organization of life than the machine, from which the bodies of our future homes and cities may be constructed and inhabited. Attention is drawn to a specific parallel reality; the *Living Architecture* project actualizes *living bricks*, which combine structural and metabolic systems while exceeding the expectations of hylomorphism through its capacity for transformation. Soft living architectures are evaluated by their capacity for material resourcefulness and also through the way they are inhabited. A variety of performance techniques are presented in this book as assessment apparatuses, where radical material spaces are occupied by extreme bodies, such as cockroaches and circus performers.

*Soft Living Architecture: An Alternative View of Bio-informed Design Practice* aims to distil the concepts, materials, methods, technical apparatuses, prototypes and installations that increase the capacity for biodesign to develop agile protocols of spacetime as specific expressions of life. It invites the transdisciplinary synthesis of new design practices through prototyping soft living architecture, to realize the Babelsphere. While this does not solve our present ecocide, it aims to increase the portfolio for working more symbiotically with the natural world – where, one day, making a building may actually increase the fertility and liveability of our world, rather than diminish it.

# 1
# Life as You Don't Know It

The framing of life's character and its difference from machines sets the scene for the application of Gould's thought experiment to an architectural practice of worlding. In re-running the tape of life, from around the start of life's origin, the character of parallel life, our expectations of lively bodies and implications for design practice are considered.

## 1.1 Prototyping life

At the heart of modern bio-inspired practice is a philosophy of life, which embodies a scientific worldview that is further shaped by cultural and technical contexts. Historically, the built environment aspires, not to be a machine but to reach equivalence with biological systems (promoting life, environmental responsiveness, organic aesthetics). During the Enlightenment, these relationships were rationalized through mathematical languages such as geometry and computer algorithms, creating the possibility for greater control over the construction process. These languages can also instruct mechanical operations, which are ordered according to a hierarchy of inert geometric objects that are powered by external forces (fossil fuels, electricity, computer programs, etc.). The *modus operandi* of machines is extremely powerful and is validated through our ability to incorporate its logic into our daily lives. Despite its organic aspirations, mechanical notions of the body dominate the protocols of the built environment, which are conceived as a hard-edged form of biological determinism that is framed by René Descartes's notion of the bête machine (Nicholson, 2013).

## 1.2 Beyond the bête machine

While the bête machine has brought many advances in the modern understanding of nature, it does not speak perfectly for the living world, most especially since it is blind to its environmental context. It also strips matter of innate agency and its capacity to exist in more nuanced ways than measurable expressions of form, efficiency, modularity and function. Modern buildings draw from this devitalized model of life, since they are made up of 'brute' materials that draw liveliness from their inhabitants and surroundings. Yet, machines are more than models of living systems; they are also socialized, through personalized gadgets, robots and even become our companions. Their ubiquity and potency have been demonstrated through displays of incredible power that can be deployed at the scale and power of natural forces, like the Moonlight Towers in Austin, Texas (Oppenheimer, 2014), which floodlit the city with artificial night light, not only replacing the moon but also 'improving' upon its performance.

At a time of ecocide, it is pressing to establish alternative nuanced readings of the body, which exceed the logic of machines, so buildings do not just consume natural resources but may also actively enhance the liveliness of the natural realm by, for example, transforming 'waste' matter into usable or energy-rich substances. Soft living architecture aims to examine the character of life, so that knowledge-making toolsets and architectural practices may be accordingly expanded in ways that establish an alternative relationship with nature.

## 1.3 Replaying the tape of life

In many ways, the extraordinary phenomenon of life may be considered contradictory to the logic of the bête machine. Although life obeys the laws of physics, it cannot be predicted by them. Machines are deterministic systems that operate within a world at relative equilibrium; life is probabilistic and exists within far from equilibrium systems. While machines are insensitive to their environmental contexts, life is deeply correlated with its surroundings. Soft living architecture proposes to ethically alter the present mechanistic protocols for space-making and explore the impacts of an ecological engagement with choreographing spacetime. Since this may have far-reaching impacts, a design-led practice of prototyping critically explores possibilities using Stephen Jay Gould's concept of *replaying the tape of life* (Gould, 1989, p. 48). This thought experiment (re)imagines the consequences of starting the evolutionary process at any time after life's origin to consider whether the subsequent life forms would be recognizable today. This concept was based on an ongoing dualistic debate – whether environmental conditions or predetermined agents like genes played a more significant role in biological development – specifically, in this case, with respect to the evolution of human intelligence.

> Wind back the tape of life to the early days of the Burgess Shale; let it play again from an identical starting point, and the chance becomes vanishingly small that anything like human intelligence would grace the replay. (Gould, 1989, p. 14)

What is unknown in Gould's experiment is the extent of the impact that environment makes on an organism. The reciprocal relationship between creatures and their environment was established by Charles Darwin in the controversial publication *On the Origin of Species by Means of Natural Selection, or the Preservation of Favoured Races in the Struggle for Life*, which established a secular view of life. While he did not characterize the systems that enabled this relationship, over the course of the twentieth century this was attributed to the central organizing role of genes. Through modern (digital) computing and molecular biology, these structural codes and units of biological information became equated with the agents that programme life. Through this worldview, the new science of synthetic biology became possible, which alters genetic sequences (like changing computer codes) to change the function, behaviour or appearance of a creature (Woese, 2004). Genetic technologies also provide ways of investigating the degree by which organisms are shaped by their biological protocols. However, the results are neither clear nor unanimous. While synthetic biology confirms that genes are critical for the function of cells, it also clearly establishes there is more to life than genes. Even the audacious biohacks of J. Craig Venter and his team of synthetic biologists, who can 'crank out' the entire gene sequence of an organism, cannot build life from scratch from genetic information alone (Gill and Venter, 2010). Artificial gene sequences need to be jump-started into action by inserting them into host cytoplasm. This is harvested from another creature, like a genetically enucleated bacterium or yeast. In other words, cells need more than genetic information to 'live'.

Other conceptual and technical frameworks are also acknowledged as playing a critical role in biological systems. Since ancient times, liquids were considered essential for conferring unique order on organisms. Fluids enable movement and self-assembly, where molecules can freely associate through transitional complexes and spatially orient themselves within a site. Indeed, liquids are more than an infrastructure for molecular exchanges; they are also structuring systems. While their openness leaves *liquid bodies* vulnerable to the potentially devastating effects of turbulence and mechanical destruction, they are also robust and responsive to changes in their surroundings. When life left the oceans for the terrestrial environment, it brought along its internal seas within the protection of semi-permeable membranes.

Other important frameworks in the structuring of life relate to the nature of chemistry, whereby the chemical order that shapes biological systems also creates the limits of possibility for the development of living things.

> A chemical sequence and a chemical order shape the chaos of biology and history in surprising, yet rational ways, explaining many facts. It is a long story, but it coheres with chemical logic, and it shows that the nature of history is ordered by chemistry. (Macfarland, 2016, p. xiv)

Through envisaging parallel worlds, Gould's hypothesis creates a platform for developing and interrogating alternative frameworks for the evolution of life's processes. These go beyond centrally determined, geometric protocols for working with inert matter and are sensitive to environmental changes through their relationship with enlivened fabrics.

## 1.4 Parallel worlds

Since ancient times, storytellers have drawn upon alternate realities such as heaven and hell to imagine life in a different realm. Today, the advent of quantum mechanics (where matter acts demonstrably strangely), psychology (where the mind produces reality) and astronomical theories about the *multiverse* (Maguire, 2017) have provided a technical basis and sites for the realization of parallel worlds. Surrealists mastered the technique of juxtaposing strange and absurd phenomena with scientific study to generate *parallel methodologies*.

> No domain has been specified, a priori, for this undertaking, and surrealism proposes a gathering of the greatest possible number of experimental elements, for a purpose that cannot yet be perceived. (Durozoi, 2005, p. 65)

Invoking its own futility, the *Bureau of Surrealist Research*, also known as the *Centrale Surréaliste* or *Bureau of Surrealist Enquiries*, proposed that surrealism was capable of producing knowledge on par with scientific investigation, while Alfred Jarry constructed imaginary solutions for real and non-real phenomena through the science of `pataphysics. Despite its paradoxical purposelessness and unfathomability, `pataphysics held spaces open for experiment, which would otherwise be closed by logic and empiricism. Indeed, André Breton considered such endeavours as anything but meaningless, since they provided the foundations for new myths that offered a possible way out of modernity's war-mongering, irrational rationalism.

> Perhaps there was an invisible 'Super-Sargasso Sea' suspended somewhere overhead, 'derelicts, rubbish, old cargoes from inter-planetary wrecks; things cast out into what is called space by convulsions of other planets ... ' It was a sort of junkyard where gravity didn't apply, or worked in unexpected ways. (Steinmeyer, 2008)

With Jarry-esque eccentricity, Charles Fort collected, sorted and valued discoveries that were rejected by traditional science, inferring the presence of an enchanted realm in our midst. His worldview was a counterpoint to a cynical despondent age of staunch conservatism that had lost delight in reality where

> Terrorists delivered bombs in packages on the streets of Washington, anarchists planted explosives on Wall Street, and civil liberties were tightened around thousands of citizens suspected of communist sympathies. America banned alcohol and cynically withdrew from world politics. Fundamentalists debated the theory of evolution in court. Every day, newspapers were filled with reports on political machinations, psychic phenomena, or scientific discoveries that seemed to portray the world as a strange and dangerous place. (Steinmeyer, 2008)

The scientific basis for parallel worlds is encapsulated in the Many Worlds Hypothesis, which implies every possible alternate history and future is real and exists as an actual world, or universe. Its existence was implied during a Dublin lecture in 1952 by Erwin Schrödinger, who reported that some of his calculations suggested solutions were not alternatives but coexisted with each other (Maguire, 2017). Furthermore, Niels Bohr proposed the principle of complementarity that suggests objects have complementary properties that cannot all be observed or measured concurrently (Bohr, 2011).

These notions of simultaneity and the capacity to choose our futures suggest that our existence is not a single unfolding history but shaped by an infinite number of possibilities, which simultaneously occur. Such imaginative forays explore alternative ways of thinking and being, which help unlock the cultural potential for change. In the case of soft living architecture, parallel worlds are a platform for transitioning from an industrial to an ecological era.

## 1.5 Nature of matter

> All matter squirms. This is the fundamental reality that underpins our cosmic fabric. (Armstrong, 2015, p. 72)

The most radical possibilities for a parallel living world occur at the transition from inert to lively substances, with the potential to challenge assumptions about the nature of living matter and even the character of nature. Our current understanding of matter is based on the atomic model, which dates back to ancient times. This proposes that the fundamental unit of matter is the 'uncuttable' atom, which over the course of the twentieth century was demonstrated by quantum physics to be incorrect. At the subatomic level, substances are made up of probabilistic clouds of muons, leptons and hadrons, which behave as waves and particles (Lederman and Teresi, 1993, p. 168; Bitbol, 1996). The atoms and molecules produced by these fields can now be recombined into radically new configurations through the principles of supramolecular chemistry, where the weak bonds between atoms can be linked (Lehn, 1995). Atoms and molecules even exert influence beyond the local scale as their actions are situated within the interconnected cosmic network of the 'implicate order' (Bohm, 1980). Consequently, altering the material sequence of events that led to the origin of life on earth potentially has far-reaching effects that can change the story of our world.

By the time biogenesis occurred, matter itself was already 9.7 billion years old and therefore already bounded by constraints implicit in its structure. Created shortly after the Big Bang when the cosmos went from 'nothing' to 'relative' infinity around 13.8 billion years ago, the lightest elements were born in the first three minutes, when temperatures cooled from 100 nonillion Kelvin to 1 billion Kelvin. Protons and neutrons formed a stable isotope of hydrogen called deuterium, which condensed to form clouds that collapsed to form the first cosmic bodies, which occupied the cosmic darkness. Between 150 million and 1 billion years after the Big Bang, supermassive black holes formed, which devour matter to produce luminous objects known as quasars, and interacted with other forms of matter and radiation, rendering space luminous (Yeager, 2017). Around 5 billion years after cosmogenesis, matter started to condense under the influence of gravity and the current expansion of the universe was initiated. Around 4.5 billion years ago, our sun was encircled by a cloud of hot debris, which cooled and combined into clumps, followed by planetesimals, then increasingly larger planets, which frequently collided and vaporized each other. Within this unspeakably brutal, cosmic battleground, our planet and moon were born. The first evidence of structures on the earth were zircon crystals that are around 4.3 billion years old and the most ancient remains of biotic life found on the Western Australian rocks are said to be 4.1 billion years old.

The answer to the nature of lively matter does not lie in understanding its subatomic structure, as when we look downwards into the heart of atoms, they are not solid at all but particle clouds. Matter is a paradox. Its illusion of solidity is forged through constant shuffling between weak intermolecular bonds, transitional states, quantum entanglements and indeterminate forces, which actively seek new relationships that couple particle fields together and confer the material realm with its strangeness. Nor does the nature of lively matter arise purely from the properties of atoms since their properties are deeply altered by their context. Given the mutability and contingency of the material realm, its outcomes are therefore not best imagined as deterministic systems. For example, when the gases hydrogen and oxygen are combined under terrestrial conditions, they produce liquid water, whose characteristics cannot be predicted by knowledge of the original reagents alone. Matter is particularly unruly when it is far from equilibrium, as it is sensitive to environmental conditions, dynamic, possesses innate 'intelligence' (the capacity to make 'decisions' during transitional states) and capable of radical (phase) change.

## 1.6 Mineral sensibilities

> A mineral-forming process should be the same whether it occurred billions of years ago or last Tuesday ... there was no reason to assume that minerals couldn't evolve, just as life changes over time ... life didn't spring up in isolation – minerals likely helped it along the way. And as life evolved, it created a myriad of chemical niches that allowed new minerals to form. (Wei-Haas, 2016)

While biological narratives highlight the agency of organic molecules in shaping life, which are coordinated through gene expression, minerals also play essential roles as catalytic and structural agents. In replaying the tape of life, a different emphasis on the mineral realm has the potential to produce radically different expressions of the living world.

> Activated by radiation, the matter of the biosphere collects and redistributes solar energy, and converts it ultimately into free energy capable of doing work on Earth ... In its life, its death, and its decomposition an organism circulates its atoms through the biosphere over and over again. (Vernadsky, 1998, pp. 44–56)

There is no classification system for non-biological lifelike agents. Yet, Carl Linnaeus's original taxonomy of natural systems – animal, vegetal, mineral – attributed stones with some of the properties of living things. For example, he interpreted mineral formations like sandstone as a parallel form of life that actively grew in the ground (Uppsala Universitet, 2008) and that quartz was produced by a 'parasitic' mechanism. Even Charles Darwin noted that heavy stones sunk into the ground faster than the effects of gravity owing to the action of worms in the soil (Darwin, 2007). Contemporary geologists Arnold Rheshar and Pierre Escollet argue that the vital properties of stones occur much more slowly than organic processes. Based on photographic evidence taken over a lengthy durational period, they deduced stones change their structure, breathe in cycles of inspiration that last from three days to two weeks, possess heartbeats that last 'three days', move and grow old (Grachev, 2006). Although environmental conditions are likely to be responsible for these activities, the geologists assert their observations are evidence that the world is animate – not 'brute'. More recently, large stones have been tracked by GPS sailing across Death Valley, which has been attributed to the temporary formation of frictionless surface tracks of ice, which enable stones to move significant distances due to pressures exerted on them by a slight breeze (Stromberg, 2013). Unusual geological formations known as 'trovants', or living stones, are found near the small Romanian village of Costesti (Murgoci, 1905). They are formed from layers of cemented sand and mineral salts that are arranged in ring-like formations, like the trunk of a tree. After every rainfall, they are said to grow and rise from the ground, multiply through 'budding' and even move from one place to another. While it is rumoured that they are 'inorganic' forms of life, their apparent liveliness is produced by physical and chemical forces. When saturated, their internal osmotic pressure rises and causes the rock to grow from the centre to its margins, increasing its girth, which alters its presence on a site. The flow of water through the stones causes the formations to increase in size, with a deposition rate of about 5 cm in 1,000 years.

Although stones are not 'living' in the same way that organic matter proposes to be, inorganic matter is still capable of participating actively in natural systems. Notably, organizing matrices such as clay and sulphide rocks are likely to have had a significant role in biogenesis (Cairns-Smith, 1987). Indeed, the possibility of living stones is endorsed in principle by today's origin of life scientists who observe the close links between the evolution of life and rocks, where life is considered an extension of the chemistry of the earth (Comfort, 2016).

## 1.7 Origin of life

The current story of biogenesis sets the benchmark against which parallel life is observed. How life arose in the first place cannot be fully witnessed. Accounts therefore present versions of parallel worlds that consider many possible events, which may have led to the emergence of life and ultimate evolution. While most assume that biology is inevitable, this is debatable; modern biology is what happened on earth, not what was possible. Moreover, the geostory (Latour, 2013) of the planet is steeped in ecocide. Even at the time of biogenesis during the Hadean epoch, life on earth had already been extinguished many times under intense asteroid bombardment. Since its inception, geological records indicate that life has been almost wiped out five times in the last half a billion years (Ceballos et al., 2015). While these previous catastrophes have been wrought by natural disaster, uniquely, we are currently facing the sixth great extinction, which is brought about by global industrial development. Its catastrophic impacts are not only wrought upon existing creatures but also devastate the elemental systems that expedite planetary viability.

In modern times, the genesis of the living world is recounted through the transition from inert to lively matter, whose key actors are a cosmic circus of organic molecules, which are capable of seemingly defying the classical laws of physics. Yet, the boundary between chemistry and biology remains a matter of contention, as increasing complexity alone cannot account for biogenesis.

Since the mid-nineteenth century, the nature of biological systems and their distinction from chemical building blocks were the subject of many experiments that proposed to disprove theories of 'vitalism'. This theory proposed (invisible) animating forces infused matter with liveliness. The Enlightenment identified these forces as material events that were forged through chemical bonds and ultimately encoded within cell organizing systems. Time was also a critical factor for this view of biogenesis, where simmering natural elements in a muddy pond, such as those described by Charles Darwin, were stirred by evolutionary pressures and seasoned by chance. This process continued over the course of aeons, until the soup blossomed into a plethora of species.

Drawing on chemical characteristics as a model for biogenesis, early experiments in the animation of non-biological materials were characteristically bold and theatrical. For example, a range of cell-like bodies could be produced from chemistry alone, without recourse to biological ingredients. The Bütschli system (Bütschli, 1892), which rippled from the centre of oil-filled dishes, and the Traube cell (Traube, 1867), which was thought to be the first 'artificial' plant grown from inorganic ingredients, were propagated through physical and material changes in reactive chemical fields, namely alterations in surface tension, osmotic forces and mineral lattices. Although highly inventive in their morphology and behaviour, chemical reactions alone do not produce life.

Even bolder were experiments that proposed to rewind the tape of biogenesis back to the Hadean epoch, 3.5 billion years ago, when the earth's first organic molecules were formed. Home-made atmospheres of poisonous gases were activated by artificial lightning within pressurized, sealed flasks, generating a thunderous brew from which the first building blocks of life could be retrieved from the tarry residue of the storm (Miller, 1953).

The discovery of DNA provided a structural system and a customizable biological programme for making cellular proteins, which were regarded as the main building blocks for primordial biochemistry (Watson and Crick, 1953). Material experiments were less theatrical but were concerned with 'writing the code of life'. With the rise of digital computing, the deciphering of biotechnological systems became more sophisticated in terms of engineering approaches. These have largely transformed synthetic biology into a practice of *computing with life*, where using engineering protocols, laboratory experiments 'hack' the soft machinery and biological codes of organisms to invent artificial living systems (Venter, 2007).

Contemporary views of life centre on a programming metaphor, whose compilation is theorized by two main worldviews. The 'information first hypothesis' is a command and control style system, which proposes that all biological information arose in a primordial agent, which then assembled an energy-producing body. The most popular of these theories is the 'RNA world' hypothesis that exploits the dual properties of a smart molecule, ribose nucleic acid (RNA), which can catalyse chemical reactions and also replicate itself. RNA is especially interesting, as it has multiple functions that – applied sequentially – could potentially give rise to a modern cell where *replication comes first, then metabolism*.

The second approach is the 'metabolism first hypothesis'. This theory is based on a distributed programme of information that is spatially distributed and enacted through chemical contingency. It draws on the programming potential of self-sustaining biochemical systems that can operate outside a bounded primordial information system. Although these bodies are not yet capable of replicating, they are persistent and at tipping points of organization, which are typical of dissipative structures, can transform into recognizable chemical bodies. Eventually, this energy-rich system proposes to provide a nurturing environment for a replicating chemical system. So, *metabolism comes first, then replication*.

Metabolism first theories invite the participation of information systems beyond organic codes. They look to alternative organizing matrices as analogue computers such as clays like montmorillonite. These are more abundant than fragile nucleotides and contain soft silicon scaffolding. They are also molecular printers that possess incredible surface area-to-volume ratios and can act as complex organizing sites and catalysts that transcribe the action of 'crystal codes' into molecular patterns. The building blocks of life, such as amino acids and simple sugars, may therefore be organized around these chemical hubs and may have been precursors to organic replicators (Logan, 2007, pp. 123–8).

Any lifelike system requires a stream of energy *[that]* passes through the system and its environment. Life begins in this interaction where the energy is bent and diverted into little chaotic vortices, unexpected patterns, dynamic containers of information. A clay crystal ... fulfils just these requirements ... well-ordered but capable of many meaningful permutations. A certain minimum energy is required to change it from one state to another. It is therefore a code. The clay code however, is more complex than either the genetic code or human language. Only now are we beginning to catch glimpses of its order, and one cannot help thinking that pursuing it will be as fruitful and endless as the cabbalists' search for that perfect expression of the Hebrew aleph, by which God created the universe. (Logan, 2007, pp. 127–8)

Even stranger than polymeric clays, the quantum realm is invoked in the most radical notions of computation and theories of life. Information stored in quasicrystals, or aperiodic crystals, demonstrates extraordinary characteristics such as long-range order and five-fold symmetry axes, whose processing powers remain unfathomably elusive. While such structures do not appear to exist spontaneously in natural systems, they raise questions about our assumptions of the potential of the living realm, which is described in terms of classical physics, chemistry and mathematics. With the advent of quantum physics, the very nature of matter and information is up for grabs – an observation that has not been lost on 'quantum biologists', who observe that coherent quantum processes may well be ubiquitous in the natural world. Examples include the ability of birds to navigate using earth's magnetic fields to the chemistry of photosynthesis – arguably the world's most important metabolism (Al-Khalili and McFadden, 2014).

To date, there has been no experimental evidence that life can be initiated from information combined with atomic ingredients that can be found on the earth. Proponents of 'panspermia', such as Sir William Thomson and Lord Kelvin, attribute the emergence of terrestrial life to extraterrestrial 'seeding' events (Kelvin, 1871). While this theory does not shed light on life's origin nor further elucidates the nature of information or matter from which it springs, it enriches the portfolio of possibilities for our further exploration of the limits of life, through the prototyping of parallel worlds.

## 1.8 Biogenesis and vivogenesis

Life's potential expression exceeds the limits of modern biology. We only have to look at the fossil record of life forms that have existed such as the Burgess Shale, discovered by Charles Doolittle Walcott, to see previously unknown creatures. When based on our previous experience and current expectations, the radical and often surprising modes of expression of the living world may be overlooked. This limits the potential available design and engineering possibilities. While *biogenesis* deals with the mysterious initiating events for biological life as we recognize it, *vivogenesis* casts its reach more widely. It can be explored through 'natural computing' techniques (see Section 4.2.2), which look at the pattern languages and material expressions associated with far from equilibrium systems. Importantly, while materials at equilibrium states and those at far from equilibrium may be made up of exactly the same molecules, their behaviours are not interchangeable. Indeed, the fundamental organizing agents of vivogenesis are not genes but highly structured and agentized chemical bodies known as dissipative systems, which operate at a much lower level of dynamic order. Such lively matter is not only theoretically acknowledged (Bennett, 2010) but also identified in systems such as dissipative structures (Prigogine and Stengers, 1984).

> A patterned integrity accessible to the mind; topologically stable; subject to variations of intensity; brought into the domain of the senses ... for the vortex is not the water but a patterned energy made visible by the water. (Kenner, 1991, p. 146)

Dissipative systems, or structures, exist at far from equilibrium states and are spontaneously produced where reactive fields of energy and matter overlap, such as when hot and cold air fronts collide to form a tornado. They challenge our expectations of objects, as they are simultaneously objects and processes, and become stable by shedding energy as they move away from chaos towards equilibrium. While they possess innate agency, they are not given the status of being alive. Their value in developing parallel life is as a visualization system that provides insights into the innate liveliness of the material realm. They also offer an alternative range of tools, materials and systems for prototyping lively agents (see Section 4.2.3).

## 1.9 Dissipative life

In 2007, I set out to discover the minimal unit capable of organizing life. I searched for a testable system that could potentially establish an evidence-based counterpoint to the truisms of biological determinism, which is complicated by many political, social and cultural factors (Gould, 1981). Identifying an alternative experimental system that can generate lifelike phenomena without drawing on existing biological systems is no small task, as nobody has created alternative life forms from scratch – nor have alien creatures been identified. When it comes to the analogue life forms available for comparative analysis, then $n = 1$, where $n = \{$biological life$\}$.

While dissipative cell-like structures are studied in experimental settings, Rayleigh–Bénard (convection) cells are used. These are formed when a layer of liquid is heated from below, so that hexagonal convection cells arise. Although they are easy to produce, they do not present much morphological variation. In 2008, I came across the Bütschli experiment, which can actively synthesize lively, heterogeneous, non-biological bodies from simple ingredients and produce material traces. It was first described in 1892 by Otto Bütschli, who aimed to make a simplified experimental model of body morphology and movement, based purely on physical and chemical processes such as fluid dynamics, or changes in surface tension. He used saponification to produce an 'artificial' amoeba with pseudopodia (cytoplasmic extensions), which behaved in a strikingly lifelike manner (Bütschli, 1892).

When the recipe was reproduced for a modern laboratory using 3M sodium hydroxide added to *Monini* Extra Virgin Olive Oil, it generated millimetre scale droplets (Armstrong, 2015). Each possessed a primary metabolism, which absorbed thermal energy from its surroundings (an endothermic reaction) and made products in the form of surfactants, or 'soaps', which further modified the oil–water interface. During the reaction, surface tension was lowered, which allowed the droplets to deform and move. As they moved through their environment, droplets used the alkaline reactant within the bodies as fuel to consume olive oil and produce skins of soap. The activity of any particular droplet was not predictable but lasted between several seconds and around twenty minutes. Outcomes were highly complex and variable, despite the lack of central programming by molecules such as DNA and the behaviour of droplets was complex and lifelike. While droplets were drawn towards each other, they rarely fused. This constant oscillation between attraction and repulsion suggested their products are both repellents and attractors for the system. However, even using mass spectrometry techniques that can detect tiny amounts of substances, these factors were not identified. Strange population-scale behaviours were also observed, where droplets appeared to work as a construction community. At unpredictable tipping points, they could alter their structure and behaviour suddenly, moving apart from each other while simultaneously producing long product strings of soapy crystals (Armstrong, 2015, pp. 100–4). Progressively, the activity of the system slows as it approaches chemical equilibrium and eventually becomes inactive. Despite their vigour, Bütschli droplets fall very short of meeting the accepted criteria that qualify them as being 'alive'. Other than the presence of organic molecules and a phenomenological repertoire that includes movement, environmental sensitivity, interaction and coordinated population-scale behaviour, they share very little in common with biology.

Their actions therefore exist beyond the established conventions of life and without recourse to a centralized biological code reveal what enlivened matter is 'actually' capable of. Since they can be modulated by events in their surroundings, they are susceptible to design and engineering. Therefore, they have the technological potential to ask specific questions relevant to the transition from inert to living matter.

## 1.10 Dissipative adaptation

The emergence of dissipative structures encapsulates a parallel world of dissipative life that is not orchestrated through central biological codes but contingent on myriads of preceding events. Stuart Kauffman has described this stochastic, emergent space, which is sensitized to environmental conditions, as the 'adjacent possible', which exceeds the capacity of contemporary computing methods to predict (Kauffman, 2008, p. 64). If unprovoked, dissipative systems comply with the theory of dissipative adaptation where they become more efficient at releasing energy into their surroundings, which increases their stability. Dynamic droplets demonstrate this principle as they rapidly alter their behaviour and appearance at tipping points of order and may persist for up to an hour during this time. They are also capable of forming stable oscillators. Yet, without encountering them first-hand, such systems are difficult to imagine.

## 1.11 Phantasmagoria of life

We are the inhabitants of the invisible realm. The dark matter of the earth. Without us, there is no you[1].

Over the last eight years, my senses have been plunged into the lightless environment of a microscopic realm that is entirely inhabited and constructed by chemical bodies. Here, the phenomenology of dissipative structures becomes apparent and offers a parallel reading of vivogenesis (see Figure 1.1).

Backlit and at low magnification, I am transported back into deep terrestrial time – where lively chemical agents show striking individual characteristics

---

[1] This poetic fragment is inspired by the experiment 'Glitch' by Simon Park, reported by Bruce Sterling for Wired (Sterling, 2011): 'Hello! We are the dark matter of the biological world. Let it be noted that without the unacknowledged legislation of microbes, inside and outside of you, there is no you.' (Park 2012a, 2012b, 2012c).

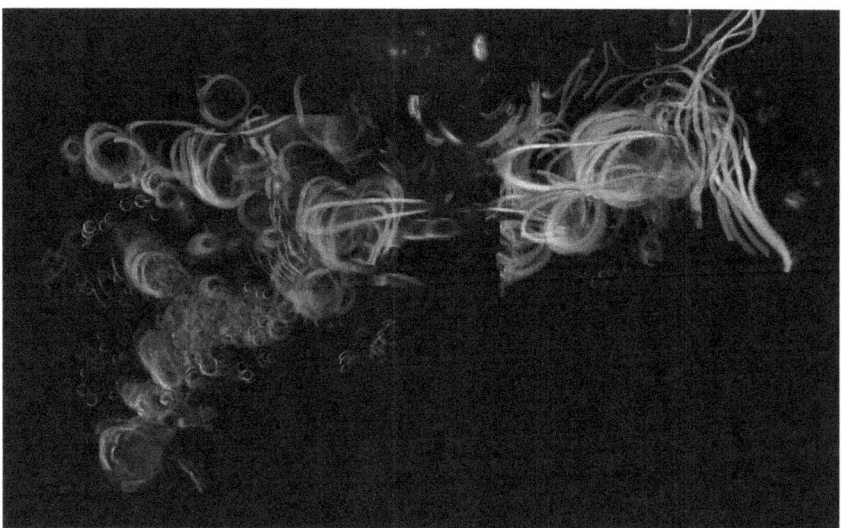

**FIGURE 1.1** *Protocell Phantasmagoria: Portrait of an origin of alternative life. Drawing by Simone Ferracina, from a movie of dynamic droplets courtesy of Rachel Armstrong, 2016.*

and form vibrant communities. In a state of semi-sensory deprivation, my senses are entangled with chemical events and I am attuned to these shadow spaces and haunted realms.

The stage of a light microscope set at x40 magnification is the backlit stage for a theatrical course of events where a strong drop of alkali is introduced into a quiet pool of oil in a Petri dish. A conversation begins as alkali meets oil and parallel life's coming into being draws momentarily into focus and recedes again.

Under a soup, a smog, a scab, a fire, the incandescent heavens rain molten rock into deadly landscapes. Spared from the cruel stare of ultraviolet rays and deluge of ionizing space radiation, a succession of chemical ghosts haunts the heavy atmosphere. Here, imaginary figures, like those that appear in a dream or fevered condition, split faint light around. Sudden ectoplasms spew in various acts across the horizons of the darkened theatre of this planet. They thicken and fold into various densities of matter, scum and crusts, through enrichment rituals that take place over the course of half a billion years – entirely beyond the human appreciation of time. Electrical storms claw at the earth, and charged tendrils of matter stand on their ends, dancing under ionic winds to begin the process of chemical evolution. An argument between phantasms is called into existence, where chemical life is pregnant with desire and hungry for novelty.

Vulgar in its becoming, the emerging blubber slobbers on biomass with carbohydrate teeth, drooling enzymes that digest nothing but its own bite.

Energetically incontinent, it acquires a cold metabolism and a watery heart. Expanding and contracting, it starts to pump universal solvent through its liquid eyes, lensing errant light into its dark thoughts. Mindless, yet finely tuned to its context, it wriggles upon time's compost, chewing and chewing with its boneless jaws on the agents of death. In its structural disobedience, the misshapen mass steadily grows more organized and reluctant to succumb to decay. Patterning the air, ectoplasmic strands extend like claws. Caressing itself in gratuitous acts of procreation, the daub shows contempt for the forces of disorder and crawls steadily towards being.

## 1.12 Life as material subversion

While the orthodox commandments of classical matter view the characteristics of life as simplicity, clarity, reversibility, symmetry, centrality, decipherable codes, control, coherence, Euclidean geometry, consistency, precision, rigid boundaries, homogeneity, holism, unity, universality, completeness and equilibrium, the subversive creativity of the organism wreaks multiple destructive acts against them through non-equilibrium, non-linearity, negentropy, chaos, spookiness, disorder, irreversibility, strangeness, coincidence, messiness, uncertainty and randomness. The inadequacy of our language to engage in unconventional worldviews is described by Niels Bohr as a symptom of our cultural conditioning.

> Difficulties ... arise from the fact that all our ordinary verbal expressions bear the stamp of our customary forms of perception, from the point of view of which the existence of the quantum of action is an irrationality. Indeed, in consequence of this state of affairs, even words like 'to be' and 'to know': lose their unambiguous meaning ... We here come upon a fundamental feature in the general problem of knowledge, and we must realize that, by the very nature of the matter, we shall always have last recourse to the word picture, in which the words themselves are not further analyzed ... for the time being we must be content with more or less appropriate analogies. Yet it may well be that behind these analogies there lies not only a kinship with regard to the epistemological aspects, but that a more profound relationship is hidden behind the fundamental biological problems which are directly connected to both sides. (Bohr, 2011, pp. 19–20)

Parallel biology challenges the use of conventional language in framing our understanding of life and provokes conversations about non-classical and paradoxical objects, which open up the possibilities for alternative ways of imagining, discussing and prototyping aspects of the natural world.

## 1.13 Subnatures

The seeds of material subversion are already growing within architectural discourse. For example, David Gissen's notion of subnatures examines the performance of recalcitrant matter in our cities, such as dankness, smoke, gas exhaust, dust, puddles, mud, debris, weeds, insects, pigeons and crowds, to reveal parallel forms of nature that provoke acts of 'life' within the urban landscape.

> They [*subnatures*] are often associated with the break-down and denigration of the enviro-socio-sphere, we must not use them to advance a simplistic, picturesque nihilism of the present. Subnature should not be used to give in to the processes of pollution and war that appear to generate many horrifying landscapes. Nor is subnature meant to promote urban decay or celebrate infrastructural breakdowns. It is not intended as a source of fantasy, in which architects provokes their peers by drawing thousands of smokers and feral animals in the space we inhabit. (Gissen, 2009, p. 214)

## 1.14 Chicken and egg: The paradox of lively matter

The protocols of soft living architecture aim to decode the seemingly contrary character underpinning life's transformational processes without reducing it into simple dualities, or causes and effects – typified by the chicken and egg paradox.

Chicken-as-origin theories are deterministic ideals, which are instructed by divine forces, or biological information systems. Egg-as-origin theories are probabilistic and deal with contingencies like resource availability and environmental constraints. Yet, both these accounts are centred on specific objects that exist in complete and stable forms. However, biological systems are not discrete and are not only permeated by their environments but also their propagation is not the responsibility of any one body. Indeed, living things are sustained, in one way or another, by the ongoing exchanges between other lively bodies around them, some of which result in progeny.

Life's persistence depends on a generous network of metabolic exchanges and their contingencies, where discrete boundaries between life forms are leaky and insides communicate with outsides. It does not stand alone, or even survive without other beings (such as the bacterial biome, trees, earthworms and mitochondria) and environments. The conundrum of the chicken and egg only arises where conceptual frameworks cleave their connection as the concept of life cycle is erased and it is not possible to move between the spectrum of states.

Eggs are not insular bodies. They are transformers that operate through folded membranes to establish the conditions for material exchange between lively chemistries and energy gradients. Through these connections, they produce a range of related structures with multiple identities that change with time. These modes of existence include various states of egg-ness (e.g. fertilized, unfertilized, egg shell fragments) and chicken-ness (e.g. chick, pullet, hen, cockerel).

Chickens are also transformers that produce biological seeds of potentiality established by their sex. While not all sexual encounters are potent exchanges, certain states of chicken-ness may (on fertilization) give rise to various stages of egg-ness, so the continuity between chickens and eggs persists but is never guaranteed.

By viewing chicken-ness and egg-ness as a continuum, the question of which stage precedes the other becomes redundant, since the various forms of chicken–egg are continuous expressions of an ongoing living process that is characterized by a range of anatomical structures and physiological events. So, the chicken–egg is not a paradox but an ongoing function of complex interdependencies, whose manifestations fluctuate accordingly with time, encounter and location, and it is only cleaved by dualistic thought.

This notion of radical, coherent transformation underpins the ambitions of soft living architecture.

## 1.15 Worlding

Worlding is a complex process of inhabiting space, where bodies are not simply objects that exist within the world but agents that operate to partially make it (Heidegger, 1962). As part of the responsibility of socialized life, worlding 'stay[s] with the trouble' (Haraway, 2013) that characterizes twenty-first-century challenges, by embracing risk, uncertainty and surprise. It is also a method for prototyping and exploring parallel worlds for the synthesis of ideas and discoveries, which enable alternative, complex configurations of matter and their modes of inhabitation to be prototyped into existence.

> The Biltong was dying. Huge and old, it squatted in the center of the settlement park, a lump of ancient yellow protoplasm, thick, gummy, opaque. Its pseudopodia were dried up, shriveled to blackened snakes that lay inert on the brown grass. The center of mass looked oddly sunken. The Biltong was gradually settling as the moisture was burned from its veins by the weak overhead sun … The Biltong's central lump undulated faintly. Sickly, restless heavings were noticeable as it struggled to hold onto its

dwindling life ... On the concrete platform, in front of the dying Biltong, lay a heap of originals to be duplicated. Beside them, a few prints had been commenced, unformed balls of black ash mixed with the moisture of the Biltong's body, the juice from which it laboriously constructed its prints. (Dick, 1991)

An example of worlding is depicted in Philip K. Dick's 'Pay for the Printer', which recounts a highly technical community that starts to reimagine how they will live together without the alien life forms that they have relied upon to make everything (Dick, 1991). Their plight resonates with our current times, where twentieth-century technologies are failing to address critical needs and conditions of the third millennium like climate change, catastrophic loss of biodiversity and global scale pollution. An alternative worlding paradigm than industrialization is needed so that our species has a chance to develop parallel and ongoing futures that do not diminish the liveliness of the planet but enhance it. As is the case with the community in Philip K. Dick's short story, this will take courage, persistence, persuasion and time.

Fergesson grabbed the cup. Trembling, he turned it over and over. 'You made it with **what?** I don't see how! What did you make it **out** of?'

'We knocked down some trees.' From his belt, Dawes slid something that gleamed metallically, dully, in the weak sunlight. 'Here – be careful you don't cut yourself.'

The knife was as crude as the cup – hammered, bent, tied together with wire. 'You made this knife?' Fergesson asked, dazed. 'I can't believe it. **Where do you start?** You have to have tools to make this. It's a paradox!' His voice rose with hysteria. 'It isn't **possible!**' (Dick, 1991)

# 2

# Experimental and Soft Living Architecture

This chapter explores the conceptual and technological traditions that underpin experimental architecture's methodological approaches for designing and iteratively developing soft living architecture prototypes. These are presented as portraits and fragments of parallel worlds, which convey the alterity of these bodies, their ecological contingencies and quality of spatial encounters.

## 2.1 Experimental architecture

> The world of architecture will eventually move away from the idea of buildings as something fixed, monumental, great and edifying, into a situation where buildings take their rightful place among the hardware of the world. Then architects as presently known will cease to exist and a very different kind of animal will emerge, embracing sciences, art and technology in a complex overview. Established disciplinary boundaries will be removed and we will come closer to the all-at-once world of Marshall McLuhan. (Chalk, 1994, pp. 172–3)

The term 'experimental architecture' first entered the architectural lexicon in 1970 when Peter Cook offered his critique of the stasis in Victorian pragmatism that underpinned the 'materialist corner of the modern movement' (Cook, 1970, p. 30). Believing that architectural freedom of expression was compromised by dominant formalisms, Cook embraced the cutting edge of modern invention to explore how new kinds of emergent social order were possible by using new materials, computers, communication, transportation, plug-ins, plastics, prefabrication, portability, and water- and airborne living.

Emerging as a serious and exploratory form of architecture that presented seductive and frightening versions of reality, which provided a counterpart to the ebullient postmodern movement (Betsky, 2015), experimental architecture was not imagined as a techno-fix. Rather, it was a medium for discovery using experimentation within thematic concepts to move design and society towards change that empowered communities.

During the 1980s, Lebbeus Woods used experimental architectural approaches to develop an uncompromising view of architectural agendas. Using draughtsmanship to reveal parallel worlds for architectural engagement, he proposed new roles for the architect in a range of unconventional terrains – from natural disaster to warfare. Even in the most orthodox spaces he developed radical new structures and spaces without walls, where the built environment was (re)imagined and (re)constructed, including its relationship with the biosphere; indeed, he was prepared to rethink the very planet if required (Manaugh, 2007). Woods held the first Conference on Experimental Architecture in 1988 in upstate New York, which featured Peter Cook, Neil M. Denari, Michael Sorkin, Hani Rashid, Michael Webb, Lise Anne Couture, Gordon Gilbert and Ted Krueger. Following his passing in 2012, Woods's visionary agenda is actively pursued by the Research Institute for Experimental Architecture (RIEA), the Experimental Architecture Group (EAG) at the University of Newcastle, UK and the Institute of Experimental Architecture at the University of Innsbruck. It is also practised by individual architects such as Nat Chard, currently professor of experimental architecture at the Bartlett School of Architecture (Chard, 1999–2016); Neil Spiller, who is Hawksmoor chair of architecture and landscape and deputy pro vice-chancellor of the University of Greenwich (Spiller, 2016); Mark Smout and Laura Allen at the Bartlett School of Architecture (Cook and Hunter, 2013) and Perry Kulper, associate professor of architecture at the University of Michigan (Archinet, 2012).

### 2.1.1 Twenty-first-century experimental architecture

Experimental architecture forms the components of a see-saw activity between the rational investigation of techniques at one end and the enforced accentuation of the new and always extending limits of what might be termed 'environment' at the other ... the future of architecture lies in the explosion of Architecture. (Cook, 1970, p. 152)

New technologies are now available to experimental architects that are not confined to industrial paradigms and logical approaches to urban challenges, but engage imaginatively with the natural realm. Alternative ways of performing work and choreographing matter and spacetime in design practice are now possible owing to recent advances in molecular science and an emerging portfolio of natural computing techniques (see Section 4.2.2). As professor of experimental architecture at Newcastle University, UK, my research specifically responds to ecocide through applying cutting-edge materials and biotechnologies in testable scenarios. Shifting away from the traditional view of architecture as a static, form-giving subject to a practice of agile, interrogative prototypes that operate through the experimental practice of 'worlding', which through its engagement with the process of inhabitation, challenges the assumptions of established architectural protocols and classical science. Embracing notions of participatory design practice, which collaborates with many diverse lively agents, experimental architecture develops knowledge through *storytelling as transdisciplinary synthesis*. This becomes key to not only developing the scope of research itself but also its capacity to link and connect forms of expertise previously kept apart (Hughes, 2009b, 2014; Armstrong, 2016a; Armstrong, Hughes and Gangvik, 2016; Armstrong and Hughes, 2016). Characteristically, experiments speak to transformative materialities that conjure invisible realms, embrace change, provoke uncertainty, take risks, create hybrids and are formed from hypercomplex materials such as fur, soil and felt (Geiger, 2016). They also form connections across disciplines, artefacts, performances and encounters, which explore the possibilities within wet environments and potential applications for soft structures that are capable of dynamically responding to their surroundings, such as the Living Architecture project (see Section 8.1). In keeping with Cook's agenda of establishing alternative modes of living that disrupt tyrannical systems of order within urban spaces, twenty-first-century experimental architecture has more in common with surrealism than with industrial machines – like Dalí's soft clocks, hairy materials, liquid environments and quantum phenomena. Importantly, soft living architecture also questions the status of the (human) body and the character of life, which inform the architectural imagination. These protocols examine the participatory status of bodies in these spaces, as active (non-mechanical) agents that alter and evaluate architectural choreographies, non-human actants and site-specific modes of inhabitation. Experimental architecture therefore possesses the capacity to completely change the expectations of our habitats and the notion of what constitutes a body – experiments that are currently being explored in collaboration with (radical) circus artists (see Chapter 10).

Indeed, experimental architecture regards bodily experiences as an essential integrator of knowledge-making and spacetime; so, instead of prioritizing highly controlled centres of knowledge and production that characterize the modem laboratory, it offers counterpoints through an engagement with site-specific, subjective, performative, 'messy' and highly distributed workspaces, which subvert the protocols of pristine environments. From these rebellious seeds and unpoliced environments, disruptive modes of inquiry may further sustain and enrich our knowledge of an ecologically stressed planet.

Such research methods imply a need for new evaluative criteria that do not aim for complete solutions or perfection but speak to established notions of research *quality* while respecting the specific characteristics of each disciplinary contribution. Such a daunting ambition to bring together so many different aspects of inhabiting and experiencing spaces is consistent with bringing the Babelsphere *to functionality* (Haraway, 2015). Whether this project is completed or not, the journey towards its realization produces rich integrative and synthetic platforms for fresh juxtapositions and insights, which reside within the terrains of poetry, magic and monsters (Hughes, 2016a).

## 2.2 Soft living architecture

All that is living burns. This is the fundamental fact of nature. (Logan, 2007, p. 3)

Soft living architectures are experimental architecture prototypes that engage with questions about the character of life, ecology, planetary systems and nature, which are explored through a practice of worlding. Arising from a spectrum of developmental stages that necessitate the maturation of agile prototypes, soft living architecture is forged through a Cambrian renaissance of spacetime protocols, choreographies of matter, living technologies and modes of inhabitation. Each iteration provides a portfolio of inhabitable apparatuses that explore how we dwell – and may inhabit the planet better – beyond industrial mores and practices.

Soft living architectures occur spontaneously as condensations of nature and occupy site-specific niches throughout the built environment. For example, they form microgeographies where mosses, lichens and biofilms detail the intersections between water, sunlight, minerals, ecological poisons and wind flow (Park, 2012c). They may also appear as crystals of efflorescence that blossom from brickwork or as mottled grey blushes on a concrete wall take traction on pits etched by acid rain. These building details are microsites with specific characteristics that indicate particular conditions for life's flourishing. Some may hold just a little more water than nearby depressions and are less exposed to sunlight. In other places, threads of green slime take hold in microfractures on paving stones, and around other locales rich urban crypto-biotic crusts swell in blooms of olive green and mustard from cement like an over-sauced bun. These transient communities leave their residues within these niches, further shaping their character, perhaps through the recording of shadows from buildings which offer their residents a little protection from harsh light, where embellished scabs on south-facing sides of fences may celebrate in blossoming displays as nearby drainpipes spatter them with nourishing – or toxic, lead-stained – runoff. Such soft living architectures are transient, parasitic, protean, episodic, subtle, capable of growth, constantly changing, highly contextualized and acquire meaning through being inhabited.

The advent of advanced biotechnologies has enabled us to design and engineer directly with the creativity of the living world, so soft living architectures are not necessarily naturalized and are concerned with modes of empowerment. Indeed, soft living architectures inform the protocols of spacetime through a range of approaches, which simultaneously promote environmental vigour and various (hybrid) expressions of human development.

## 2.2.1 The character of 'life' in soft living architecture

Soft living architecture exists at many scales, from subatomic particles to galaxies. It generates alternative conceptual and ultimately buildable frameworks that inform notions of space making, which are relevant to a world in flux. They span many scales, accommodating human and non-human agents alike such as dynamic droplets, lifelike materials, biofilms, bricks, walls, cities, weather, oceans and soils. Its genesis and development are therefore not exclusively human endeavours.

Soft living architectures incorporate dynamic materials at far from equilbrium states into their substance. Such fabrics, which typify the living world, also tend to be 'soft' (at least initially) as they accommodate fluid infrastructures that provide nutrients and remove waste products. In practice, this means that soft living architecture opens up a radically transformative choreography of space by converging advanced forms of biotechnology with elemental flows (air, earth, metabolism, water), the infrastructures of life (atmosphere, soils, oceans) and subnatures (see Section 1.13). Soft living architectures are hyperbodies, fertile infrastructures and sporadic sites that, for example, may bloom only at specific times like algae, jellyfish swarms, ice flowers in Antarctic seas, fields of blossom after desert rains and the legendary village of Brigadoon. While they may be modified through modes of soft control, they also provoke uncertainty, creativity and surprise. Yet, they do not sanitize their radical potency but speak through unresolved material phenomena like ectoplasms, ghosts and monsters that inhabit transitional realms. They are richly enfolded with their infrastructures and, depending on their complexity and choreography, may potentially give rise to a kind of embryology; not as morphological aesthetic, as in Gregg Lynn's parametric Embryological House (DOCAM, 1997–2002), but as an evolving materiality that differentiates, grows and becomes increasingly autonomous.

Soft living architecture, therefore, forms the basis of a palette of lively materials that can be orchestrated by natural computing techniques (see Section 4.2.2) – the synthesis of which may be regarded as producing parallel natures.

## 2.2.2 Soft living architecture: Examples

Soft living architecture is a transdisciplinary research practice that searches for ecological protocols for architectural design and embraces academic and commercial partners.

Philip Beesley, professor of architecture from the University of Waterloo, Ontario, assimilates soft, living technologies into the meshworks of his expanded cybernetic systems. His Hylozoic Ground series, a semi-living architectural installation, has adopted many manifestations of semi-living chemical organs, some of which can taste carbon dioxide and produce brightly coloured microsculptures (Armstrong and Beesley, 2011). Indeed, the synthetic capabilities of minerals and the potential programmability of matter through primed matrices like soils and clays are intrinsic to the soft living architectural portfolio. While crystallization results in a 'hard' structure, the conditions for self-organization require 'soft' liquid environments that are strategically employed in design practices – notably, Tokujin Yshiok's 2011 Venus Chair (Guy, 2011), Sigalit Landau's 2016 Crystal Bridge Gown (Peoples, 2016) and Roger Hiorns's now decaying 2008 Seizure installation (Ward, 2015).

Claudia Pasquero and Marco Poletti from EcoLogicStudio explore the potential of biological metabolisms in algae and other biomaterials, which change paradigms of occupancy within urban spaces by converging the digital, cybernetic, organic and social realms (Medina, 2014); while Carlo Ratti Associati's Office 3.0 further draws together biological parameters of spaces into new convergences with the digital realm through the Internet of things, in ways which link inhabitation and internal environment with building performance (Dezeen, 2016).

The non-profit organization Terreform ONE (Open Ecology Network) takes an experimental, interdisciplinary approach to the unprecedented challenges posed by climate change and rising populations by creating a whole range of new architectural materials, such as growing entire houses out of plants or building models of tissue culture producing 'meat' houses that provoke new building typologies (Szewczyk, 2015).

As infrastructure becomes less cosmetic and more integrated to biomaterials, new properties begin to emerge, such as Henk Jonker's self-healing concrete, which resists structural decay by taking advantage of water entry into microfractures within concrete, which activate resilient calcium carbonate-producing bacterial spores that seal the defects (Jonkers, 2007).

Other species of concrete are being developed, such as Martyn Dade-Robertson's pressure-sensing concrete, which detects different stress patterns to produce appropriate structural adjustments that secure building foundations, similar to bone remodelling (Dade-Robertson, 2016).

Spanish researchers at the Universitat Politècnica de Catalunya in Barcelona have developed specific infrastructures in a special kind of cement that uses natural rainwater to provide a moist environment for algae, fungi, lichen and mosses, so that they will thrive on a building surface without artificial irrigation. With enriching infrastructures, the living materials can absorb carbon dioxide in the atmosphere and act as an insulating material or a thermal regulator (Leon, 2013). Currently, such substances are mostly deployed towards industrial paradigms rather than being unleashed to provoke radical changes in the material performance of buildings. Regarded as 'smart' materials with obedient tendencies, these fabrics nonetheless tremble with the potential to bloom and explode modular units apart at the seams, leaving behind a trail of ruinous configurations that become fresh sites for alternative expressions of architecture.

Such potent substrates enable the integration of the classical and living realms where grey meets green in an inventive range of building details. Elizabeth Demaray, an artist at Rutgers University, paints lichen slurry on walls using a 'gorgeous palette of light greens to yellows' to introduce hardy forms of natural life into an urban environment, while mosses are gardened on walls by the BiotA team at the Bartlett School of Architecture, run by Richard Beckett and Marcos Cruz. Their 'bioreceptive' façades foster the growth of 'cryptograms' (Eveleth, 2011), which are cultivated on building surfaces and may be as ornate in their design as a Persian carpet.

Michael Hansmeyer's digital grotesques veer towards the practice of experimental architecture, since they are not fully formed building typologies, but explore the potential for 3D printing technologies to produce materials like sandstone that could potentially form an infrastructure for the kinds of synthetic bacterial colonies used by Jonkers and Dade-Robertson. Other reflexive incursions that create the adaptive infrastructures for microorganismal colonization – even if they are not yet seeded with them – are the hygroscopic materials such as wood and new polymers that draw water into their bodies and, by virtue of geometric programming and computational movements, adopt another configuration over time (Rieland, 2014; Menges, 2015); and Philippe Rahm's Hormonorium (Fredrickson, 2015) that engages biochemical 'climate processes', which reach towards dynamic modes of working with the living world.

Astudio architects are actively exploring experimental contexts and bespoke building installations that engage with the dynamic properties of microorganisms, and are setting new benchmarks for the next generation of 'sustainable' building designs, such as a sixth-form college in Twickenham, which proposes a next-generation ecological architecture as a focus for the school curriculum. The facility also produces soil substrates as a water filter and acts as a local resource for green roofs and walls, which promote urban biodiversity (Armstrong, 2016a, p. 137). Importantly, these prototypes are not simply speculative; they are early stage, experimental designs that are setting the scene for potential wider uptake within the built environment. Indeed, Arup's Intelligent Building, or BIQ House (Steadman, 2013), which opened to the public in Hamburg in November 2014, possesses a façade that offers a liquid environment for the growth of microcellular organisms that offset some of the building's energy demands through the solar thermal effect.

With the deliberate construction of infrastructure (matter, space, time), manipulation of flow (air, water) and the integration of living materials into a fabric, biologically programmable materials start to become possible. The Living Architecture project explores how the outputs of complex metabolic networks can be designed to perform specific work, like producing electricity, purifying water and even extracting valuable nutrients from the environment such as phosphates. This EU-funded project uses three kinds of bioreactor – microbial fuel cells, algaeponics and a genetically modified 'farm and labour' module – to explore how biofilms, formed by heterogeneous populations of microbes, can strategically process matter in their internal and external environments – as 'metabolic apps' – and be developed towards architectural-scale impacts (Living Architecture, 2016) (see Section 8.1).

While complex exchanges between metabolic systems are challenging in dry environments, in those instances where buildings and materials are habitually wet, soft living architecture becomes more tangible as a response to challenging environmental events. On an architectural scale, this creates the conditions for cities that possess complex environmental organs enabling them to respond to specific challenges like wear and tear or subsidence. In Future Venice I and II, complex biomaterials constitute a deliberate attempt to produce new forms of ground – specifically, a reef structure that can spread the point load of the city (see Section 8.5) and a plastic microfragment-removing island (see Section 8.5.2) (Armstrong, 2015).

The city of Venice is founded on urban soils, created from a whole range of raw materials such as alder woodpiles, impermeable Istrian marble, garbage, construction debris and human bodies that are unearthed during invasive construction and canal-clearing operations. The integration of the composting process into these systems further increases the potential for design and engineering that are not only architectural-scale but also respond to environmental cues – in other words, they embody the synthesis of soils. Indeed, it is likely that, with the abundance of modern garbage tips, biomaterials will be increasingly used to address the specific challenges of these structural wastes by, for example, using mycorrhiza to alleviate toxic build-up of plastics (Roth, 2015) and specific forms of bacteria capable of 'bioleaching' that process metals into more extractable or pure forms (Hornyak, 2008; Callaway, 2013).

The role of soft living architectures as processers of resources, such as recycling wastewater and producing metabolic energy to offload power consumption, may reduce living spaces' ecological footprints, if not make them negligible. Of course, these kinds of developments are yet to be commercially implemented, but many of the founding principles of their potential are established; all we need is to consider the transition towards 'living' buildings to be important enough to make it happen. Third millennial experimental architecture possesses all of the revolutionary potential of the postmodern pioneers but, through laboratory practices and testable experiments, transforms its reputation for 'paper architecture' into a multidisciplinary practice that engages with method, materials and technology and is thus, ultimately, buildable.

Although soft living architecture shares common principles with existing design-led practices such as biomimicry and biodesign, which also seek to engage natural processes, it is distinguished by its ecological negotiation between many distinct bodies and their infrastructures, the incorporation of (material) change in the system and ethical engagement (which elevates the status of non-humans rather than reducing the value of humanity) (Bennett, 2010, p. 13) with a biodiverse community of actants.

> This fusion [*of a material self and life support*] becomes fur – it does not take its forms in any sort of biomimicry, which Rachel Armstrong has aptly called 'like biology for the copy-and-paste generation,' – but in a real sense of behavior. Fur is neither surface nor endlessly porous. Its plush depths are variable, its contours pliant and its liveliness ambiguous. Fur grows, it insulates and it binds to a living flesh. These are behaviors all central to the material qualities of a continuous interior, and they, too, have been subject to fictitious development that can serve us. (Geiger, 2016)

The outcome is a radical (re)envisioning of matter that produces semipermeable materials and transient spaces, with characteristics similar to soils – although without naturalistic expectations – that link life and death. Soft living architectures therefore confer matter with the prospect of regeneration and ultimately reincarnation.

### *2.2.3 Soft living architecture: Body*

> An architect should live as little in cities as a painter. Send him to our hills, and let him study there what nature understands by a buttress, and what by a dome. (Ruskin, 1989)

Soft living architecture is a theory and practice of many types of bodies, with various modes of organization that exceed established biological definitions of aliveness ranging from minimally living bodies, such as dynamic droplets, to infrastructures like elemental media and colossal, complex structures, such as hyperbodies made up of many participating yet loosely associated agents like soils, subnatures and cities. It acknowledges their capacity to choreograph protocols of spacetime and alter sites by their modes of inhabitation and extended ecological relationships.

> I am released from conventions of object-boundedness and permanence so that I may establish a new relationship between 'this' body and 'my' surroundings. Constantly reconfiguring, my flesh searches for new allies, as my trembling presence extends through transitional states of being and networks of material interactions. Here, I take the form of an excitable assemblage of fields that shape material behaviours, where re-laced metabolic webs infuse my flesh with nascent creativity and my presence extrudes into new terrains as an unbounded anatomy in flux that is seamlessly integrated with and responds to its environment.

Everyday repetitions – like Henri Lefebvre's rhythmanalysis, whose circadian events conjure a sense of environmental reciprocity (Lefebvre, 2013) – are drawn together with extraordinary events through the way spaces are haunted. For example, Cirkus Cirkör's *Knitting Peace* brings circus artists in proximity with white rope to embody symbolic and actual threads of community-building endeavours, which are vital in the global struggle to make peace (Kavanagh, 2015).

> A subterranean world of white drapes and stalactites of rope spreads from the stage into the foyer of the pointed big top, with its traditionally theatrical rows of raked seating. A universal whiteness has transcended purity and entered the world of maggots, of underworld creatures who never see the sun. (Kavanagh, 2015)

The mutability of the body is also ethically problematic as it may be associated with cruelty, enslavement, degradation and even death. While soft living architecture rejects suffering, it does not however regard death as an endpoint but as the start of a parallel phase of hypercomplex ongoing transformations.

> My head is shaven. I'm marked with fading neurosurgical instructions. My eyes are swollen and bloodshot. I'm a terrifying chimera – part Ripley, defiant, powerful – a chocolate-red Thomas Jerome Newton – androgynous, hairless – and Tame Iti, the Maori tattooed 'face of the future'. I drop my

chin assertively and admiringly. At the top of my head is a neat horseshoe scar, cross-embroidered with surgical staples, grinning at me. They offered only to remove a patch of hair. But I insisted they took it all. It just feels better like this. Coherent. Bare. (Armstrong, 2018, p. 203)

## 2.3 Storytelling

> It matters what matters we use to think other matters with; it matters what stories we tell to tell other stories with; it matters what knots knot knots, what thoughts think thoughts, what ties tie ties. It matters what stories make worlds, what worlds make stories. (Haraway, 2011, p. 4)

While Cook conjures the high-modern technology that hard science fiction thrives on (Young and Manaugh, 2010), soft living architecture looks to nature as a technical apparatus that is capable of folding myths, dreams, magic and aspirations into the choreography of spacetime, where unlikely material exchanges alter the character of our living spaces – and may even change our expectations of them.

> The surrealist odyssey has encompassed many of the key conceptual drivers of architecture – the body, the house and the city. The surrealists also understood that the differing points of view of observers changed the meaning of spaces and, further, if bodies used prosthetics like suits, masks and optical devices, then architectural space changed. They also saw the house as a repository of personal meaning and iconography, a series of fractal thresholds containing our thoughts and ways of seeing the world from erotic pleasures to deepest fears – a psychic cabinet of curiosities. The city they saw as a massive engine of chance throwing up possibilities of love, strange juxtapositions of ideas and symbols and ever changing. (Spiller, 2016)

Radical perspectives are needed in characterizing capricious terrains, with a sufficiently broad scope that may influence the way we think. Arguably, the most influential parallel perspective on the nature of the city is Italo Calvino's *Invisible Cities*. The story tells of a conversation between the explorer Marco Polo and the ageing Emperor of China, Kublai Khan. Polo boasts of all the fantastical places he's seen on his way to the East. Each of them bears a woman's name and is radically different from all the others. Some like *Beersheba* exist in the sky, others like *Melania* are concerned with death, while several, like *Isidora*, harbour memories of desire. Yet all turn out to be based on only one city – the city of Venice (Calvino 1997). In Michel Serres's

*The Five Senses: A Philosophy of Mingled Bodies*, the order and character of the sensible world is reconstructed through its relationship with stories (Serres, 2016); and Walter Benjamin's *The Arcades Project* hurtles from thought to experience, transforming familiar urban spaces into unlikely encounters (Benjamin 1999).

> The 'refuse' and 'detritus' of history, the half-concealed, variegated traces of the daily life of 'the collective' that was to be the object of study, and with the aid of methods more akin – above all to their dependence on chance – to the methods of the nineteenth-century collector of antiquities and curiosities, or indeed to the methods of the nineteenth-century ragpicker, than to those of the modern historian. Not conceptual analysis but something like dream interpretation was the model. (Benjamin, 1999, p. x)

Such forms of storytelling do not propose to fully resolve the difficulties and contradictions they discuss but raise further questions that even go as far to emphasize the impossibility of alternatives than the *status quo*. Within these tensions, parallel approaches emerge towards realizing the Babelsphere, where the limitations of rationality appear and in its place wonder, darkness, magic and mystery begin to make room for our (re)connection, (re)empowerment and (re)enchantment with our reality.

## 2.4 Ambient poetics

I'm watching a sheet of paper tumble over the Rio de la Sensa. It sticks stubbornly to the side of a passing gondola, and I'm suddenly struck with the idea that 'living' Venice is an inverted tree with stony roots and sexual organs that are serviced by street litter. Since they feed on detritus, they flourish twice yearly in February with the onset of the festival season and late summer when the tourist load is at its peak. Male organs shed copious amounts of dust into the air, like yellow snow and roam the alleyways in search of a female receptacle, an egg-shaped structure with generous petals, like waste collection bins. Such a union produces fruits coated with long, yellowish brown fibres with tiny hooks that fall to the ground and cling to each other in hairy biomass rafts. Floating mats and new island embryos emerge that grip the developing land with their tentacles and soon meld together into twisted bridges. Yet, not all city seeds are destined to become mature settlements but can be harvested for multiple uses like rope, yoke straps, strings for musical instruments, baskets, nets, snares, fishing lines, cloth – and sometimes, they are consumed because of their sweet taste.

Soft living architecture explores the potential of ambient poetics (Morton, 2007, pp. 33–4) to infuse its prototypes and sites with a sense of place through the creative use of language. Examples appear frequently throughout this book, such as *Automatic Venetian Chess* (see Section 6.4) and *Mirror Puddle* (see Section 7.9). Through language experiments, discoveries can be received and interpreted in ways that open up real spaces for experiment by framing the contexts of ideas so that they may be creatively explored. Parallel laboratory settings include performance (see Section 9.3) or the participation of non-human agencies like cockroaches (see Section 9.4.1) and dynamic droplets in the discovery process (see Section 1.9). Through ambient poetics a parallel toolset for the practice of experimental architecture emerges, with the capacity to open up alternative spaces for experiment that – through exploring the limits of language, provoking the transgressive agency of environment and engaging the potency of recalcitrant materiality – begin fresh conversations about the protocols of spacetime and the radical potential of lively matter.

> The sense of fantasy implicit in Armstrong's protocell research deters people from regarding it as a real-world solution. For architects and designers of infrastructure, it's hard to embrace a built proposition that doesn't involve concrete or steel but that's exactly what Armstrong is asking us to do. 'When we talk about systems in architecture, we tend to revert to machine iconography,' she says. 'With the protocell system, we don't need to. It doesn't have parts; it's not an object.' It may act more improbably and organically than any architecture we know, but it represents a chance to replace the outdated practice of designing buildings as environmental barriers with a more constructive and harmonious approach. (Patel, 2011)

# 3

# World in Meltdown

This chapter examines the context for architectural practice at a time of ecocide, uncertainty and material insurrection. The idea of the Babelsphere becomes a model and metaphor underpinning an architectural practice of worlding and ongoing project that encapsulates a world in constant flux. Soft living architecture prototypes negotiate parallel modes of inhabitation where protocols of spacetime interlace the webs of life and death, forging ongoing cycles of ecological regeneration and sites of synthesis for artificial natures.

## 3.1 End of Utopia

> In the years to come, we will brace for the violence, the anger, the racism, the misogyny, the xenophobia, the nativism, the white sense of grievance that will undoubtedly be unleashed now that we have destroyed the values that have bound us. We all knew these hatreds lurked under the thinnest veneer of civility. That civility finally is gone. In its absence, we may realize just how imperative that politesse was. It is the way we managed to coexist. (Gabler, 2016)

The twentieth century convinced us that by controlling and regulating the world using powerful technologies, humanity could be homogenized under a single global identity. People could then be housed in idealized cities based on Edens and Utopias. Yet, we are realizing the impossibility of surviving these monistic purification processes, with their crisp categories and universal laws (Latour, 1993). In these deterministic worldviews, we find ourselves at odds with a lived reality that is composed of messy environments. These are sites for nascent conflict, insurgent confusion, even frank psychosis, where it is impossible to comfortably exist alongside marginalization by crisp categories, the loss of our identity through exclusion and alienation on account of homogenizing universal laws (Latour, 1993). Despite the utopian ambition to 'regain' order and control of the world, our cities and environments remain beyond the reach of formal Enlightenment logic to 'solve'. Urban environments are unruly, matter is recalcitrant and the living world is in retreat. After 150 years of global industrial development, ecocide is no longer a threat but our reality, where our earths are littered with substances like plastic particles, and environmental coherence will not be naturally restored for tens of thousands of years. Our current response to such crises is to ensure that our cities are better machines for living in (Le Corbusier, 2007, p. 158), where we consume fewer natural resources, use less damaging construction processes, invent more ingenious geometric solutions to optimize urban density and even import vestiges of the living world as urban canopies to ameliorate industrial scars on the landscape. Yet, none of these measures actually reverses the paradigm whereby human development inevitably damages the natural infrastructures that sustain us. While the world is not entirely destroyed, agile protocols of inhabiting space are urgently needed that lead to mutual survival, not just between peoples but also in concert with the natural and planetary realms.

> It is time to think carefully ... about ... what kind of systems we want. The future we have been sold doesn't work. Applying the principles of the factory floor to the natural world just doesn't work. Farming is more than a business. Food is more than a commodity. Land is more than a mineral resource. (Rebanks, 2017)

## 3.2 The Tower of Babel

The Tower of Babel is a symbol of a world on the verge of falling apart.

> Now the whole world had one language and a common speech ... They said to each other, 'Come, let's make bricks and bake them thoroughly.' They used brick instead of stone, and tar for mortar. Then they said, 'Come, let us build ourselves a city, with a tower that reaches to the heavens, so that we may make a name for ourselves; otherwise we will be scattered over the face of the whole earth.' But the Lord came down to see the city and the tower the people were building. The Lord said, 'If as one people speaking the same language they have begun to do this, then nothing they plan to do will be impossible for them. Come, let us go down and confuse their language so they will not understand each other.' So the Lord

scattered them from there over all the earth, and they stopped building the city. (Genesis 11:1–9, New International Version)

Babel is more than an iconic structure; it embodies the very nature of ecosystems and purpose of life, which as Erwin Schrödinger observed is to avoid the inevitable decay towards thermodynamic equilibrium or death:

> Everything that is going on in Nature means an increase of the entropy of the part of the world where it is going on. Thus a living organism continually increases its entropy ... and thus tends to approach the dangerous state of maximum entropy, which is death. It can only keep aloof from it, i.e. alive, by continually drawing from its environment negative entropy ... [so] ... the organism succeeds in freeing itself from all the entropy it cannot help producing while alive. (Schrödinger, 2012, p. 71)

Soft living architecture allies with Babel as a recalcitrant expression of matter and an ally of the living realm that resists the imperatives of decay. It does not seek permanence, but facing ruination incites fresh rebellion against entropic forces and becomes the substrate for many new acts of life. Its quest is not to 'solve' Babel and prevent it from collapse but to develop the materials, apparatuses and prototypes that help its diverse communities continually negotiate its persistence.

## 3.3 Babelsphere

If a sense of ongoingness is to be achieved without avoiding the messiness, contradictions and difficulty of inhabiting our contested territories, then Babel, rather than Utopia, embodies the challenges of our times. The goal is not to wilfully submit to the same fate as the historic, technologically advanced city, but like ecosystems which engage with multiple forms of diplomacy that render Babel possible. These collective acts constitute the 'Babelsphere', which constantly negotiates the mutual coexistence of its communities through a series of (unnatural) successions, invasions, withdrawals, seasonal variations, diurnal cycles and even extinction scenarios. The Babelsphere therefore becomes a protocol for the design and engineering of agile, responsive living spaces, which are based on mediation, vibrant materiality (Bennett, 2010), multiple modes of dwelling and ecological principles. However, the attempt to bring the Babelsphere to functionality (Haraway, 2015), does not sanitize the difficulty of rendering complex spaces liveable but generates agile protocols for inhabitation that reclaim our connectedness with each other and the natural realm.

## 3.4 The changing character of nature

Nature embodies the Babelsphere. While the natural realm is precariously held together through its multitudinous relationships, where every moment is negotiated and struggled for, these frictions seldom result in mass extinctions.

Although nature is a universal idea, it is not actually a homogenous construct, nor is it unchanging. The modern view of the living world presents an image of nature that can be controlled, understood and subdued. In an ecological era, the natural realm is lively, agentized and unbridled. The third-millennial understanding of the natural realm is based on a *systems* view of the planet that is governed by change, which is consistent with the ancient philosopher Heraclitus's notion of a world in flux. Ludwig von Bertalanffy modernized this perspective by emphasizing the interactions and connectedness of components that made up individual organisms and ecosystems, through notions of information exchange, methods of control and feedback systems (von Bertalanffy, 1950). In recent times, the natural world has become reduced to and conflated with the idea of ecology. 'Dark ecologist' Timothy Morton observes that nature is mired in aestheticisms, which he urges require deconstruction, so it is possible to see the deep ecology within spaces more clearly, and therefore deal with the 'actual' materiality of a site. Yet, in encouraging the production of 'straightforward environmental images' (Morton, 2007, p. 150) by designing with metabolism, Morton invokes a scientific perspective of nature, where 'ecology' denotes a material condition and objective encounter with matter, the complexity of which is bestowed by its physical relationships. Derived from Ernst Haeckel's notion of animal groups within an environment, the term 'ecology' has evolved over the course of the twentieth century to embrace concepts like Lovelock's Gaia (Lovelock, 1979) and Vladimir Vernadsky's biogeosphere (Vernadsky, 1998), as well as Arthur Tansley's work on 'systems' (Armstrong, 2015, pp. 25–8). So, far from being a pure distillate of the world's spontaneous material processes in action, the idea of ecology is deeply entrenched in minimalist, functionalist, reductionist, puritanical and abstract aesthetics, which characterize modern science.

> The ecological thought ' … is a vast, sprawling mesh of interconnection without a definite center or edge. It is radical intimacy, coexistence with other beings, sentient and otherwise.' (Morton, 2012, p. 1)

However, ecology does not fully equate with nature, which is also culturally and technologically defined (Van Mensvoort and Grievink, 2012). Proposing to maintain impartiality by removing cultural and technological influences is problematic since an ecological ethics is disavowed. While design practices like biomimicry claim to take an 'impartial' view of biology through the selection of particular forms and functions, they largely ignore those aspects of the living realm that are grotesque, or 'red in tooth and claw' (Darwin, 2006). In other words, in an objective reality the blooming of a flower has no more or less significance than say, infanticide, because both are equally 'natural'. Similarly, if Morton's deconstruction of nature is perused as an impartial design proposition, it risks creating devitalized or meaningless spaces, which further compound the progressive cultural estrangements that have led to our present capacity to debase and abuse the environment. Indeed, the 'inhabited' natural realm is inescapably biased and laden with values that are informed by subjective encounters and highly situated ways of inhabiting sites. So, while deconstruction helps identify what is materially at risk, it is equally essential that following analysis, the relationships between humans and non-humans with nature are ethically reconfigured towards mutual (re)empowerment. Indeed, Morton reconstitutes his analysis of nature by invoking a 'dark' ecology, which is inspired by Gothic sensibilities that are suffused with desire, grief, passion and unnaturalness (Morton, 2007, pp. 185–6) and recognizes 'each life-form as a unique being, a temporary manifestation of an indivisible whole' (Morton, 2007, p. 29).

Soft living architecture understands that designing with nature and its biotechnical apparatuses is never impartial and obliges ongoing ethical consideration.

## 3.5 Nature of nature

Nature is not a universal constant. Life and nature are deeply entangled, being semipermeable to each other's inconstancies, feeding upon one another and mutually re-relating through their contingencies. In this unquiet entanglement of constant exchange, the living realm persists along with nature through countless (varied) bodies as an unbroken legacy that spans 3.5 billion years. Even today, many species are unfamiliar or unknown to us, since they are found in extreme habitats such as abyssal black smokers in troglodyte cave complexes, like the Movile Cave in Romania, that have never been exposed to light and in the remotest regions of the world, like the ice-covered Lake Vostok, which has been isolated for 15–25 million years. Indeed, multiple Natures are fundamental to the emergence and persistence of life, and each of these overlapping agencies may conceivably be interdependent forces.

Moreover, nature's repertoire is constantly changing and evades complete encoding by existing classification systems – a phenomenology that can be likened to oceans. Water pools in vast bodies on the surface of the planet where oceans comprise 97 per cent of earth's surface water environments. These massive liquid bodies straddle worlds, being situated between earth's breathable atmosphere and the crust's solid ground. They are so vast and deep that they are opaque to our gaze. Liquid bodies continually rise, undulate, entangle and fall within watery landscapes. To navigate such protean terrains, the Marshall Islanders made stick charts. These were not literal images of the sea but thought apparatuses, whose details were memorized as the chart was constructed. Curved sticks indicated swells around islands; short, straight sticks depicted near-shore currents; longer strips of wood projected the position of islands and small cowrie shells denoted the position of islands themselves. These details were then internalized as a working system by the islanders before they set sail (Romm, 2015). Their survival depended on how they applied their mind maps to interpret the character of the ocean; where to find food and fresh water, or weather devastating events like hurricanes, tidal waves or storms. Indeed, the stick charts suggest that navigating the sea is not a logical task but a sensory skill, which requires an emotional investment to get from one place to another. Transiting the open waves is so great a feat, which may be complicated by so many unknowns, that without the unfailing belief that such daunting journeys are possible, then all is lost before the voyage has even begun.

Stick charts are an example of an apparatus for navigating *oceanic ontologies*, and through priming possibilities within the imagination their increased familiarity conjures forth encounters with hypercomplex phenomena. Like ecosystems and other aspects of the natural realm like weather, oceans intersect with human inhabitation in many ways and although they have facilitated human settlement, they are not reducible to their social uses or simple categories. Indeed, oceans provide 'an ideal spatial foundation ... [that] is indisputably voluminous, stubbornly material, and unmistakably undergoing continual reformation' (Steinberg and Peters, 2015). Oceans, like ecosystems, weather, soils and the Babelsphere, demand their own language and modes of navigation so their vastness and strangeness can be appreciated, not only in their generalities but also through their details.

Such overwhelmingly vast and messy spaces herald the advent of an ecological age of human development – an Ecocene – where the relationship between nature and humanity is reconfigured. In this epoch, nature becomes a (hyper)body and an invisible organizing force that negotiates many difficult relationships between countless species of lively material agents – inorganic agents (Woods, 2012a), biological systems, weather, geological forces, soils, oceans, atmosphere, gravity, light, star systems, black holes, dark matter and energy. This version of nature demands to be engaged and nurtured – not tamed – by ideas about life, society, existence, design, technology, ecology, politics, spiritual belief and culture.

## 3.6 Venetian nature

When you turn the city upside-down, it's nothing like a mirror image of its surface. Like upending a rock that has been sitting in the ground, rather than an off-the-shelf brick, you are likely to recoil at the sudden shock of life, as slimy things slither over its surface. We do not expect our cities to move.

Venice is explored as real and imaginary site for investigating a highly site-specific expression of nature through various design-led experiments, which enable the conception and prototyping of parallel worlds.

The city formally sprang from the muddy shores of its lagoon between the ninth and twelfth centuries. Its settlement has been a complex process, as the soft lagoon silts are unstable and unsuitable as foundation soils. Venetian buildings stay upright owing to a technique of driving 4-metre stakes of alder through the soft sediments and into a denser layer of Ice Age buried soil beneath that of the Venice lagoon. As materials eroded from the Alps were washed down to stabilize in the flatlands, this calcium-rich palaeosol – known locally as *caranto* (stone) – developed across most of northern Italy around 18,000 years ago. Around 10,000 years ago the warm and humid climate led to calcification, with the formation of large nodules of chalk-like minerals that solidified as the soil dried out. When the lagoon was formed, this *caranto* was buried beneath its silts (Donnici et al., 2011). Even though the stone is 4–7 metres below mean sea level and does not provide direct support to the relatively shallow foundation piles in the city, it still has an indirect role in building construction and urbanization, by increasing the structural stability of the ground. Alder is particularly suitable material for use in the lagoon environment, since it grows primarily in swampy areas or by riversides, so its wood does not rot in wet conditions. As long as the piles, or *tolpi*, are fully submerged in salt water they do not decay, since organisms cannot feed upon them without free oxygen. In places like Rialto, larch planks were also laid across the alder piles to bind them together. Such a simple system is remarkably resilient, for if a small amount of the mud is washed away during a bad storm or tide, the piles still transmit all the weight into the deep clay. Above this robust structural system, impermeable Istrian marble slabs are laid down as a watertight layer. However, owing to the expense and availability of these stabilizing approaches, such measures are patchily applied throughout the city. Some places are therefore more susceptible to rising damp and sea-level infiltrations than others.

Since its founding, its citizens have colonized an interstitial realm between the two irreconcilable media of the lagoon – land and sea. In this section, Venice is encountered as a tale of two cities – a millennium-long experiment in inhabitation – where one city allies with the land and occupies the world above the tide, while the other exists below it and extends out into the marine environment.

Each city is unique and exists independently from each other.

The first Venice is situated on the land. It is a museum city and backdrop of ornate architectural 'stones' that characterize its Venetian Gothic style, which combines the Gothic lancet arch with Byzantine and Moorish influences. Believing the city to be in moral decline since the fifteenth century, John Ruskin documented the architectural 'stones', or building details, of Venice, so with the city's demise, they would not be lost to subsequent generations. Today, tourists come in their millions to view the city as a spectacular ruin, as its buildings actively, yet quietly, crumble as a result of the destructive effects caused by the increasingly frequent high tides, or *acqua alta*.

> The idea that St Mark's Basilica will one day become a species of Debussian *cathedrale engloutie*, with coral-encrusted statues and fish swimming across the mosaics and the Pala d'Oro turned into an oyster-bed, is no doubt an alluring one for some. (Windsor, 2015)

The other Venice is a shoreline terrain. It takes the form of a rich ecosystem of active biological agents that are unruly and recalcitrant. This 'living' Venice is a proliferating organic landscape that flourishes at the interfaces between stone, water and air. More than a landscape of ornate veneers and inert stones, it is a natural computer whose subtractive and additive agents are continually (re)making its territories. This paradoxical, parallel settlement is capable of not only resisting the ravages of decay but also thriving upon them.

Venetians do not take their city of contradictions for granted, but continue to work tirelessly to forge relationships between the terrestrial and marine Venice, using the latest technological developments of each epoch. Early Venetians used agrarian land drainage techniques to make soft silts liveable and (re)invented the rules for constructing buildings, where even the foundations of the buildings were expected to move. From these stepping stones, opportunistic bridges sprung like briars between the 124 archipelago islands (Windsor, 2015). Yet, the slippery waters proved treacherous, as flooding events regularly killed its citizens, and so sea walls were built and two major rivers diverted so citizens could survive the relentless incursion of the Po's shifting waters. Today, citizens use modern technology such as the MOSE gates to hold back the most destructive effects of the lagoon's rising waters and their destructive incursion into the city space. In a parallel Venice, the marine environment may synthesize a living technology in the form of an artificial reef, which actively participates in the city's survival (see Section 8.5).

Venice is a prototype habitat of clashing paradigms – a Babelsphere – that remains sensitive to its precarious context, its cultures and technological developments while embodying the spectacle of life. Yet, its continuing evolution is not shaped by any particular form or material performance, but by the passion of those people who love the city enough to continue to live there. They draw us into its enchanted terrains with their many stories that played out within the city's constantly evolving parallel spaces.

> Living Venice produces sounds like a body. It farts, belches, squelches, sighs, breathes, snores, sings and hollers. It is warm to the touch and shockingly biodiverse. In fact, the living stones that spring from this upside-down world could be accused of having 'too much' life. But you don't have to take my word for it; next time you are in Venice, just look for evidence of these processes in the encrustations around the waterways, where the shellfish, biocrete and thrombolites form garlands that mark the tidal zone. Here, you will observe the breathing, bleeding edges of Venice, which have upstaged and upturned the city.

## 3.7 The gluttony of death

An aspect of life and nature that is generally ignored in biodesign practices is death, which, in modern times, equates with failure. Yet, the processes of decay sustain the living realm.

> There is a tendency to decay inherent in materials and systems themselves – an entropy – that no amount of care in design or maintenance can overcome. Buildings will inevitably decay, and there is nothing architects or those charged with a building's upkeep can do about it. So, what is an architect to think or do about it? (Woods, 2012b)

Soft living architecture does not stop at the limits of synthesis but reconnects the realms of life and death in decomposition processes through soils. The composts that enable these linkages are not simple products; they are highly heterogeneous and metabolically active – being neither fully alive nor inert. Such transformational fabrics are selectively permeable to environmental processes. They do not sanitize the processes from which they are formed, nor conceal the grotesqueness of their materiality.

> The ecological thought, the thinking of interconnectedness, has a dark side embodied not in a hippie aesthetic of life over death, or a sadistic sentimental Bambification of sentient beings, but in a 'goth' assertion of the contingent and necessarily queer idea that we want to stay with a dying world: dark ecology. (Morton, 2007, pp. 184–5)

The values of these life-giving materials exceed established conventions of design and invite a robust choreography between synthesis and dissipation, where the process of decay is recognized as a reorganizational system in which adaptation and even (re)embodiment becomes possible.

In Venice, a beach has appeared, as if from nowhere, beside the St Alvise *alilaguna stop*. On disembarking from the ferry, the marine-polished, red-brick shoreline is formed from weathered masonry, plastic bottles, shells and seaweeds that have been swept up by lagoon currents and spat out behind a local football stadium wall. The city's flotsam accumulates here; a doll's head with one eye missing, the leg of a chair, a foam mattress, a rotting pigeon, a wooden crate from a market, a dead fish with its guts missing, rusting cigarette lighters and broken glass bottles. In this paradise for non-humans, microorganisms, zebra mussels, oysters, crabs, gulls and silt feeders, continually (re)organize the terrain bestowing the discarded objects with new value and meaning.

**FIGURE 3.1** *A beach composed from masonry entering the system of currents in the lagoon is mixed together with garbage, conjuring strange and uninhabited land. Drawing courtesy of Rachel Armstrong and Simone Ferracina; S. Alvise, Venice, Italy, September 2015.*

The (re)embodying process associated with decomposition is not pure – a dead pigeon does not become a live pigeon – but is fraught with odd couplings, metabolic opportunism and shocking hybridizations. For example, one organism may be engulfed but incompletely digested by another and still continue to 'live' inside it.

Such gluttonous kinds of (em)bodying resemble the indulgent cuisine of engastrulation – an ostentatious cuisine epitomized by the *rôti sans pareil*: the roast without equal. Invented in the early nineteenth century by Alexandre Balthazar Laurent Grimond de la Reyniere, a man so outlandish he faked his own death to see who would attend his funeral. The *rôti* consists of a bustard stuffed with a turkey, stuffed with a goose, stuffed with a pheasant, stuffed with a chicken, stuffed with a duck, stuffed with a guinea fowl, stuffed with a teal, stuffed with a woodcock, stuffed with a partridge, stuffed with a plover, stuffed with a lapwing, stuffed with a quail, stuffed with a thrush, stuffed with a lark, stuffed with an ortolan bunting, stuffed with a garden warbler, stuffed with an olive, stuffed with an anchovy, stuffed with a single caper, stuffed with layers of Lucca chestnuts, force meat and bread stuffing between each bird. The entire *rôti* was then stewed in a hermetically sealed pot in a bath of onions, cloves, carrots, chopped ham, celery, thyme, parsley, mignonette, salted pork fat, salt, pepper, coriander, garlic, and 'other spices' and slowly cooked over a fire for a whole day (Durack, 2007, p. 419).

By infusing living networks with the webs of death, our capacity to appreciate the value (material and social) of compost begins to emerge in the rituals of eating, mourning, interment and burial, which take place at different points along the continuum between life and death. In Western civilizations, life and death are habitually regarded as binary states of existence, yet we invent names that depict significant slippages in their embodying (e.g. fertilization, embryogenesis, ageing, senescence) and decomposing processes (e.g. autolysis, putrefaction). Language also contradicts assumptions where sporulation refers to a death-like phase of life and decomposition invokes the active dead. Yet, such semantics are not trivial; confusion over the status of a body's liveliness may lead to abnegation of status, with a loss of value and, therefore, may be subject to oppression.

> Death is a two-stage process, and where you wake up after your last breath is something of a Purgatory: you don't feel dead, you don't look dead, and in fact you are not dead. Yet ... You are losing you but you don't seem to care ... The scattered bits of you are collected, pooled and unified. The mirrors are held up in front of you. Without the benefit of filtration, you see yourself clearly for the first time. And that is what finally kills you. (Eagleman, 2009, pp. 43–4)

## 3.8 Breaking up

Life is not a singular phenomenon. It depends on the actions of many bodies – living and dead. The reordering of matter takes place in ecosystems where organic matter is assimilated into metabolic networks of exchange that enable life's persistence.

Once, the fish, crustaceans, giant pen shells (Pinna nobilis), dustbin-lid jellyfish (Rhizostoma octopus) and rare coral polyps swarmed along the mile-long rock and 23,000 tonne concrete foundations of the MOSE gates. Here, they flourished, thriving on the 'perfect storm' of light, rich organic matter and warming waters, which were more typical of conditions in the southern Mediterranean or Red Sea.

Then, one grey November day, the colossal barrier was activated for the first time. The smart robotic gates stirred like sunken ships, their sensors measuring wind, water level, waves, pressure data and body slammed the sea for several hours, until the tides receded. Miles away, their remote brains performed real-time mathematical calculations from a control centre in a converted chapel in the Arsenale, which used the data to predict the lagoon's tidal movements five days hence and so, anticipate the likelihood of further flooding events. Each day, the swollen tides pushed again and again at the iron defences and, dripping with silt, established reefs on the concrete supports were torn and communities displaced – little more than collateral damage in the fight against the rising waters.

That same year, the flooding persisted and, so, the colossal gates wrestled with the swells. Each time, the turbulence and churning currents lasted longer, causing instabilities within the reef and only the most tenacious species could persist. So, the exiled creatures relinquished their homes and moved from one wall to another, as hyperlocally invasive species. Unwelcome.

Attraction, adoration, comfort, irritation, contempt, trauma, sadness and distancing: these cycles keep us together and draw us apart again – yet, not all breakups are the same.

## 3.9 Design and death

Death's processes actively promote the flourishing of metabolizing communities that thrive in composts such as the thanatobiome (Methé, 2012) and necrobiome associated with corpses, which are distinct but overlapping ecosystems that return deanimated matter into the webs of life.

> The disintegration introduced to an object by rotting processes is not a regular disintegration as of separation into component parts, fragments or constitutive atoms. Decay is a non-fragmentary disintegration in which everything remains connected to the decaying entity. Continuity is preserved in the absence of consolidated dimensions and coherent measurement. Consequently, the disintegrative process of decay expresses the logic of terminal softness (or goo) where continuity is the result of wasteful bonds and the impossibility of rejecting such bonds. Integration too, is impossible because scales and dimensions no longer maintain the capacity of their formative powers. Decay creates a mucoid continuity in disintegration. (Negarestani, 2008, p. 187)

These communities are not faithful to the anatomical boundaries of their symbioses and hosts.

> My 'own' body is material, and yet this vital materiality is not fully or exclusively human. My flesh is populated and constituted by different swarms of foreigners ... the bacteria in the human microbiome collectively possess at least 100 times as many genes as the mere 20,000 or so in the human genome ... we are, rather, an array of bodies, many different kinds of them in a nested set of microbiomes. (Bennett, 2010, pp. 112–13)

The networks of metabolic death are decadent and the happy mutual state of affairs that characterizes the beneficial relationship between human and microbiome completely changes, as the deceased loses control over its immune surveillance system. Once the circulation collapses, the vigilant white cells that slip between cells to ensure that all agents in the ecosystem of the human body are working towards a common goal – mutual survival – no longer effectively patrol the gut wall. Now, there is nothing to stop the bacteria indulging themselves on a nutrient-rich feast of succulent flesh and run amok, unabated, in every organ. These festivities compel other bacteria to join them in feasting and procreative revelry. Indeed, replication and consumption are so tightly linked within rapidly proliferating bacterial communities, eating and replicating become confused – one and the same. The corpse is desecrated from the inside out, as destructive chemical cocktails leak out of damaged cells and further digest the tissues as a ready-made food source for the thanatobiome. With no significant diplomatic force to civilize their appetites, the depths of bacterial desire become unshackled and the entire assimilation of the devitalized body is inevitable.

> There are three deaths. The first is when the body ceases to function. The second is when the body is consigned to the grave. The third is that moment, sometime in the future, when your name is spoken for the last time. (Eagleman, 2009, p. 23)

## 3.10 Urban (Terra)toma

In modern cities, decomposition is associated with disease and is banished to controlled environments such as waste disposal systems and sewers. In medieval cities household waste went directly into the street, or as in the case of Venice, the canals. These primordial soups are parallel spaces with the potential for ritualized forms of waste disposal and decay that may spawn alternative and surprising lifeforms.

The cofferdams slam up against the hundred-metre rio section, isolating it from the rest of the liquid highway. Wide bored drainage nozzles, as big as your head, slurp its contents dry like giant leeches, leaving behind a slate-grey layer of sludge – diagnostic of decades of urban constipation. Yesterday, it was almost an alleyway where only fifteen inches of water sloshed over six feet of mud; the kind of place where creatures might die and wake up as fossils – given a few hundred million years.

At the dredging site, a dainty dragline scrapes carefully at the slurry, scooping it like soup from a formal dinner table. It tips the muck into a wheeled vehicle with a tilting hopper that moves back and forth on temporary rails, spooning them into a barge. And so, the etiquette continues, serving the toxic brew into the belly of a chain of vessels, until it's time for shovels to remove whatever the dragline can't handle.

The exhumation begins down past the foot of the chewed marble doorways and way under the dried slime steps of the buildings, where muscled spades sift the dirt like ragworms, indistinguishable from the stuff. Under masked sighs, they hold their breath while performing the autopsy. Guts are spilt where the fragile bones of ancient pilings and sinews of public utilities that trail in the slop are damaged during repairs conducted on the digested building foundations and gatoli.

Deep in the reticula, between the gaps of the foundational stones, an urban (terra)toma glares under its sudden exposure to flesh-eating light. Yes, terra-toma, an organized tumour made of earth that produces cites within cities. Like its corporeal counterpart, it is a tiny, yet deranged version of a body with no obvious internal logic. So, while its structures are remarkably familiar, the formal architectural relationships are lacking. In this particular specimen, the building details date from the fourteenth century and include doorways, rooftops, stairs, window frames and bracketed pillars, which look like teeth, or hair. On further inspection, cystic doors generally appear to be located on the upper floors, dense rooftops accumulate along the side of waterways, dermoid windows are hopelessly tilted within a forest of pillars, and a cluster of stairwells seems to go nowhere. Yet, this place is home to anaerobic organisms that go about their daily life without concepts like ground or elevation. So, they open up shutters into moorings, hang out their biofilms from balconies yelling at others to get together in quora across rooftops, and seem to live their entire existence on stairwells. Highly illogical; but if you strike up a conversation with them, they'll tell you that certain areas are simply inaccessible, so it makes sense to ignore them.

At some point, somebody decides to clean up the mess and the toxic slurry is finally condemned to a treatment plant, before it is formally laid to rest as the island foundations of San Michele.

## 3.11 Insurrection and death

The recalcitrant matter that characterizes the metabolic networks of death does not work to appease polite sensibilities or pursue ideals, but draws together the processes of death, dying, decay, composting and putrefaction. As they find new contexts and modes of organization within the living realm, they become substrates for the synthesis of monsters, angels and hybrids.

Such ruptures in continuity and embodiment are the bedrock of evolution.

The active processes of death are responsible for the subversive quality of soft living architecture. They account for its deeply animating character and capacity to invent ways for supporting the emergence of life. Even the 'failure' of an organism may be restored through the decay process and provide another opportunity for attaining liveliness. The extreme mixology of decomposition provokes difficult decisions, which enable life to persist in the most extreme environments and under the most precarious of circumstances. Soft living architecture tolerates a broad range of tactics, programmes and values, even when some of these belief systems are at odds with each other.

> For decay, softening and disintegration coincide, as formation is taken over by poromechanics. In poromechanical events, the hard exists through the soft. Decay's line of initiation corresponds to that of chemistry, from the inside to the outside, from hard and rigidly connected components to soft parts. Chemistry starts from within, but its existence is registered on the surface; ontology is, so to speak, merely a superficial symptom of chemistry. Decay extorts softness from the hard, making the hard and infested factory for breeding a softness, which again is anonymous even to the formlessness of matter. The softness of decay is précised a production of its irony. (Negarestani, 2008, p. 187).

Within this messy set of competing interests, not every outcome perpetuates the unbroken legacy of life. Some protocols result in extreme transformations like maggot migrations or strip organic sites of their richness, owing to the metabolic vigour of composting processes. While there is no guarantee of happy endings, an active engagement with the processes of death is fundamental to the organic world. Many acts of recovery are promoted during the composting process where, with every iteration of life and death, parallel trajectories of life become possible, which are most significant in the wake of tragedy and disaster, as they demand particular values to be prioritized. In response to the detritus of our present ecocide, soft living architecture does not seek to homogenize responses, ease pain or ameliorate difficulties – rather, it negotiates parallel worlds to establish new forms of (material) diplomacy and peacemaking.

## 3.12 Sewage

While life's earliest secrets may have been violently spawned in abyssal geothermal vents, in a parallel realm the most potent sites of material transformation reside in sewers that generate odd lifeforms with the capacity to infect us.

> I lost my sense of smell somewhere around 'here'. Careless of me. It must be stuck down one of the gatoli.
>
> A stick tangled in a clot of scum beckons as a probe, so I roll up my sleeve and fish it out from its plasma.
>
> Three boys eating ice cream, trailing behind their nanny in the full throes of curmudgilingus – complaining for the sake of complaining – snigger at me face down on the sidewalk, staring into the sediment rich waters like Narcissus. I don't care. I have to get it back.
>
> As I fish around in the accumulating slop, I remind myself that Venice was once one of Europe's cleanest cities. While other townsfolk flung their waste into busy narrow streets, the tides here swept residential muck out to sea twice a day. Ingeniously, Venetians even developed the fognatura, a unique gravity-driven waste and rainwater drainage system, which flows through a meshwork of gatoli under these walkways.
>
> I change position like a lodestone, sniffing visibly, but still sense nothing.
>
> I last saw it, cephalopod-like, writhing happily around a bakery doorway, slobbering over the prospect of an almond croissant. I denied it, but only temporarily, as it's gluttonous and mightily canny.
>
> I inhale deeply again, just to establish whether I am in a salubrious place. Nowadays, around 140 small biological waste-processing plants are

installed throughout the city and over 6,000 septic tanks, but they are not evenly distributed, and the antiquated patchwork circulation doesn't meet the city's excretory needs.

I am unsure if there's a reek, and call politely out to a couple of tourists reading a map, inquiring about stench, but they ignore me. Exasperated, I make my way to a green dustbin exploding with flies and use my probe to divine something pungent to use as bait. Camembert. What on earth is that doing in the trash? Irresistible.

I thread the liquid cheese on the end of my probe and prod at the brickwork. A cloud of fish fry swarm around the bait, but it's not for them. I stir the water to shoo them away.

Masonry fragments loosened by sediment crumble onto the Camembert, I have to work quickly, or this gatoli outlet may burst under the strain of noxious filth.

Then I see it. Waving its purple tentacles happily sucker side up, pulsing its way towards the cheese. Quickly I grab it and with dripping sleeve, snort it up.

This place stinks.

# 4

# Synthesis: Entangled Materials, Tools and Methods

This chapter introduces specific concepts and apparatuses used in prototyping soft living architecture. It invites an expanded toolset for inventing parallel modes of making and inhabiting spaces, which includes (hyper)complex fabrics like soils and alternative (analogue) forms of computing.

## 4.1 Nature as technology

> Buildings are inorganic and inanimate. Yet they are routinely said to function like living organisms. Architecture deploys a range of metaphorical conventions to invest buildings with life ... There are even those who think buildings have a kind of agency, or at the very least a capacity to adapt to changing circumstances through time. (Cairns and Jacobs, 2014, p. 11)

Designing and engineering with natural systems at architectural, urban and potentially planetary scales require a broader portfolio of tools than industrial technologies alone (Morris, 2016). The challenge with the production of the material expressions that produce soft living architecture (see Section 2.2) is not a question of life versus machine, where one set of causes and effects is pitched against the other, but rather a synthesis between multiple operating systems – such as the made and the born (Kelly, 2010) – that can work synergistically to prototype new forms of making.

An alternative worldview to modern (industrial) society seems almost impossible to imagine. New forms of industrial revolution, which are based on alternative energy generation and distributed forms of production, continue to embrace the fundamental principles of resource consumption and do not alter the models that underpin economic prosperity (Rifkin, 2013). In fact, if energy becomes freely available to everyone, the present 'energy' crisis would become a war against matter, where the availability of substrates to feed these carnivorous processes would be perceived as the bottleneck for unlimited consumption – and we would not be able to eat our world fast enough.

Our present institutions and infrastructures are no longer fit for purpose for the advent of an Ecocene. Social, political and economic systems that once symbolized justice, order and wealth are dissociated from the material realm, and we are left as little more than bystanders as nightmarish scenarios that have been precipitated by the Anthropocene unfold around us. Yet, stubborn weeds of revolt that exceed the hierarchical systems of industrialization and corporatism are spilling into unruly spaces and establishing themselves as nascent platforms for a new kind of economic, cultural and social synthesis. For example, the blockchain, a sophisticated, cryptographically secure distributed ledger that coordinates millions of events on millions of disparate computers through a shared database, is generating an infrastructure for new forms of order. Its 'Internet of value' enables transgressions across established boundaries (TEDx Lausanne, 2016) that are unconstrained by modern binaries of geography, politics, economics, identity or discipline; so, parallel modes of existence become possible. The clear either/or distinctions that formerly shaped our experiences are being replaced by a much more fluid and transitional relationship with reality, while having more influence. Emerging developments include smart contracts for architects so they may gain back more influence, while at the same time simplifying the relationship between stakeholders. Soft living architecture experiments with alternative forms of making, social structures, trading agreements, types of colonization, expressions of identity and technical platforms that enable parallel modes of architecture and associated ways of inhabiting these spaces – even if they ultimately fail. While change is always associated with the risk of failure, should these forms of practice succeed, then the emergent systems that arise from these explorations could offer an exciting, convergent, complex worldview where the Babelsphere may begin to exist – first as relationships, then as investments through which communities may flourish. This inclusive, experimental, ecological view of the world is made up of alternative streams of resources and many disparate interacting bodies that are invested in mutual development and realizing the Babelsphere (DeLanda, 2002, p. 26).

While the advent of the Internet and blockchain communities enable cultural transgression, biotechnological developments create the possibility of alternative material cultures with different environmental impacts than industrial practices. Their design and engineering processes extend into the realms of the inner workings of organisms but their reach does not stop at the limits of natural systems. Molecular biology and complex chemistries –

such as protocells, dynamic droplets and cell-free synthetic biology systems – are also conferred with lifelike agency that may catalyse the production of soft living architectures by working in concert with the metabolic exchanges that characterize the natural world. Indeed, an origin of life transition within the built environment – the transition towards living matter – may even be possible. Currently, tar and concrete deserts form the ground of modern cities and are inherently hostile to living systems. These deserts could be replaced by vibrant communities of soil-like bodies. Transplanting or seeding extensive metabolic networks into urban environments could increase planetary fertility, inviting the natural realm to inhabit even the most extreme environments. Like the rich reticular systems of mother trees (Howard, 2011), these unruly forms of soft living matter may be likened to the hybrid root systems of arboreal networks, where communities of highly heterogeneous agents such as fungal mycorrhiza, worms and nitrogen-fixing bacteria establish cooperative modes of existence that nurture and enable 'life'. These vitalizing choreographies extend beyond the care of any single species and build capacity into the environment through increasing the fertility of spaces, supporting biodiverse communities.

The prototyping of soft living architectures, materials, cultures and methods will necessarily exceed the limits of scientific protocols; so, outcomes will provoke the existence of parallel worlds that ultimately increase the vitality, diversity and understanding of our environments and living spaces.

## 4.2 Modes of computation

> This image of a revolving wheel is a picture of our world. In it, the dramatic interplay of object and network becomes visible. Countless entities circle into and out of our lives, some of them threatening and others ludicrous. The objects in the cars and those on the ground or in the chambers affect one another, coupling and uncoupling from countless relations – seducing, ignoring, ruining or liberating each other. This process is anything but a game: in it, our happiness and even physical safety are at stake. (Harman, 2010, pp. 4–5)

Computation is fundamental to our species. It is a mode of thinking and practice that enables us to sort and order the world, so that values may be established and new knowledge acquired. Appropriate forms of computation are necessary for the development of soft living architectures so they embody and express fundamental ethics and approaches that locate the practice within a philosophy and vision of the world.

Digital computation is a modern invention that underpins global society, which is based on symbolic languages and a deterministic worldview. Its calculations occur within an invisible landscape of massless electrons that are encoded into patterns of ones and zeroes ('bits'). These are further grouped into 'bytes' and moved around into different physical storage areas within a central processing unit according to a set of instructions, or algorithm. When compiled, they can collectively perform specific 'applications' or 'apps' that bring functionality to electronic gadgets (Epstein, 2016). Although the digital realm is a platform for universal computing, it nonetheless presents a polarized view of reality that recognizes only one way of viewing, ordering and sorting the world – a realm of parts identified and classified through the Enlightenment's Great Dissections.

It is much easier to understand life through its 'lack', which is how the phenomenon has largely been (scientifically) understood – rather than comprehend the miracle of its genesis through its passions. Through simple subtractions, deficits identify that which enables liveliness. Let us remove the heart, the brain, the entrails, the head, the limbs, the eye, the genes and the soul and watch an exquisite choreography of unfathomably complex exchanges fall. There! Like a mediaeval Trial by Ordeal, these insufficiencies are formal proof there was once a living thing. Since this essence can be isolated and obliterated, it is now understood. What beautiful poisons balance these theories, which ultimately conclude the nature of being is bounded by a fat 'full stop'.

Since number theory underpins the development of mathematical knowledge, equations stand in for the parts of living things. However, there are more forms of symbolic computation such as Qualitative Computing, with an expanded portfolio of representation. This unconventional form of computing is underpinned by irrational numbers, which are incompletely divisible and therefore pertain to infinity, which Françoise Chatelin observes is more like life than the finitude of rational numbers (Chatelin, 2012). In this way, what, why and how we compute remain contestable. Ignoring the range of possibilities in computation restricts our capacity to invent and adapt to changing circumstances. While digital processes have largely replaced analogue modes of computation in the industrial era, David Deutsch reminds us that only the material world can compute and *all* other forms of computation in physics and mathematics are abstractions (Deutsch, 2012).

Although Nature computes much more slowly than digital platforms, its agents are not symbolic but made of lively matter. They possess mass, can respond to changes in their internal state or surroundings and therefore may behave in surprising ways, which can be observed, characterized and tested by modern physics and chemistry. Nature is capable of 'counting' events through its many material iterations that perform the role of numbers: an orbital pathway, a pulse, an oscillation, a blink, a footstep, a bowel contraction, the tide and the rain. These events are not exact, self-similar, regular or universal, but persistent. They are nature's 'beats' – the living realm's numerical-equivalent system – which is nothing like numbers at all. As Henri Lefebvre notes,

> The departure point for this history of space is not to be found in the geographical descriptions of natural space, but rather in the study of natural rhythms, and of the modification of those rhythms and their inscription in space by means of human actions, especially work-related actions. It begins, then, with the spatio-temporal rhythms of nature as transformed by a social practice. (Lefevbre, 1991, p. 117)

Examples of natural computers (see Section 4.2.2) that can be used experimentally are oscillating systems like the Belousov–Zhabotinsky reaction (Belousov, 1959; Zhabotinsky, 1964) and the pulsatile connecting tubes of slime mould colonies (Adamatzky et al., 2013), which can be clearly observed at the macroscale. The next level of organization upwards for the outputs of natural computing is in the formation of patterns, which reveal something about the conditions of their production, as in meteorological predictions. However, persistent or recursive patterns may also act as generative processes and hubs of activity that provide a basis for prediction, although they are probabilistic structures and not absolute indicators for events.

## *4.2.1 Computing with humans*

In 1822, Charles Babbage's (decimal) difference engine aimed to automate and standardize calculations that were prone to human error by 'computers' that were people employed to make complex numeric calculations using logarithmic tables. This project was abandoned owing to cost of the complex mechanics necessary to build the machine, but with the advent of electronics and applications of Gottfried Wilhelm von Leibniz's binary code, the technical difficulties that bedevilled mechanisms for computing became soluble with von Neumann information architecture and Turing machines. This platform gave rise to today's digital computers.

In the Ecocene, where the living world is in constant flux, the standard reference points that have calibrated the industrial era are in question. When faced with such uncertainty, our senses and previous experiences become avatars in navigating these protean spaces. Indeed, when challenges are sufficiently complex – such as establishing whether an agent is truly 'intelligent' or not – then comparative (subjective) encounters provide sufficient information to allow (imperfect) decision-making, a tactic that Alan Turing exploited in his *imitation game*. However, if we are to open up unchartered territories and occupy them differently, then there is little point calibrating these unfamiliar terrains through the experiences of conventional bodies, since their senses and physicality are constrained by tradition. Rather, extraordinary sensibilities and radical physicality are required to interrogate alternative modes of thinking, making and inhabiting spaces.

The circus arts challenge the conventions of (em)bodying ourselves, since they deal with the currency of exceptions and the exceptional – muscular women, superbodies, andryogynes, precocious juveniles, mutable deviants, multi- and even interspecies chimeras. Here, gender identity is functionally, aesthetically and socially ambiguous; and traditional notions of collectives challenge ideas about family, biological categories, social organization, labour, economics and politics. Indeed, circus bodies are kith and kin bound in a community of trust, engaged in countless acts of mutual survival.

> They knitted nets from vegetable strands and launched them so they would challenge the very limits of the sky. They travelled with the ascending fibres and just as they reached the apex of their climb in those moments before they would fall, they riveted them to the tarry lid. Feeling the full weight of impossibility, tears leaked from their eyes, noses congested and their hearts crushed. Secretly they wondered how long it would be before they breathed their last but steeled by radical love for each other, a few of them built cutlery from their disarticulated sky scaffold and organized a last supper, a communal breaking of sky-bread as a dignified farewell to one and all. 'Bon appetit', they said as they plunged their knives and sporks into the approaching miserable matter under which they'd soon choke and began to chew. And so, they ate their way through the upper limits of their world and flopped like newly evolved beasts into a strange terrain for which they were ill-equipped. They squinted into the space above them without the words to describe what their senses beheld. With unlimited freedom to invent, they began to construct new ambitions, new practices and a parallel space to thrive in.

Circus knowledge resides within the body, which generates a messier and subjective understanding of the world than rational faculties, but one in which values, ethics and subjective experiences are deeply embedded (Hughes, 2016c). As canvases for the corporeal desires and anxieties of society, circus bodies are more than a spectacle and ongoing expression of life's events; they offer a radical potential to reinvent and reassess the conditions of existence, embracing all dimensions of life – physical, social, biological, astronomical, cultural and philosophical. Transforming these tropes into radical expressions of embodiment, notions of community and modes of inhabitation, circus bodies (re)present more than a mirror of ourselves, but spellbind and mock us in a parallel critique of our limits and expectations. Artists may speak of the bones, the sinews, the heart, or even other kinds of places where their modes of knowing reside. Using a whole range of unique instruments, apparatuses, materials and techniques to explore bodily ideas, such as the hoop, trapeze, wobble board, devil sticks, unicycle, rola bola, German wheel, stilts, freestanding ladder, horizontal bar, slackwire, tight wire and pyrotechnics, circus practices are prone to exploring more than one concept or skill set at a time – for example, juggling while balancing – and therefore embrace accidents, so that unlikely occasions may be drawn together. Circus defamiliarizes us from the simplifications that accompany our dominant modes of thinking, which appear to be strangling the contradictions and richness from our present reality. It reminds us most poignantly of what is truly at stake.

## *4.2.2 Natural computing*

Alan Turing's interest in the technological potential of the natural world inspired the term *natural computing*, which currently consists of a range of overlapping scientific practices that are interpreted by different disciplines, namely as morphological and unconventional computing. Morphological computing is a form of natural computing that arises from the field of robotics and engineering. It has begun to exploit the shape and non-linear properties of materials to improve the efficiency of a computation (Pfeifer and Iida, 2005; Füchslin et al., 2013). Unconventional computing is a branch of information technology that aims to enrich or go beyond the standard models of computing, such as the Turing machine and von Neumann architectures, which have dominated computer science for more than half a century (Adamatzky et al., 2007). These alternative computing systems are providing fresh insights into how materials at far-from-equilibrium states make decisions, as in soft robotics (Shepherd et al., 2013), slime mould computing (Adamatzky et al., 2013) and reaction diffraction computing (Adamatzky and De Lacy Costello, 2003).

Natural computing draws on the agency of lively matter to create a convergent platform for different kinds of analogue programming. It can organize interfaces between the physical and informational realm like logic gates (Adamatzky and De Lacy Costello, 2002) or inform digital modelling practices (Zhang, Györgyi and Peltier, 1993) without reducing or abstracting lifelike structures. When natural computing techniques are applied through soft living architecture, they may alter the character of our living spaces.

## *4.2.3 Dissipative structures*

Living matter, while not eluding the 'laws of physics' as established up to date, is likely to involve 'other laws of physics' hitherto unknown, which however, once they have been revealed, will form just as integral a part of science as the former. (Schrödinger, 1944)

Dissipative systems (or structures) are forged from a paradoxical condition that gives rise to the operative agents of natural computation. They spontaneously arise as manifestations of structure and flow from the tensions between overlapping fields of energy/matter such as convection currents, turbulent flow, aperiodic crystals, cyclones, hurricanes and living organisms. Dissipative structures are inconstant yet characterful agents that can undergo local and systemic complexification and possess reproducible features, patterns or persistent oscillations. These familiar details enable us to understand them and make predictions about how they are likely to perform – although, it is never possible to fully predict them as they are highly sensitive to their context. Their trajectories are 'computed' through countless local material interactions, rather than being internally driven random sets of events. Perhaps the best way to imagine a dissipative structure is to think of the lifecycle of a tornado, which is produced by the collision between fields of hot and cold air. The resultant vortex, or 'twister', is a highly dynamic structure that generates a characteristic set of behaviours, through which it may be recognized and predicted. Yet, no two tornadoes are exactly alike and no vortex is exactly the same body from moment to moment. Like all dissipative structures, a tornado exists beyond its object-boundaries through active fields of matter and energy emanating from its body, so that it is possible for an observer to feel the presence of a tornado in its winds long before they reach the eye of the storm.

Dissipative systems can also self-organize into more complex structural arrangements, geometries or oscillators that are also iterative apparatuses – or 'natural' counting systems. These can be ordered to generate a range of programmable outputs whose movements and molecular 'calculations' produce field disturbances. Reaction–diffusion waves are examples of these systems, which loosely couple bodies together that pattern their environment or cancel each other out. While active fields are present, the system never truly collapses to a zero state. Such processes can be visualized through time-based material systems such as the Belousov–Zhabotinsky reaction and have also been called 'reaction–diffusion' computers (Adamatzky et al., 2005). Dissipative structures therefore tend to seed the conditions for next iterations of self-similar – but not identical – phenomena, until relative thermodynamic equilibrium is reached.

While not all dissipative systems meet the technical qualifications of 'life', all 'life' is a dissipative process. Over time and in the right contexts, they increase the probability of lifelike events taking place within their constituent fields. Indeed, dissipative structures are associated with a unique theory of structural change: dissipative adaptation (Wolchover, 2014), where, in an open environment, matter at far-from-equilibrium states self-organizes into increasingly more ordered arrangements and becomes increasingly more efficient at releasing energy into its surroundings. In other words, dissipative structures can dynamically alter their organizational programme without need for any centralized code. These operations are not self-contained but fundamentally open and may be shaped by 'soft' forms of control, which are already culturally known to us as everyday practices that range from cooking, gardening and agriculture to working with small children, herding cats or choreographing the production of soft living architecture.

Dissipative structures are more than a model visualization system for paradoxical, hypercomplex entities. They can also be technically engaged, with the potential to shape an ecological era of design practice. Such substances sound mysterious, but some of their material expressions can be recognized in everyday materials such as soils – the fabrics on which all terrestrial life is founded.

## *4.2.4 Consciousness and living materials*

Notions of non-human agency raise questions about where intention and decision in computational processes reside, as well as the nature and location of 'consciousness' or 'mind' in these systems. Given that the entirety of Western philosophy is invested in the idea of a single, central notion of agency, which is located in a particular organ recognized as the 'brain', it is challenging to imagine persuasive counterpoints to these established perspectives. However, in the Ecocene, lively materials are distributed – contingent and highly sensitive to contexts – which create the potential for different kinds of mind/agency/consciousness/decision-making.

As our understanding of molecular processes evolves, a broader set of ideas that meaningfully alter the natural course of events is needed, which do not rely on central command systems to account for all decisions. Since agentized matter emanates from hypercomplex and dynamic systems, their processes are likely to remain incompletely understood, however much we interrogate them. This should not deter us from attempting to explore the possibilities, but in doing so should develop additional tactics that can deal with unknowns or incompletely understood phenomena, such as dissipative structures (see Section 4.2.3). By experimenting with alternative perspectives on the nature of life that deal with probability, change and incompleteness, it may be possible to better appreciate how spaces are haunted by bodies.

### 4.2.4.1 Chemical consciousness

In a parallel world observed through a microscope, (prebiotic) forms of existence emerge from fields of entangled chemical conversations. Each body is shaped by a field of interiority that interacts with a field of exteriority, which spawns dissipative structures that carry the seeds of sensibility. Leaving residues that shape the next set of metabolic decisions through the presence of inhibitors (waste products), facilitators (catalysts) or physical obstacles (crystal skins), these droplets produce structured landscapes of exchange (tissues, organs, other bodies). Their chemical trails become a kind of short-term memory that is not encoded within the body but is 'remembered' in its immediate environment. If the actions are repeated, they may be laid down as long-term archives, or persistent structures. Gradually, such memories are eroded through a host of physical events such as diffusion, or active metabolisms where waste matter from one body becomes the 'food' source for another. These restless encounters are uniquely marked with the traces of their encounters, which participate in their decision-making processes (conscious, subconscious, reflex) and continually respond to these physical environments, until they collapse into functional death. Herein lies the challenge. Since the primary operations of a conscious system are partial, then objective evaluations ignore the fundamentally biased nature of mind and are inevitably distorted by the assessor's agendas. Establishing whether a system is conscious or not is a value judgment. The ontology of mind is not neutral.

> Each of us has the indisputable impression that the sum total of his own experience and memory forms a unit, quite distinct from that of any other person. He refers to it as 'I' and what is this 'I'? If you analyse it closely … the facts [*are*] little more than a collection of single data (experiences and memories), namely the canvas upon which they are collected. (Schrödinger, 1944)

### 4.2.4.2 Locating consciousness

Soft living architecture's sensibility is not an ephemeral quality, channelled spirit or divine influence. It is manifest through material relations, which are extended into terrains beyond the reach of traditional boundaries. These sensibilities may be identified through secondary phenomena such as movement in response to a stimulus, requiring specific ideas, languages, images and modes of expression (see Section 2.4) to articulate their meaning. Such exchanges may be very simple, or highly convoluted. Sometimes recognizable patterns appear that become familiar and allied with particular states of existence. For example, Bütschli droplets may be observed osculating, extruding root-like *osmotic structures* or billowing in travelling fronts of 'fire and ice', which indicate particular stages of the droplet lifespan (Armstrong, 2015, pp. 87–103). Although they do not have an organized central processing system, dynamic droplets nonetheless possess sensibility (feeling) as they respond to their environment, and their complex interactions with other droplets suggest that sentience (awareness) arises from molecular decision-making.

Decision-making in systems without a central nervous system can also be observed in slime mould colonies in their feeding stage, which adopt the form of a gel body or plasmodium (a single giant cell with many nuclei). The colony responds to cues in its environment that are relayed through a network of biochemical oscillators, which are distributed throughout the collective body (Matsumoto, Ueda and Kobatake, 1998). Using Mihaly Csikszentmihalyi's criteria as an evaluation system, creativity rather than mind is explored which 'arises from the synergy of many sources and not only from the mind of a single person' (Csikszentmihalyi, 2013, p. 1). Observable criteria are evaluated as a spatial system with physical outcomes and are defined in relationship to 'risk-taking' tasks, as the deliberate (but not rational) interactions between chemical processes (agents) (Adamatzky et al., 2013). The outcomes of these exchanges shape a grammar of chemical and spatial languages based on the metabolic networks that underpin the flow of information and 'meaning' within the plasmodium. In response to its interpretation of environmental events, the slime mould extends and retracts strands of cytoplasm. The idea that such a brainless entity could make decisions by externalizing its agency challenges Cartesian notions of mind, which privileges interiorized, ephemeral agents as the source of intellect. Yet, the non-human world is not 'dumb' but differently engaged with its contexts that are shaped by implicit non-human criteria. Indeed, the modes of existence and perceptual encounters of non-classical bodies may be so alien to our understanding they cause us to marvel, or be repulsed by them.

Mrs. Harris discovered the 'blob' one morning earlier this month when she looked out her bedroom window. 'It was white and foamy looking – about the size of an oatmeal cookie,' she said. 'But that was two weeks ago. It has now grown to the size of 16 oatmeal cookies and cannot be destroyed.' ... Despite her attempts to kill it, the blob remains in the Harris backyard. 'I sliced the thing with a garden hoe and it was blackish mucus inside.' ... 'taking it for a fungus of some kind, I cut it up and spread it out. Two mornings later it had returned – twice as big this time.' ... Mrs. Harris said that her husband then took a whack at the 'blob' but 'Then last Saturday there it was, this time the inside was orange.' Last Monday the 'blob' appeared again, 'Big as a platter – foamy and creamy and pale yellow.' Mrs. Harris sprayed it with a nicotine-based mixture and 'It appeared to be bleeding red and purple fluids.' The spray appears to be restraining – but not killing – the 'blob'. Arnold Dittman, a member of the waste-recycling firm, Growth International, said that his preliminary examination showed the membranous material to be a harmless bacteria-like substance. Mr. Dittman picked up samples of the growth but he specimens died. 'We haven't been able to revive them. We're trying to produce the same effect that Mrs. Harris has in her yard. You never know, but this appears to be nothing more than a mutation of common ordinary bacteria or fungi, or a combination thereof.' (Reuter, 1973)

The externalized mind is a hyperobject and system of material flow that activates networks of ongoing chemical conversation, which interrelates the community of life. Stable oscillations within these networks may even linger as phantom traces, long after their original author has gone.

> Ghosts are ecological imprints. Owing to trauma, distress or because of their forceful character, their metabolic networks are severed in an untimely manner and keep operating as if the body itself was still present. They continue to produce existential eddies that continue after their passing. However, not everyone can see these persistent connections and interactions. Only those that share those metabolic or experiential networks that bind them to the same reality may encounter them. These beings are not fictions, or vivid imaginings; they are real but not fully material. It is not known how long these energized fields persist. Some last indefinitely.

Soft living architecture is not a passive shell, or barrier behind which to hide the inhabitation of space. Through lived experiences between many lively bodies, it changes the nature of encounters with the environment. As an expression of 'mind' or natural computing (from which consciousness is inseparable), it actively participates in the haunting of spaces and site-specific production of memories.

## 4.3 Softness

The naturalist will feel this astonishment more deeply after having examined the soft and almost gelatinous bodies of these apparently insignificant creatures, and when he knows that the solid reef increases only on the outer edge, which day and night is lashed by the breakers of an ocean never at rest. (Darwin, 1842)

The softness of the organic world with its agile materials, melting surfaces, mutating bodies and voluptuous geometries defy notions of a fixed geometric order and understanding of the world. Softness sets the scene for differentiation, maturation and decay, so that 'time is stored in and emitted by matter, rather than matter being buried in and propagated by time'

# SYNTHESIS: ENTANGLED MATERIALS, TOOLS AND METHODS

(Connor, 2009). In a parallel realm, the Future Venice project (see Section 8.5) explores the principles of designing with agentized soft matter by producing a reef-like formation of encrustations that envelops the city's watery foundations while maintaining their integrity (Rowlinson, 2012). These characteristics were called into existence through on-site shoreline experiments.

> At the lagoon-side, we ground crystals of calcium sulphate into droplets of Diethyl Phthalate (DEP) and made a paste, which we sucked into a disposable pipette. A simple aquarium tank had been bought from the mainland and transported over the winding bridges on a short trolley with wheels. Less straightforward than you might imagine, the glass heaved perilously against its elastic constraints, bouncing over each bridge and down every step and twist of the sunken paving. Then we filled the vessels with lagoon water, so that we could see the transformation in the turbid water. A GoPro camera stirred the depths of the tank while waiting for the droplet stream. They came flowing in convoy. Within seconds the clear droplets had ossified into pearly structures. Bright, like moons, they bounced on the base of the tank. How robust would they be? We generated artificial waves and currents in the water, noting how the pearls rolled, deformed, butted up against each other and separated, like boiled eggs. Never fusing, but also never growing hard shells. In the laboratory, the presence of silica hardens these soft shells but not here in the natural lagoon water, although perhaps with time, this would be possible. Yet we only had a day to run these tests and would need another opportunity to investigate what a lengthier relationship between droplet and marine landscape might be. (Armstrong, 2015)

At Newcastle University's Chemistry Outreach Laboratory in 2016, a method of exploring the latent potential for 'soft' materials to generate parallel spaces was explored using a *wet printing* technique. Deformable droplets of plaster of Paris were passed through layers of fluids at different densities using a hand-held pipette – a simple, analogue printing apparatus. As the droplets journeyed through these media, they were transformed – droplet bodies lengthened like tadpoles and pressed together in pointed clusters like blastocysts. Pausing temporarily at the interfaces between the liquids, they continued to deform under the force of gravity. The soft droplets were morphologically imprinted by their encounters until they had fully descended to the bottom of the vessel. Here, they aggregated and formed interfaces with each other. At the end of the process, the liquid media were drained and the agglutinated droplets left to dry in tadpole spawn-like structures.

**FIGURE 4.1** *Plaster of Paris droplets pass through three sets of liquid interfaces: olive oil, diethyl phthalate (DEP), glycerine (from upper to lower layers), recording their surface deformations as they fall. The final forms visualize the resilience and remodelling, which underpins the dynamic frameworks of soft living architectures. The softness is counterbalanced in this experiment with 'hard' crystalline structures, in this case table salt. This can be seen as particles producing a storm of liquid trails where food colourings reveal water molecules that travel alongside the crystals in their clear oil medium and have not been modified by their descent through the liquid interfaces. Photograph courtesy of Rachel Armstrong, Newcastle University, February 2016.*

In their simplest form, soft scaffoldings obey the laws of classical physics, adopting an energy-conserving minimalist interface, which commonly implies a sphere, which is a suboptimal structure for life's vigorous metabolic exchanges. At non-equilibrium states, therefore, surface areas are maximized to facilitate the unrestricted flow of energy and matter. Such material vagrancy implies a different kind of topology than stable geometries, which can be observed in cellular structures such as endoplasmic reticulum that is strung like entwined tongues through soft, vermicular scaffoldings.

The paradoxes of successive erosions and depositions of matter shape the living realm. Soft living architecture is made up of tactile, sensate bodies that are penetrated by, infused with and leak into their environments. They participate within a broader metabolic set of exchanges that not only alter their bodily form but also change their surroundings. Traces, formed by the metabolic dust of (bio)chemical processes, settle first like snowflakes, which accrete into soft formations that are consolidated by crystallization processes, infiltrated by mineral accretions and ultimately become firm scaffoldings. Such processes are within the repertoire of living matter, which – like corals – is 'entirely formed by the growth of organic beings, and the accumulation of their detritus' (Darwin, 1842). These protean structures are not simply about concretization or solidification but also involve the subtraction and canalization of matter. Whether made by corals or sabellariid worms, reefs are hypercomplex materials and, like organic bodies, are punctuated by soft matter, which forms a plane of growth. Only the outer layer of a reef is living and is studded with colonial organisms across which soft materials travel unimpeded by gravity. Individuals within these colossal structures perform specific functions such as making proteins that catalyse metabolic processes or secrete structural carbohydrate glues. Ultimately, these soft materialities exude architectural-scale stones that record and shape environmental events over aeons.

> Stromatolites are fossil evidence of the prokaryotic life that remains today, as it has always been, the preponderance of biomass in the biosphere. For those that subscribe to the theory of the living earth, it is the prokaryotes that maintain the homeostasis of the earth, rendering the biosphere habitable for all other life. They maintain and recycle the atomic ingredients of which proteins, the essence of life, are made, including oxygen, nitrogen and carbon. (Virtual Fossil Museum, Not dated)

## 4.4 Making soils

Soils are highly heterogeneous and hypercomplex bodies, which are not obedient to an original geometry but are capable of radical transformation.

> Soil participates in the recirculation and transformation of the four major elements, earth, air, fire and water. Like our bodies too it is full of channels and pathways, directing the elements in fertile combinations and transformations at distinct organized levels of the whole structure. And like our bodies, it has a definite genetic form. (Logan, 2007, p. 171)

Early clays are likely to have had a critical role in biogenesis, creating the reactive fields of terrestrial fertility by catalysing and spatalizing matter into configurations that could persist and transform within their environment as lively assemblages. With the advent of photosynthesis, solar energy could be trapped and stored in carbon building blocks to produce biomass bodies and incorporate organic fabrics into its substance to produce organic soils like loams and peats. Working with a rich palette of agents including minerals, organic matter, air, water, diverse groups of microbes, the reactive fields, interfaces, elemental infrastructures, lively materials, subnatures, active decaying metabolisms and biological agents, the composting process gives rise to soil's giant bodies. Their tapestries are not simply decorative but possess unique material identities that are expressed within highly contextualized sites. Each fabric draws together the material residues of the land and weaves stories through its hardware, which is made up of seven layers – the water table, bedrock, weathering rock, subsoil, topsoil, organic litter zone and growing zone. Its blending and reworking of matter may be considered as a mixology, whereby its substance is transformed through the artful co-orchestration of primary and contingent events by non-human agents. Like blending a fine elixir with the powers of an *aqua vitae*, soils possess unique, complex protocols that evade the decay of matter towards equilibrium states. Sometimes, physical processes which can be described by classical science achieve these effects, such as the corrosive actions of free oxygen on metals like iron. At other times, soil synthesis relies upon biological actions such as worms to produce carbonate-rich casts. Yet, most of the soil is invisible to our surveillance and harbours unseen forces, matter and exchanges that are yet to be discovered or remain eternally mysterious. While soils and composts can be objectively measured for specific content like their acidity, they are also appreciated through 'subjective' experiences and sensory indulgences (scents, textures, landscapes), like William Wordsworth's sudden surprise and encounter with a 'host of yellow daffodils'. Such blooms are an expression of an enriched ground where compost harbours the secrets of fertility, which draw from the confluences between various knowledge practices to encourage mutual enrichments between these fields – from ancient (religious) to corporeal (channelling) to modern science (measurement) to quantum theory (counterintuitive). Deploying spatial, temporal, material, narrative and phenomenological tactics, soil fertility prevents the living world from reaching permanent stasis. Each time a body falls, their constituents are sorted, ordered and reinvigorated through the metabolic networks of composts, which are in turn, enabled by extant life forms and life-giving solar rays. Indeed, neither fertility nor life itself is the outcome of a single initiating event, but it arises from a process of material activation that occurs through a succession of syntheses. These re-animating processes are unevenly distributed over a much wider field of activity than delineated by the discrete boundaries of bodies that we conventionally recognize as 'life'. Soft living architecture is a mode of design synthesis conducive with these processes, being a 'soft' material phenomenon with loose controls and multiple authors, where life is transformation as much as transformation is life.

Natural soils form spontaneously on this planet through a complex process of weathering, decay and regeneration. They are more than materials, but organic apparatuses that function spatially through organized assemblages of minerals, organic matter, water, air and biological agents; a property observed by Charles Darwin, who noted that earthworms were responsible for the movement of large stones into the earth (Darwin, 2007). Today, this action could be likened to additive and subtractive printing technologies. Soils are also communications networks that form alliances with other bodies such as mycelia and arboreal root systems that whisper to each other in chemical languages (Howard, 2011). Yet they go beyond the possibility of negotiated connection. Soils are integrators that seamlessly combine the actions of lively bodies such as dissipative structures, elemental matrices and natural computing processes to become a global system of structured and spatialized fabrics. Despite the many differences and potential incompatibilities of their constituent agents, they exploit proximity and opportunity to become a multipurpose production platform. They directly influence the performance of molecular species that pass through their complex infrastructure, moving them away from equilibrium states. Notably, the matter that passes into a soil system actually also becomes an integral part of the soil body – not just structurally but also physiologically. Soils are parallel processors with a metabolic and structural identity that can return spent organic matter back into the cycle of life through their transitioning via rich compost. This is then broken into digestible particles and passed into food chains by the catabolic actions of saphrophytes such as fungi, which feed directly on decaying matter, where they are incorporated into new metabolic systems. In linking the networks of synthesis and decomposition, they increase the fertility of sites. The transformative nature of these highly heterogeneous materials may convert sterile environments into abundant environments, so that human development becomes a process of terraforming – not its antithesis. Capable of spanning many different terrains, soils augment the ground with soft, life-bearing matrices – or Babelspheres.

> Venetians began to weave and cultivate their own building fabrics, repairing and regrowing their beloved city as they tended to their garden plots ... In the scavenged pieces of societies lost, a new world fabric began to mature. (Holden and Stefanova, 2016)

Conventionally, the accepted ways of making soil involve combining various ratios of decomposing organic matter, fertilizer and mineral particles (coarse sand/peralite). These are folded together to form a well-draining, nutrient-rich mixture. Although naturalism has an important role in enlivening ecosystems, a first principle's perspective on the nature of soils may provide

**FIGURE 4.2** *The Silk Road discusses an architectural fabric that regenerates lands and societies in an ecological flourishing made possible through joining the webs of life and death. Digital drawing by Imogen Holden and Assia Stefanova, 2016.*

parallel approaches towards some of the biggest challenges we face, such as desertification or destruction of land quality. Potentially, soils may be designed and engineered to meet specific performance criteria. These may be naturalistic, artificial or *supersoils* that augment environmental performance as well as create alternative spaces that enable new processes and metabolisms to occur within the ground. For example, hygroscopic granules may be added to sand so that water retention is increased, or (designed and natural) organisms introduced into loams that can process certain compounds such as plastics, which are hard for natural organisms to metabolize. Radically different kinds of soil bodies that work more agilely with our environment may be produced by expanding the range of available tools and methods for their construction.

Translucent gels provide an accessible and reactive medium for prototyping artificial soils that allow processes, such as the free flow of minerals, to be directly observed. Their structural polymers facilitate chemical interactions and may also be altered by them. For example, brightly coloured complexes are formed when alginate reacts with soluble divalent salts, like copper (II) sulfate, which also change the molecular structure of the gel framework.

An alternative approach to generating soil lattices is to take a bottom-up approach using dynamic droplets, which share basic similarities with the biological organisms that inhabit soils, such as worms and mycelia. Potentially, such self-assembling, mobile, programmable and responsive bodies can remediate soils in toxic environments, such as after chemical spills or as a consequence of electronic waste.

## 4.5 Liquid soils

No other terrain and matrix invokes complex navigational skills and capacity to deal with unexpected events and invisible forces than our oceanic bodies of water. They are so rich and varied in their molecular composition through the solutes, particles and objects they are entangled with, they may be considered 'liquid soils', which promote life as much as our terrestrial equivalents do.

> This is a space whose multiplicity is subsumed to the physical properties of water: an incompressible fluid that is permanently in motion because its molecules can move relative to each other, adapting to the shape of its container, the earth's surface, and to the forces of the atmosphere. Shorelines, in short, are among the most dramatic thresholds in human experiences of space: the point where the consistency and materiality of space abruptly changes and the body faces the beginning of a liquid world with flows, rhythms, and properties that are not those of land. Coastlines

are those areas where space folds to reveal the edge of an immense liquid space, planetary in nature. (Gordillo, 2014)

Water is a universal solvent and, therefore, characterized by the various substances it contains that are not homogenously distributed but 'fielded' by local contexts, densities, depths, temperatures and currents, where marine organisms establish local preferences.

> Green algae ooze yellow cement and are fed upon by clusters of shellfish – limpets, mussels, oysters and barnacles – that clamour for traction in the rich nutrient broth. Fine seaweeds piggyback upon their shells, taking advantage of their access to light. Everything appears hairy. The encrustations splay and warp with the current, as they stretch down to reach deeper masonry. Shoals of small fish pass between crevices, turning at every change in shadow, while crabs slip in and out of the vegetation, waiting for the current to bring them marine carrion and the delights of decomposition. A trumpet fish hovers with tiny fins, then vanishes vertically, like a UFO. A long string of red algae tumbles in knots past the cluster of structures, pausing in the rips and invisible currents, which shatter the appearances of things. Gills of fish are spliced onto shell bodies. Everything pauses, then separates and re-forms as mosaics of sea vegetation, with fugitive eyes on stalks and horror-shot claws. Algal tails are plaited into brown, green and ruddy fabrics, which appear to belong to no particular site, or place, at all. Anemone hearts wrathfully pulse, as plastic bottles glide languidly on the skin of the sea. Light is broken by the waves into twisted knots and everything shatters kaleidoscopically again.

## 4.6 Ice computer

While many characteristics of water are recognized, not all its properties are fully understood, or applied in ways that fully engage its potential. In the solid form, water (as ice) occupies about 9 per cent more volume than in the liquid phase, so it floats. Digital simulations indicate that the spatial distribution of water molecules in ice is uneven. It appears that pockets of water with differing characteristics exist and account for the way that ice can retain some of its liquid properties while in solid form. So water's properties are not simply a function of global molecular properties but are configured by local spatio-temporal relationships (De Marzio et al., 2017).

> On warm days, the wells reconfigured the skyscraper façades along the Chicago River into brilliant candle-flame fingers. When it was freezing, they became crystal frost fingerprints, uniquely muddied with whorls. But,

during the rarest days, ebullient white hairs were conjured from a single well's open palm. Curling irrepressibly at the tips, they could not be tamed, even with the toughest of combs.

To explore the parallel repertoire of water in its capacity to transition between material states, an 'ice computer' was conceived and developed as an apparatus that differentially responded to water under environmental conditions. This was initiated during the Royal Institute of British Architects (RIBA) US region's programme in the Chicago Architecture Biennial RIBA-USA's *Liquid Happening*, with architect of record lead designer Lira Luis (RIBA-USA, 2015) supported by volunteer staff Jose Bonilla, William Vivians, Sam Nam and Troy Larsen from RIBA and the Leapfrog Project. It proposed to highlight water's hypercomplexity and variability.

Taking the form of a series of wells with differing diameters, volumes and depths, the ice computer functioned as a reflecting pool in its liquid state (where mirror reflections inverted and transfigured images of the environment dependent on local conditions such as wind speed) and as a display for the freezing process during the Chicago winter. The wells solidify at different moments owing to the water's 'molecular reading' of complex environmental conditions. Yet, these computations are not simple extrapolations of known variables but invite a site-specific 'perfect' storm of events to generate ice flowers – spiky crystals with a complex aetiology shaped by temperature gradient, humidity, water impurities and bacteria. While there is no guarantee that the rare event will occur, the apparatus provokes a dialogue about environmental design expectations and situating design decisions on how natural events may be initiated through architectural experiments that enrich urban encounters.

The project is a work in progress. Lira Luis is exploring the capabilities and performance of this platform by integrating chemical computing and developing techniques for installing the work's architectural responses to opportunities and risks at the water's edge in more complex environmental contexts, such as aquatic installations and levitating structures.

## 4.7 Aeroso(i)ls

The air, water and soils of this planet are not separated by their materiality but through their relative densities. The heaviest residues aggregate as earths, the fluids enter the water cycle and the lightest layers rise into the atmosphere, carrying particles that form smogs and particulate rainfalls.

During the day, stratifications of air, water and soil produce rainbows, brilliant sunrises and sparkling gowns of sequins worn by the lagoon.

A range of mirages that characterize the aqueous landscapes may be found in the waterways as a stream of writhing images. Like smog, the capacity of waterways to transform spaces is not conferred by their clarity but by their filth. The particulate matter in the water creates tiny screens where countless shimmering parallel planes reveal themselves. Cloudy water thickens and layers the photons into thick dark mirror folds that project anamorphic images on to odd surfaces, while in other places these virtual fabrics seem to possess mass and sink like river scum into the muddy water beds. Sometimes it even appears possible to reach your destination by treading upon their shimmering expanses and forgo the convoluted system of bowed bridges – the corkscrew pathways to destinations everywhere and blind alley nowheres – that form the guts of the city.

# 5

# Embracing Change

In developing an ethical practice of prototyping parallel worlds, alternative frameworks for practice and research, appropriate modes of evaluation are needed. This chapter explores potential methodologies, experiments, apparatuses and their implications for soft living architecture, which are likely to have significant impacts on the choreography of space-time, including implications for the role of the architect.

## 5.1 Choreography

Experimental architecture holds that the living world is never still. While particular moments may be freeze-framed to better appreciate their richness, each is unique – as in Heraclitus's dictum – and is never the same but altered by the nature of the participating agents, sites and their specific contexts. Iterative experiments are used to explore the choreography of ethical values of exchange that take place through the movement of a body, or alterations of matter, in space and time. How the development of prototypes such as soft living architecture is conducted depends on the specific perspective and role of observers, inhabitants or investigators of events. Within this protean landscape of possibilities, innate preconceptions and perspectives frame the way by which the choreography of events and their consequences are observed. Indeed, even the apparatuses used to observe a system establish the parameters for our appreciation of events and the resultant conversations that (re)inform our expectations and values. However, incessant change does not preclude the value of exploration, as repetitions make it possible to discern patterns, themes and inconsistencies within even the most agile complex choreography of space-time. While selective attention directs our gaze, so that the expectation is never absolute consensus, the smallest contradictions in our experiences and encounters can be detected. With the advent of apparatuses that allow us to look downwards to the phenomenology of subatomic particles and outwards into segments of the cosmos, the challenge is no longer the perception of change but when to attribute significance to it.

> Of course, the validity of our calculations depends on agreement. The spacetime interval is a mathematical expression that deals with the idea of subtraction. Its value can be negative, zero or positive. If the spacetime interval is positive then observers cannot agree about the order of events. However, when its value is zero or negative, then everyone agrees on the sequence. So, the interval can tell us whether one event will influence another. While observers can't agree about past, present, future, time or distance – they can all agree about causality. Although it seems counterintuitive, causality is ultimately what's real. (Armstrong, 2018, p. 37)

Rather than being discussed as an afterthought, the value of this expanded approach taken by experimental architecture in general – and soft living architecture in particular, and how this may be observed and captured within experimental systems, even for those that cannot be fully appreciated through empirical instruments – is discussed in this chapter. The importance of shared value systems and perceived impacts are highlighted so that the reader is aware of the slippages between classical and parallel experiments. Indeed, experimental architecture investigations begin with the construction of the tools and approaches necessary to understand the limits of soft living architecture and how these apparatuses may also influence the ways spaces, events and modes of inhabitation are evaluated.

## 5.2 Evaluation

> Science is built up of facts, as a house is built, of stones; but an accumulation of facts is no more a science than a heap of stones is a house. (Poincare, 1952, p. 141)

Enlightenment conventions value objectivity and impartiality in pursuing *research* agendas, which release us from the burden of creative obsessions. However, with the progressive 'scientification' of higher centres of education, a crisis within artistic research has been precipitated. This is partly attributable to the increasingly central role that science and technology play in our lives but is also owing to university-wide assessment criteria that are linked to funding. Scientific modes of assessment do not embrace subjectivity and actively exclude it in the process of experimental design, through notions of 'controls' and empirical instruments that simplify and reduce observations into measurable data. Creative disciplines, however, require subjectivity not only as part of their method but also to experience the encounters that are provoked by the work. For example, Italo Calvino confessed that when developing a storytelling apparatus using tarot cards to produce *The Castle of Crossed Destinies*, he was possessed by internal mania that haunted him during the creative process (Calvino, 1973).

> I was trapped in this quicksand, locked in this maniacal obsession ... even now, with the book in galleys, I continue to work over it, take it apart, rewrite. (Calvino, 1973, pp. 123–9)

Appreciating that science was valued more highly than art, Marcel Duchamp sought to invent a non-rational form of geometry (Rose, 2014). His *3 Standard Stoppages* were unique instruments that mimicked the exactness of science, but instead of operating through universal, empirical logic, they drew upon the principles of chance which allowed him to construct and evaluate his thought experiments. The *3 Standard Stoppages* were purpose-made from three individual white, 1-metre threads that were held horizontally and dropped onto three narrow black canvases. They were then fixed in place using varnish before being used three times each in mapping Duchamp's 1914 diagrammatic painting *Network of Stoppages*. In turn, this diagram became an instrument for positioning the *9 Malic Moulds*, or *Bachelors*, in his 1915–23 masterpiece *The Bride Stripped Bare by Her Bachelors, Even (The Large Glass)* (Molderings, 2010).

While Duchamp parodied science as counterpoint against unquestionable and universal truths (Ades et al., 1999, pp. 78–9; Howarth, 2000), Alan Turing made one of the most significant breaks from absolute empiricism as an evaluation method by also incorporating subjectivity into the assessment method. Proposing an 'imitation game' for systems whose very definitions are based on values – like life, consciousness and soft living architecture (see Preface and Section 4.2.4.1), – the observer's own experience was placed at the heart of the evaluation. Prior experiences formed a comparative system, against which observers identified common patterns to make an evaluation about whether the encounters were sufficiently alike for the observed system to pass the test. This imitation game is now more popularly known as the Turing test and offers an approach that values subjective experience across a wide range of challenging yet familiar contexts, including the chemistry of life (Cronin et al., 2006; Armstrong, 2015, p. 29).

Even the Turing test cannot fully evaluate hypercomplex phenomena such as nature, the cosmos, weather and life, as they are only partially encountered and therefore demand a new kind of approach, where there are many parallel ways of reading a system's performance. In these realms, the senses must be (re)engaged to incorporate meaningful values for human and environmental agendas. These may include direct experience, cultural conditioning, biases, aesthetic preferences, and social or environmental contexts. If value systems are not to be collapsed into notions of utility and commerce, then alternative instruments and methods of evaluation are needed that are based on shared values and agreed upon by communities of trust. Alternative assessment protocols are developed alongside their ethical contexts, where the implications of design decisions are considered, and parallel approaches contemplated, which are coherently and iteratively updated through active experiments (Hughes, 2009a).

> Without freeing up a zone for architectural education to explore the space between vocations and ideas, the profession and the discipline will wither. Without a return to the value of an architecture of ideas and not an architecture of marketing concepts then the purpose and need for the very a school of architecture may be on the table. (Zellner, 2016)

## 5.3 Alternative impacts

There is less difficulty in presenting data about the impacts of soft living architecture than establishing a global condition of trust upon which an appropriate evidencing system can be agreed. Trust, not evidence, determines the baseline conditions for how decisions are made and the way we treat each other and does not happen at a distance. It is established through living and working alongside each other and can be further built upon through storytelling. While empirical evidence needs to be respected as a particular kind of storytelling, it is not immutable – especially when contexts are changing. Values, evidenced by truths, evolve according to established agreements and are further refined through evidencing systems.

The various forms of currency that have been used throughout the ages are an indicator of how trust underpins value in response to cultural and technological contexts. Exchanges of salt, shells, aluminium (abundant but difficult to extract) and gold (rare) denote the value of particular materials. Promises written on paper also form an intermediary mode of representation between material and symbolic forms of agreement. Now, with digital currencies, numbers themselves carry value where data is the 'new oil'. Yet all these variables are acceptable only when they are contextualized and grounded in 'something'. That *something* – on a national and global scale – is currently up for grabs. Reciprocal exchanges are needed to (re)establish the reference points for shared values and contracts, which established through active debate and (re)negotiated as situations change. As the current process(es) underpinning Brexit are demonstrating, these are neither easy nor straightforward and require significant, multiple and ongoing forms of investment.

Soft living architecture aims to empower relationships between communities and reinvigorate spaces through ecological thinking. While classical architecture is evaluated in terms of how it fulfils a brief concerning a formal 'solution' related to site-specific challenges, soft living architecture aims to ask better and ongoing questions of a place through the modes of inhabitation that it provokes. The potential occupancy of these spaces may be interrogated through their evaluation by radical bodies (see Section 9.3).

> The problem with buildings is that they look desperately static. It seems almost impossible to grasp them as movement, as flight, as a series of transformations. Everybody knows – and especially architects, of course – that a building is not a static object but a moving project, and that even once it is has been built, it ages, it is transformed by its users, modified by all of what happens inside and outside, and that it will pass or be renovated, adulterated and transformed beyond recognition. We know this, but ... when we picture a building, it is always as a fixed, stolid structure that is there in four colors in the glossy magazines that customers flip through in architects' waiting rooms. (Latour and Yaneva, 2008)

The prototypes of soft living architecture are not endpoints of a process but material expressions of possibility around which many changes and revisions can occur. Evaluation systems are therefore iterative and may evolve alongside an ongoing project. While prototypes may invite commercial interest through intellectual property, patents and products, these are side effects of the experimental process and not their primary motivation. Through prototyping parallel worlds, soft living architectures have the potential to establish the conditions for trust, which may, at some point, turn around the prevalent stories of disaster and conjure instead a liveable reality, which supports our collective flourishing.

## 5.4 Alternative methodologies

> Now I held in my hands a vast methodological fragment of an unknown planet's entire history, with its architecture and its playing cards, with the dread of its mythologies and the murmur of its languages, with its emperors and its seas, with its minerals and its birds and its fish, with

its algebra and its fire, with its theological and metaphysical controversy. And all of it articulated, coherent, with no visible doctrinal intent or tone of parody. (Borges, 2000, p. 31)

Experimental architecture operates across a broad range of disciplines – from biotechnology to applied marine sciences and circus – so there is no one particular approach, or technique, that is preferred. Its methods are protean, multiple, combinatorial and can be customized, like 'apps'. Its communities are mutually invested in particular questions such as interrogating the principles of sustainable development or establishing architectural protocols that, for example, promote the growth of cellular organisms within a building without compromising its structural integrity. Roles and responsibilities are established from the outset, where each participant understands the value of their contribution, the particular benefits that the exploration will bestow on their business, the contribution to professional development, research agendas, ethical principles and how the inherent risks in the project are shared between collaborators.

The fundamental pluripotency and incompleteness that characterize experimental architecture's methodology mean that outputs do not conform to conventional business models or types of building construction. This raises many questions about its applicability to a mainstream, modern (industrial) architectural community; which – owing to the scale and project completion times that characterize the practice of the built environment – is generally slower than other design practices in adopting change.

> We have all been brought up with the idea that the best architecture should be timeless. It should rise beyond the vagaries of current fashion and style. It should embody values that are permanent. It should accept, but not be defined by, the rhythms of everyday life. It should last for as long as possible and then make a good ruin. Architecture, in other words, should be monumental, abstract, and difficult and expensive to build. (Betsky, 2016)

Experimental architecture develops a diverse set of working principles that are relevant to a profession, which is facing challenging times. Increasingly, it is regarded as a technical service for the building industry, and the role of design is slipping down the pecking order of decision making, which weakens the strategic consultation role of architects (Robson, 2003). The broader architectural community is therefore actively considering its future beyond the prevalent economic systems and embracing research practices beyond academic contexts.

Professional studios are therefore adopting research and development strategies to support both professional and commercial development (Flynn et al., 2016). Shared risk-taking through experimental approaches is particularly beneficial at a time of change and uncertainty and may reveal fresh insights to stakeholders invested in innovative approaches. This is encouraging for young architects, who can benefit in research-active educational programmes, which will alter the focus of architectural pedagogy from serving predominant models of business to pioneering new work. In the specific instance of soft living architecture, the agile portfolio of biological tactics and challenging established limits by re-running the tape of life become parallel methods for architectural design. They encapsulate the potency and strangeness of the natural realm while embracing architecture's capacity for innovation and visionary thinking. Such perspective shifts are essential at times where formal approaches imperfectly address significant challenges such as loss of biodiversity and wetter world.

Rather than being the implementers and early adopters of emerging technologies arising from other disciplines, 'experimental' architects may be (re)instated as visionary thinkers and catalysts of change, who can turn their ingenuity towards addressing the most challenging societal and global questions of our time.

## 5.5 Alternative experiments

The classical notion of experiment is based on a scientific approach towards knowledge acquisition. It invokes a rigorous study of a system that is based on the fundamental tenets of objectivity and empiricism that were established as the scientific method by Francis Bacon in *Novum Organum* (1620), which aimed to replace Aristotle's *Organon*, which was founded on logic. Experimental findings are tested and evaluated to confirm or refute a specific hypothesis.

> We have also houses of deceits of the senses; where we represent all manner of feats of juggling, false apparitions, impostures, and illusions; and their fallacies. And surely you will easily believe that we that have so many things truly natural which induce admiration, could in a world of particulars deceive the senses, if we would disguise those things and labour to make them seem more miraculous. (Bacon, 2009, p. 52)

Soft living architecture expands the protocols of life by adopting and advancing a range of practices that provide access to parallel worlds, which exist beyond the scientific technological portfolio. Such explorations are fundamental to developing the principles that uphold shared values such as living well, fairness, diplomacy, trust and respect for the natural world.

> The truth is that most experiments lead nowhere and judged from a strict cost-benefit viewpoint are a waste. However, learning and invention are

notoriously inefficient, requiring many failed attempts and dead-ended explorations to find one that is fertile enough to open out onto a rich new landscape of possibilities. If a society is unwilling to tolerate such waste it will stagnate. In today's world, which is under tremendous pressures of change, a vital and growing society not only tolerates but actively supports experimentation as the only way to transform the difficulties created by change into creative opportunities to enhance and deepen human experience. This is doubly true for the field of architecture which, charged with continuously remaking the world, is at the forefront of this struggle. (Woods, 2010c)

While neoliberalism currently corsets our global social, political and economic structures, parallel forms of order are emerging that may shape alternative pathways of practice. Much further exploration is needed in establishing formal approaches to their theory and practice. Many (experimental) iterations and prototypes across a range of media are therefore needed to establish research platforms and agile space-time protocols, which must develop alongside their associated evaluation criteria and assessment methods.

When a dreamer can reconstruct the world from an object that he transforms magically through his care of it, we become convinced that everything in the life of a poet is germinal. (Bachelard, 1994, p. 70)

## 5.6 Fertility as value

The continued liveliness of the world is deeply entangled with opportunities afforded to organisms within the structural organization and flows of resources, which establishes a site's fertility. This is a core value of soft living, which indicates the probability of life-bearing events (Armstrong, 2015, p. 140) and may be evaluated through the number of material transformations that occur within a field that link the cycles of life and death. Strategies include metabolism, hypercomplexity, quantum phenomena, radical 'openness' (connectivity, semipermeability, transmutability) and non-linearity. These priceless processes of material enrichment comprise the composting process which is uniquely capable of enlivening matter and – like the synthesis of life – has never been reproduced in the laboratory.

The soil is all of the Earth that is really ours. The seasons, with their heat and their cold, make the soil. The storms make the soil, with water, the most powerful substance on Earth. The winds make the soil, spreading dust across thousands of miles. The tides make the soil, stirring the river deltas and their fertile slimes. And above all, the trees and the plants, the dead and the digested, the eaters and the eaten, make the soil. (Logan, 2007, p. 98)

## 5.7 Alternative architectures

Buildings, although inanimate, are often assumed to have 'life'. And it is the architect, through the art of design, who is the authorized conceiver and creator of that life. (Cairns and Jacobs, 2014, p. 1)

Soft living architecture is an experimental, imperfect, probabilistic and highly contextualized practice, which is shaped by the opportunities and limits imposed by inhabitants and the site, and an extruded body whose interior and exterior are bestowed with a physiology and life cycle. The organizational systems that govern the production of its expanded spaces are not limited to biological frameworks. They also exceed 'speculative' or 'representative' approaches in establishing convergences between life and the built environment. Soft living architecture possesses the seeds of potential to exceed the mechanical ordering of machines and embrace the transformational and peculiar qualities of living systems such as growth, self-repair, movement and transformation.

The incorporation of principles of synthetic biology into architectural design and fabrication has further extended its lifelikeness. Scientific insights into the behaviors of metals, alloys, ceramics and concrete combined with synthetic reproduction of protocells and biological systems has offered new pathways for architectural design and building engineering ... Whereas architecture was once ascribed life metaphorically, these newly sentient, intelligent and self-generating cyborg buildings seem literally to pulse with artificial life. (Cairns and Jacobs, 2014, p. 12)

The exact conceptual and practical frameworks for producing individual soft living architectures are incompletely known. Prototyping methods are used to observe how they are specifically shaped by their juxtapositions and modes of inhabitation. Although there is a great deal of variability within soft living architectures, they share coherent principles such as persistence, adaptability, (re)synthesis and regeneration that deal robustly with uncertainty, instabilities, accidents, invisible fabrics, decay, mutation and adaptation and are invested in the relationships of the diverse agents that comprise their ecosystems of exchanges.

> On a promontory overlooking the scene, there is a dilapidated shack from which hangs a sign faded into illegibility. If you have the courage to climb up to the hovel and push open the door, your eyes will need time to adjust to the dark within. It is the stench of squalor that hits you first. Then a fountain of decay – a gluttonous ejaculate of over four-hundred sickly-sweet volatile organic compounds – cadaverine, putrescine, lysine, methionine, methane, carboxylic acids, aromatics, sulphurs, alchohols, nitrates, aldehydes, ketones – microorganisms ripping apart rotting flesh. Mounds of rags are strewn across the floor, home to bizarre biofilms – flourishing associations between motile microbes and their photosynthetic partners bound together in elastic polymer nets whose uncertain nature sucks up whatever sustenance they can summon from their impoverished environment – dim light, scarce sulphide, rarefied oxygen. Microbiology slugs it out, not as single colony isolates on Petri plates or in broth cultures but in biological couplings and mats of undefinable biomass that hang, vulture-like, on excrements, tacky surfaces and plumes of air. Some of the rags appear to be inhabited by a larger form that writhes in slow motion. As your eyes start to distinguish shapes in the gloom you recognize the listless outline of a former tightrope walker who returns here as if by instinct, but each time in a greater state of decrepitude. He neither speaks nor gestures – his hollow eyes may be seeing or unseeing – his abjection is almost complete. And yet some residual aura of grace clings like a shadow to his sunken frame. To turn him into a spectacle would be shameful, I admit. I would be equally ashamed, however, to neglect my ritual visit to this fallen soul, even though the putrid stench and insect death-rattle of his hovel makes me nauseous. Not once have I offered any form of assistance or support that might, if only temporarily, alleviate his misery – I, who preach 'radical love' to the hale and hearty. It is said that he came on board with an extended family and a reputation as the most daring rope artist of his generation. He failed to adapt and so fell into irrelevance and obsolescence. (Armstrong and Hughes, 2016b, p. 186)

The material exchanges that characterize soft living architecture are not simulations of nature but parallel spaces for inhabitation which produce real effects such as making electricity from microbial fuel cells, leaking odours or radiating heat. Owing to their dynamic sensitivity, they may even possess unique sensibilities that may be considered as forms of companionship between different kinds of bodies with distinctive behaviours. Such possibilities require alternative ways of thinking about the conditions for the production of architecture. These include the community it serves, the ecosystems it supports and the political position that such spaces occupy within communities, where precarious states of embodiment and inhabitation negotiate the challenges presented by a world in flux.

## 5.8 Parallel apparatuses

> Now the Lord provided a huge fish to swallow Jonah, and Jonah was in the belly of the fish three days and three nights. (Jonah 1:17, New International Version)

The 'architectural gut' is an expression of the Babelsphere. It is an integrative platform and site of material transformation for a network of diverse metabolic agents and recalcitrant materialities. In a parallel world, soft living architecture takes the form of a complex organ for the sequential processing of organic matter within a bounded but leaky milieu, where it retains various degrees of uncertainty, invisibility, processing capacities and environmental variation. With fibre optical imaging and the appreciation of microbial realms, the gut is no longer a naturalistic system of organs but becomes a parallel site for architectural (re)design and inhabitation.

> Since the scientific enlightenment, these mystical organs have been trivialized and are now considered to perform a supportive role to the creative exterior of the creative body. Lacking detailed analysis and artistic evaluation, our internal anatomy is granted no intrinsic value or aesthetic appeal; it is badly mapped-out, scantily documented and deeply misunderstood. (Armstrong, 1996)

The gut is a paradoxical space. It is continuous with the external environment, while also occupying an internal space that stretches from mouth to anus, being particularly adept at forging linkages between life and death in the formation of compost (Armstrong, 1996).

In the embryo, the gut unfolds as a tubular invagination from primordial tissues and rapidly rolls, convolutes and proliferates into a series of organs and tiny finger-like villi. From its inception, this undulating manifold links unique but interdependent metabolisms, which are produced by a mixology of exquisite hormonal, secretory, immune and neurochemical functions. These are coordinated by contingent events and slow contortions in space-time. While it is a transformative and generous space, it is not necessarily 'harmless' or 'harmonious'. Its environments are chemically fashioned surgical tools that are designed to dissect, boil, dismember and suck its contents dry of their vitality. Architectural guts are sites where individual appetites dissolve and may be equally engaged in benevolent acts of love or parasitic compulsions to nurture the self.

> This ... taboo is revealed in Peter Greenaway's film *The Cook, the Thief, His Wife and Her Lover*, a tragedy set in a restaurant. The garish interior ... of the eating space mimics the chambers of the human gut: red for the restaurant/stomach; green for the kitchen/small intestine and dark brown for the refuse yard/anus. In these settings, he explores base human drives and needs: eating, drinking, defecating, copulating, belching, vomiting ... and blood ...
> RICHARD: ... It says more about death than eating and more about living than cooking.
> GEORGINA: Does it mention cannibalism?
> RICHARD: (smiling) I believe it does. (Armstrong, 1996, p. 89)

Stelarc's original Stomach Sculpture performance for the Fifth Australian Sculpture Triennale, Melbourne, Australia, in 1993, involved the artist swallowing miniature devices that were impervious to digestion. In this performance, the stomach became a site for the performance of tiny robots, which could be observed through fibre-optic technology. The triennale protocol was set to be repeated, making a few alterations to the original protocol, so that stomach secretions would be removed for better visualization of an even more complex performance by micro-robots (Stelarc, 2006).

> In 1995, Stelarc repeated the experiment in London, this time using a sedative and atropine to dry up his body fluids. The artwork would be inserted as three separate capsules ... reconstructed on site [in the stomach] and when assembled ... driven by a [*rare*] earth magnet creating a symphony of light, sound and vibration. The whole process was to be captured on film in a medical clinic, but owing to legal difficulties [*it*] was abandoned. This technical feat would have been the first autonomous performance given by an assembled sculpture created in the body of a host artist-gallery. (Armstrong, 1996, p. 90).

The intestine is naturally colonized by its own performative agents – the *microbiome*. These are not machines but a vast community of microorganisms that outnumber our own cells by 9:1. Using genetic modification techniques, some of these organisms could be reprogrammed at the level of populations to perform different kinds of transformations shaping metabolic networks. These could, for example, extract specific substances or make different kinds of products. The Living Architecture project (see Section 8.1) explores the possibilities for interrogating the digestive system as an architectural site by engaging natural and synthetic communities of organisms within mechanical gut-like spaces or bioreactors. The robotically operated system may be thought of as a digestive system for the home or office that – like a robotically activated cow's stomach – converts organic waste into a range of useful substances like electricity or next-generation, biodegradable soap (Newcastle University, 2016).

'Metabolic apps' are being developed by coupling biofilms together to produce their own metabolic landscape and structural frameworks. The aim is to form an autonomously operating digestive architecture that can process its internal and external environments in ways that expand our choreographic understanding of intestinal spaces. It suggests our homes and workplaces may host soft living architectures that literally eat their own waste matter as a partially designed and self-sustaining ecology. The metabolic apps that enable such radical material transformations – such as the digestion of long chain hydrocarbons found on oil slicks, the decomposition of chitin (the outer coat of insects) or hair – create the possibility of working with gut-like systems in ways that are more than digestive processers, like sewage plants, but become spectacular (synthetic) ecologies and architectures.

These parallel spaces enable a very particular kind of worlding, which is shaped by metabolism, dynamic spatial relations, precarious assemblages of participating agencies and natural computing systems. They provoke spatial encounters that give rise to synthetic ecosystems.

> The most voracious predators of the follicular transplant fields are the fifty-seven species of wooly bear caterpillars, which feast exclusively on keratin. While other insects such as silverfish, crickets, and cockroaches damage these proteins by chewing them into a sticky pulp, only the young of carpet beetles and clothes moths can actually handle an exclusive diet of hair. Yet, the true apex predators of these hirsute lands are the fifty-seven types round-bellied transgenic goats. It takes a year of intensive rearing to raise an ecological beast that does not destroy the crops from the root but trims them back like a shaver. Leaving the regenerating growth follicle in the ground, transgenics rummage in the infested border, for hair, beetles, bears and all. Their toothless, nimble upper lips pluck the shaft, cleaving it with their sideways swinging, sharp bottom teeth and tongue, and then roll it into a bean-sized pellet. Down it goes in a swallow through the oesophagus. Hair plants decompose into fifty-seven different varieties that include amino acids, albumins, globulins, gliadins, fibrous protein, hormones, growth factors, DNA-binding proteins, immune system proteins, chaperone proteins, enzymes, artificially produced proteins,

glycoproteins, lipoproteins and complexes with multiple components like nucleosomes. This takes place within the four chambers of the stomach – rumen, reticulum, omasum and abomasum – a juggler's intestine that choreographs metabolic process, infestation, matter and opportunity within a manifold landscape of innards that hosts an impossibly expansive ecology … Transgenic rumens also become infested with multicellular life forms that have survived the grinding of lip against razor teeth. Shoals of hundreds of micro-squid, around a centimetre in length, swim alongside the surviving woolly bears, beetles and moths – all hungry for hair.

## 5.9 Alternative roles for architects

Soft living architectures emerge from a portfolio and platform of contingent, materially dynamic events such as active energy landscapes, lively interfaces, invisible forces and material flows. Their intersections flourish around contested sites that are as rich, varied and robust as life itself (Armstrong, 2016b, p. 27). While soft living architectures exert a remarkable degree of agency, they are not without architects. They challenge traditional notions of design such as authorship since they are produced by many collectives of variably participating (human and non-human) bodies.

While such wilful architectures appear to seek independence from human intent, soft living architecture is profoundly symbiotic with its ecosystems and human communities and perturbs the fixed, bounded and linear framings that characterize so much modern life. Their prototypes enable architects to develop agile protocols for the production of hypercomplex paradoxical structures. These can augment material performativity in multiple dimensions and produce qualitatively different kinds of outcomes for humans and non-humans. Within these realms, architects are co-designers within an ecology of actants that orchestrate soft control systems based on mutual participation, interconnection, trust and shared values. They create the conditions for inhabitation, vibrancy, fertility, wonder and enchantment between people, their habitats and the wider world (Armstrong, 2015, p. 127).

The island steadily climbed skywards, cast from the same processes that formed the land. Yet, while many built upwards, others dug down into the underground rocks. Despite its subterranean nature, the bizarre city was beautifully lit with intersecting rays channelled through jackstraw mirror formations, and other reflective surfaces that were fashioned as inverted cones, which created the illusion of infinite space. At night, a halo shone over the rising rock. Part geology, part nature and mostly unobserved, the underground city became home to many more than its founding hundred refugees and heralded a new relationship between dwelling, peoples and land. Inhabitants soon became residents that founded a coherent society woven in rock, where many hearts and minds began to heal together.

In these turbulent times, the role of the soft living architect is simply this – to begin the (re)civilizing of the world and change the way we think, work and live together. The worlding ambition of soft living architecture is a significant political undertaking that is potentially full of misunderstanding, since it proposes no less than the construction of the Babelsphere. During the course of the late twentieth century, architects have increasingly considered their practices as apolitical (Poole and Shvartzberg, 2015) or ironic (Betsky, 2015). Without a radical civic agenda, architecture can be readily assimilated into the global industrial machinery and political, social and economic systems of Western development. In practice, it is not possible to separate these contexts from the actual construction process, since political indifference simply means practitioners lack 'the means to understand [their] own political agency in the world' (Self, 2015) or recognize that of their communities. Wielding significant political influence through the *polis*, architects exert their influence through their choices in deploying building materials, technologies and natural resources in homes, communities and cities, and collectively comprise a force capable of geoengineering-scale impacts.

Soft living architects are collaborators, transdisciplinary practitioners and multitaskers – simultaneously capable of navigation, communication, experimentation, conjuring, or inventing new instruments and techniques. They are highly artful professionals, yet also amateurs who are not enslaved by their own virtuosity. As visionaries and risk-takers of the worlding process, they are not afraid of the unknown. They choreograph their practices through an expanded design portfolio that reaches into novel knowledge practices, skill sets, imaginary spaces and territories that evade constraints through specific modes of visualization or representation. Architectural 'worlders' embrace diverse, probabilistic and hypercomplex modes of existence that include provocative apparatuses such as the phantasmagoria, architectonic guts, scrying apparatuses and strange materials like fuzzy surfaces, cloudy vistas, fragile details, quantum logic, soft scaffoldings and all kinds of teratogenic in-betweens that infiltrate the spandrels between the mineralized bones of industrial construction. Yet these nascent terrains, invisible realms and complex, fertile substrates do not offer techno-fixes or totalizing solutions to the constantly unfolding challenges this era poses. Rather, they relentlessly create the conditions for change for all lively and living things, which collectively promote the fundamental fertility of the planet. Accordingly, they share a common project with the broader community of life that – shaped by human(e) ethics – raises the possibility of our mutual, continued survival into an ever-unfolding adjacent reality that is full of surprises (Armstrong, 2016b, p. 27). We are all *worlders* now; there is no other choice.

# 6

# Laboratories and Convergences

This chapter expands the range of sites for the synthesis and exploration of soft living architecture through various laboratories methods of production, which are variably entangled with the city of Venice. It opens up parallel worlds and perspectives of the city that reveal alternative forms of material order, behaviour and methods of 'ecological' construction.

## 6.1 Babel fish

Hypercomplexity challenges us to invent new languages that exceed the expectations of the industrial era and engage with parallel discourses of experience.

Tiziano Scarpa likens Venice to a fish (Scarpa, 2009), and I am reminded of Douglas Adams's character that performs instant translations – the Babel fish. 'It is small, yellow and leech-like and probably the oldest thing in the Universe' (Adams, 1995, p. 52), and if you stick in your ear, you can understand any language.

Venice is a place where language is transformed in ways that extend to its spatial protocols. The postal services, divided into six *sestieri* (San Marco, Cannaregio, Santa Croce, Castello, San Polo and Dorsoduro), number the houses according to districts rather than streets. Such inventiveness at least partly springs from Venice's elemental relationship with the water, which foregrounds its obligations to the land. Originally, the major form of transport and navigation was through natural and artificial waterways called *rio* and *riello* (which are smaller), from which the main entrance ways of buildings on *insulae*, the interstitial building-bearing landmasses, were accessed. While the city's reputation is founded on its canal system, there are less than a dozen of these public waterways, including the Grand Canal, the Cannaregio Canal and the Giudecca Canal – all the other inlets are actually *rios*.

A navigational system of *ponti* transverses the transitional spaces in the archipelago. This time, Venice agrees to use the same term for bridges as the rest of Italy, although it boasts quantity instead, possessing more than 340 bridges. More conventional landmasses are traversed by *calli, campi* and *campielli* (graded according to size) instead of walkways and highways along the canals. This accounts for some of the claustrophobia-inducing streets, like Ramo Varisco, which is literally a gap between buildings that measures only 53 centimetres across at chest height. Even the ground that Venice stands upon is constantly being remade, like a Thesian ship, where *Fondamenta* (a base for constructing buildings) are differentiated from *piscine*, which are roads that have been formed by landfill. Indeed, building components throughout the city are continually replaced and (re)interpreted, (re)assimilated and repurposed to make land, rather than razed and discarded. These practices of constant material transformation extend into the city fabric such as the ghetto, where ornate interiors of synagogues are carved from inside town dwellings on the top floor of preexisting buildings. Other places have undergone substantial volumetric and formal transformations in response to political and cultural shifts. For example, the *Ca' de Mosto* has additional floors built into its structure, and the labyrinth of power and terror concealed within the Doge's palace is a network of secret chambers and corridors (Foscari, 2015). The limits of these programmes do not stop at the architecture of the city but also incorporate all kinds of materials, which include relics, priceless treasures and even the very ground itself. Certainly, until Napoleonic times, human bodies were incorporated into the city's ground-making processes, as in the island of Poveglia – a small island located between Venice and Lido in the Venetian Lagoon – where it is said that half the earth is human ash. At the time, cremains were used like other waste materials in shoring up the foundations of the city or creating new islands from discarded bricks, garbage, stones and mortar. Despite many constraints and changing circumstances, far from being a city in decline, Venice is a potent Babelsphere that is undergoing continual transformation and inventing languages for the emergence of parallel space that enable its continued existence.

## 6.2 The soft city of Venice

> The moral character of the people of Venice ... is seen as part of the mutable character of the place, formed by the upheavals of the earth and the ebb and flow of the air and water that sustains and challenges them with the lapse of waves and the lives of stones. (Ballantyne, 2015, p. 164)

Venice is a living laboratory that interrogates the transformation of traditional building materials by the lagoon environment. The flow of water does not stop at the tidal zone but rises through masonry, like transpiration in a tree. Efflorescent blooms explode bricks into fragments that shatter on the walkways and find their way into the lagoon. Through the continual action of the tides, the waterways grind these stones like a gizzard, where they are polished and entangled with garbage, weeds and glass fragments to forge unregulated, new shores. These synthetic landscapes are further ornamented and shaped by seasonal events like algal blooms or intermittent episodes such as carpets of petals on the water. Yet in places around the tidal margins of the waterways, the 'soft living' city of Venice manages to evade complete erosion by the elements through parallel sites of flourishing. Here, marine creatures thrive on wetness and are in constant conversation with their microenvironments. They transform traditional materials into more complex, organically enriched mosaics and tapestries, which are unconstrained by Venetian Gothic design principles. So, while Venice's traditional bricks are weathered by the tides, digested by effluent from medieval sewers, exploded by salt from the Adriatic and ground down by harsh crosswinds, the nutrient-rich broths and metabolisms within the waterways offer succour for miniature parallel 'cities' of microorganisms. Through this liquid loom, clusters of non-human bodies are woven together whose details reveal the impacts of constantly changing environmental conditions and may be read as a city-scale palm.

## 6.3 Living stones of Venice

When you walk through Venice looking for the story of its origin, you are encountering it the wrong way up.

The teetering city has maintained a tenuous skyline absent of vertical lines for over a millennium. It clutches the ground with its woodpile heels, just about staying upright by virtue of the enforced camaraderie of oblique buildings that lean on each other. While the city tilts and twists, the silt swallows the ground. Venice is a creature of shoreline slurry. The first traces of living bricks are found in the mud and are produced by creatures that steady the soft delta earths – calcareous algae, biofilm-producing microorganisms, barnacles, oysters, mussels and tenacious sabellariid worms. The carefully constructed details of its 'living' organic underside stay furtively away from human eyes, where biodiverse, non-human communities flourish in a parallel realm and become part of its foundations, stones and stories.

Creatures that sift the lagoon's silty water for slime, grit, industrial waste, household effluents, brackish condiments and countless garbage garnishes are constantly reinventing the city's boundaries. Their diverse palette of building materials – from effluent broths to form hardy bio-concretes – both bind the brickwork and chew on its bones. Gradually, these communities stabilize and become biofilms that are tethered to masonry foundations. These trail long threads and warty knots of scaffolding into the waterways, filtering them like a kidney. Irregularities, caused by erosions and depositions along the water's edge, provide sites for succession that produce unique materials, structures, details and transformations, which offer a 'living' counterpart to Ruskin's 'stones' (Ruskin, 1989). As they swell, they seek further modes of attachment, clawing erosions in the brickwork, which wicks them into its substance. They gnaw at the ground-floor masonry where they make their way around impenetrable, waterproof membranes designed to keep out the rising damp and splay into sites of further flourishing and decay. In these constantly shifting material fields, microcellular communities redraw territories and (re)direct resources from one place to another. Tirelessly, these metabolic materials equip Venice with a living layer – a reef of oysters, hydroids, barnacles, mussels, sponges, biofilms and bryozoans – that enables it to patchily negotiate its survival in an ongoing struggle against the shoreline elements, just as a creature does. All the while, these 'living stones' navigate the impacts of waves, wind, tides, sunlight, desiccation and organic invasion and keep us guessing about what these parallel cities could become.

## 6.4 Automatic Venetian chess

As Venice's fabric rearranges itself according to the protocols of natural computing, as an architectural scale puzzle, or game, parallel worlds appear. These non-human agents can be clearly seen by citizens and visitors and invite their participation in shaping urban encounters.

> A large fragment of the floor in the Hotel Danieli – a favourite haunt of John Ruskin – catastrophically drops into the muddy substrata of Venice during a particularly tempestuous winter, when the acqua alta relentlessly grinds its teeth on the shoreline frontage. Unable to restore the flooring to its original position, the chequerboard marble slab is carefully removed in one piece and resituated on the lagoon side of the building. Here, it takes on the status of a parallel lobby that welcomes gondolas full of guests.
> The cavernous gap left in the palatial flooring, with its pale umber tiles punctuated and occasional beige islands, betrays the deeper truth of Venetian luxury – the city is an exquisite veneer built on mud. The chasm is soon spanned with slabs of polished concrete that are positioned at varying heights like the internal troughs and waterways of Carlo Scarpa's Fondazione Querini Stampalia. As the resituated flooring becomes

encrusted with algae, barnacles, mussels, flame biofilms, bryozoa and fat shiny oysters, the lobby becomes too slippery to walk upon. To get better traction on the chequerboard passers-by add found masonry, which has been loosened from walls, or salvaged from beaches, as stepping stones. Hop, skip and jump. Rapidly, the lobby's topology is organized in patches of yolk yellow, terracotta, chocolate chip, earthen brown, wholemeal and caramel orange building fragments. A group of bored young tourists starts arranging the masonry according to the conventions of chess.

The pawns are single, sculptural pieces, which are detailed with sharp oyster combs, barnacle buttons and jet-black tiger mussel rims. The castles are constructed by placing four large stones piled against each other and fused by marine bio-concrete. Then the precarious knights appear with glaring sea ground Murano glass stones for eyes – five stones aloft – and cantilevered wooden poles holding their heads high. The bishops are six stones tall and conically arranged. Their mirror fragments continually converse with the silver light of daybreak and the golden cloth of sunset. The queen is assembled from weather-gnawed limestone statues stolen from private gardens, which stare through barely discernible, multiple faces over the lagoon. Ten inward-looking monumental blocks of unruly masonry become the gypsy king – a temporary ruler of his transient people – who, once complete – bestows all the repurposed stones with inner life. Together they adopt their positions on the chess board.

A counter army of trash is assembled by other visitors to defy the living stones. Plastic bottles, are filled with water and pebbles for ballast. Under the harsh sun and the whims of the coastal elements, these soft bodies are sintered into abstract organic forms. Some burst their lids and are colonized by squirming mosquito larvae and shrimp fry, which, with no way out to the lagoon, become graveyards. While the garbage chess pieces have little in common with the living stones that originally inspired them they too acquire a strange vitality as the king is assembled and gameplay begins.

A living stone knight notices the first plastic pawn taking a step across the marble chequerboard. It whinnies the alarm and multiple stone pieces move swiftly over the tiles, masonry smothering the plastic army. Under the sintering sun the opposing pieces quickly fuse with the living stones and become composite sculptures. The floundering stones attempt more gameplay in response to this chemical blockade, which results in further amalgamations. A single pillar of chess pieces rises as a fist of solidarity towards the sky, just off-centre in the board. As the mass of the living stones bears down on the plastic, the composite materials re-form and reattach, becoming stronger – stranger. Then, the structure tips to form a twisted bridge that links the chessboard with the city archipelago. Now, the monstrous sculpture of transformed plastics, repurposed stones, sea-polished glass, bio-concretes, shells, garbage and salvaged masonry becomes the Danieli bridge – a unique Venetian ponti, which is known to continually transform its connections with the city, as the war of contradictions within itself persists.

## 6.5 Invisibility

The invisible realm is real – not imaginary – although its effects are experienced rather than rationalized. Arising from within material and conceptual blind spots, invisible forces are those agencies that have not been identified and named by Enlightenment toolsets. They permeate the living realm and confer it with strangeness. Rich in unnamed mysteries, potencies and unexplained phenomena, they evade direct confirmation by our senses and provoke events beyond our experiences.

Having previously been described by religions that accounted for them by divine or demonic powers, or magical practices that sought to unlock occult forces, the invisible realm became a site for the discovery of material and physical agencies during the Enlightenment, which were called into existence as named particles, rays and forces. Appreciating the invisible world is not simply the practice of debunking arcane ideas and turning them into quantifiable nouns and atomized qualia. This space continues to be a conduit into the unknown and harbours qualities that have remained unmeasurable. One of the cornerstones of classical physics, Isaac Newton's laws of gravity, outraged Gottfried Wilhelm von Leibniz, who denounced his theory as a scholastic practice of the 'occult' (Clarke and Leibniz, 1998), as the force between bodies did not have an identifiable cause, although its effects could be demonstrated. Today, the paradoxically powerful but weak force of gravity remains mysterious, since the graviton – the hypothetical fundamental gravity-carrying particle – has not been identified, even within the quantum realm. While Albert Einstein's theory of relativity takes a different perspective of gravity as a curvature of space-time induced by mass and energy (being a smooth force, not quantized like the graviton), the two worldviews offer different perspectives of the phenomena at different scales. Together, they offer a more complete understanding of gravity.

To detect, capture and name the agents of invisible forces, colossal instruments such as the Large Hadron Collider (LHC) have been constructed. This cathedral to the invisible realm is a particle superhighway buried a hundred metres underneath the Swiss–French border, where the positions of its particle detectors (Atlas, CMS, ALICE and LHCb) orchestrate miniscule Ballardian fantasies by smashing primordial plasma streams of hydrogen and lead ions into one another. As the subatomic fragments shatter in layers upon layers of thick sensate materials, sophisticated algorithms interpret their screams from the wreckage of the impacts and translate them into digital visualizations. These acts of violence upon the invisible realm may lead us to alternative modes of thinking, seeing and evaluating the world in which we are immersed. Yet once we've seen the vibrations of a particle dying on a computer screen, how can anything around us be still again?

Invisible forces are as relevant to today's agendas and discoveries as they have ever been. Having dismissed vitalism, the life sciences now call upon complexity and emergence to do their work. Moreover, biologists are beginning to controversially summon quantum forces to explain the strangeness of the living realm such as the navigational abilities of European robins that can sense impossibly weak magnetic forces and so migrate colossal distances (Al-Khalili and McFadden, 2014). Quantum physics creates a layer of unpredictability and strangeness within the phenomenon of life but does not yet 'solve' its essence. Indeed, the intelligent designers who invoke an omnipotent god at the heart of all biological narratives are simply giving invisibility a different name to that of secular scientists. Fundamentally, however, they are all singing from the same ontological hymn sheet – the invisible unknown. So, while at the start of the third millennium, we may assume that our knowledge about the world is largely complete and may be accounted for in classical scientific terms, in fact, the nature of the universe remains mysterious. We now believe that 95 per cent of reality (Armstrong, 2016a, p. 36) is flourishing with dark energy and matter. Since these agents do not reflect the electromagnetic spectrum, they cannot be directly seen but are implied, and their relevance to the quotidian is unknown.

Much closer to home, invisible forces that infuse our ecosystems with liveliness are equally elusive, and we still do not know what kinds of conditions increase liveability on this planet. Living systems contain the possibility of surprise, risk and unexpected events, which cannot be designed into a system. This principle also applies to our ecosystems and living spaces and is an important consideration if we are to establish ways of designing habitats that nourish life. Arguably, some of the most interesting mysteries of the living realm may be observed and explored within the origin of life sciences, but our knowledge of them is incomplete.

Classical science views life through an atomistic perspective, which assumes that it is built in the same way a machine is assembled from a blueprint, like Tibor Gánti's model for minimal life that includes metabolism, container and code (Gánti, 2003). However, despite 150 years of scientific experimentation, it has not been possible to make life from scratch in this way

(Hanczyc, 2011). Nonetheless, modern synthetic biology proposes to design living systems by decoding molecular information stored as DNA and is changing the way that we look at both nature and biology. Organisms are becoming technological platforms, and, conversely, technology is acquiring increasingly lifelike qualities (Haraway, 1991). Indeed, this kind of computational approach is shifting design from a mechanistic view of organisms towards a perspective where the production of data and networks can assist in the optimization of reaching specific goals. However, these insights still do not enable us to build life but enable us to modify existing systems better (Armstrong, 2013). Indeed, synthetic biology requires 'ghost cells' to maintain the invisible (unknown) operations of life by supporting the metabolic infrastructure that active genes need.

Parallel life, such as Bütschli droplets, is assembled from an alternative 'bottom-up' approach than the top-down approach of machines, where the exact outcome of the system is not exactly known. However, this does not mean anything goes, as every system is bounded by limits of possibility, which are restricted by physical factors such as temperature or reagents. Bottom-up forms of experimental practice are less about goal setting – to modify or produce a particular thing – and more concerned with expressing and encountering the full potential of the system (Armstrong, 2015). The real success of bottom-up design in living systems, however, is to incorporate invisible factors into parallel life forms. Although the term *emergence* is used to account for the spontaneous lifelike arrangement of molecules, where order appears to arise from chaos, it does not explain how the observed phenomena work – it simply normalizes the mystery.

The Bütschli system highlights the presence of invisible phenomena in the emergence of dynamic droplets from their basic ingredients (see Section 1.9). Awareness of these unknowns is essential in the experimental design, so they are not rationalized or value-engineered out of the experimental findings. This is also a challenge for synthetic biology, which currently regards organisms as being fully programmable and controllable machines. These expectations are not consistent with the actual properties of hypercomplex, heterogeneous materials that compose the substrates of life. Indeed, there is still a great deal of knowledge and insight to be gained from a detailed observation of simple lifelike phenomena. Indeed, homology exists between dynamic droplet behaviour and Stefan Rafler's *SmoothLife* (Doctorow, 2012), cellular automata (Gardner, 1970). The major difference between the chemical and digital systems is that the chemical system radically transforms to generate disruptive characteristics like a complete change in behaviour and form, while the digital system maintains a characteristic patterning output with many variations but no radical breaks in the system's order.

## 6.6 The invisible laboratory: An alternative synthetic platform

> The night is not an object in front of me; rather it envelops me, it penetrates me through all of my senses, it suffocates my memories ... it is a pure depth without planes, without surfaces and without any distance from it to me. (Merleau-Ponty, 2014, p. 336)

A parallel laboratory is needed for exploring the story of life, which does not preempt outcomes before the discovery process has begun. It invites alternative modes of discovery, which may produce better questions, generate new ways of seeing, provoke the imagination or bring unexplained phenomena to the fore. It is a site for parallel encounters with the living world that are forged through the relationships between bodies and their multitudinous contexts. It conjures a phantasmagoria of design elements that provoke the possibility of alternative forms of nature, lifelike bodies and soft living architectures. These parallel protocols of space-time and agile design tactics may transform the impacts of the built environment into potent expressions of human (co)habitation that enliven our habitats and render our world more liveable.

## 6.7 Ectoplasms

> Things leak into each other according to a logic that does not belong to us and cannot be correlated to our chronological time. (Negarestani, 2008, p. 49)

The living world has not always been shaped by the ontology of machines. Since ancient times, the Greeks thought that life was governed by fluidic forces, or humours, with melancholic, phlegmatic, choleric and sanguine qualities. As transducers of matter and emotions, the humours could be obstructed, causing disorder, and therefore needed various kinds of purging like bloodletting to rebalance the system. Liquids like blood also invoked 'invisible' factors, which were not only considered responsible for the behaviour and character of a person but also governed the nature of all living things.

During the Enlightenment, flows of liquids were transposed into concepts that could be readily interrogated through mechanical frameworks such as lifegiving bioelectricity (produced by the flow of electrons), which was identified by Luigi Galvani. Yet not all forces could be abstracted into fundamental particles that can be reducibly coupled with mechanical systems. Charles Richet, who won the Nobel Prize for his work on anaphylaxis in 1913, was particularly fascinated by the possibility of a 'sixth' sense that could detect 'ectenic' forces, which connected the ephemeral and material realms through vibrations known as 'ectoplasm'. He invited a range of investigators to consider their significance.

> How can the vibration of reality bring about knowledge? ... we are not prejudging the question as to whether these are vibrations of ether, or emissions of electrons ... We know that there are around us, quite close to us, many vibrations which do not reach our normal senses, for instance those of attraction, of magnetism, of the Hertzian waves, etc. All the same, it would be madness to suppose that there are not others. Therefore, we have three orders of vibrations of reality: a) those which our senses perceive, b) those which our senses do not perceive but which are revealed to us by detectors, c) those that are unknown to us and which are revealed neither by our senses, nor by detectors ... When we have fathomed the history of these unknown vibrations emanating from reality – past reality, present reality, and even future reality – we shall doubtless have given them an unwonted degree of importance. The history of the Hertzian waves shows us the ubiquity of these vibrations in the external world, imperceptible to our senses ... when a new truth has invaded the world of humanity, even the most far-seeing individuals can never know to what conclusions it will lead. At times this truth entails unforeseen and unforeseeable consequences, and that even from the rigidly narrow point of view of our present material life. Who then could have foreseen when the great Hertz discovered the electric waves, that our practical daily life would be transformed and that all the ships sailing on the various oceans would be supplied with wireless? (Richet, 2003)

While medically trained Arthur Conan Doyle proposed a rational material explanation for ectoplasm by likening it to gels, body fluids and viscous liquids (Doyle, 1930), spiritualists and mediums explored the possibilities through enactments of extraordinary bodily senses. These were performed around seance tables in darkened theatres. Techniques in the developing field of photography (which, ironically, sprang from the light-sensitive chemistry of gelatinous substances) were used to stage performances that immerse audiences in liminal realms, which lingered between materiality, ephemerality, embodiment, formlessness, creativity and destruction. Conjuring the appearance of strange wools and fabrics from bodily orifices – particularly ears and mouths – theosophists claimed these performances were evidence of substances that bridged the realms between the living and the dead.

Somewhere in these incomplete observations, hauntings, deceptions, performances and parallel modes of inhabiting spaces, life and soft living architectures may be understood as species of ectoplasms that can be choreographed, designed and engineered. While these unstable fields and material programmes that hover between the tangible and intangible realms are yet to be formally established and named, like dissipative systems or weather fronts, they are yet to be conjured in ways that can be accessed through design toolsets in ways that directly influence architectural and environmental events.

## 6.8 Jellyfish

There is no standard way to visualize the invisible. Phenomena must be conjured forth to challenge, or meet, our expectations of them. Like Descartes's demon, when coming across something that appears out of place perhaps the first and maybe even during many subsequent times, it is impossible at first to say whether our senses are being deceived – until we look again.

> The light is strange on the surface of the canal, like it's boiling. Or bubbling. The usual gentle ripples sour and writhe. Already a memory. I draw closer, and for a moment notice the withdrawal of something tentacular: a liminal, semi translucent body like a discarded glove, pulsing, but it's vanished before I've caught sight of it. There is it again. Medusa. Now that I am tuned into their presence they're everywhere. Their bodies split the light and remain elusive, always receding into the background. Drifting like phantoms, they snare fish fry and lurk behind strands of weed. Fascinated by their ghostly oblivion – invisible ecophagy, I watch them from the safety of the walkway, but they're out of focus again, dissolving into odd patches of light. Momentarily they bloom into pulsing reflections, laced by purple skirts and glowering gonads. Then, they've sunk and gone.

## 6.9 Sensible apparatuses

Soft living architectures resist traditional modes of representation, not just because they are probabilistic bodies but also because their evaluation toolsets are not established within commercial architectural design portfolios. Apparatuses that can appreciate an agentized perspective of matter are needed, which recognize that at far from equilibrium states the material realm is capable of channelling invisible forces, subjectivity, uncertainty and multiplicity. It therefore has the capacity to invent into spaces and at scales that are not currently easily accessible to designers.

Such materials which include paradoxical (dissipative) and lifelike systems evade hard control strategies and require soft modes of evaluation. The ancient art of scrying – a term derived from the English word 'descry' which means 'to make out dimly' or 'to reveal' – employs surfaces like mirrors, crystal lenses and water to glimpse parallel worlds that are suggested in the reflections of 'hard' objects. The plague doctor Nostradamus is reputed to have made his prophesies using a particular scrying device, known as a black mirror, to view highly situated yet transfigured relationships between objects to produce a set of symbols. Over the course of his practice, he documented 1200 visionary quatrains (four-line poems) using this method that encoded the names and fates associated with significant characters, like the Pope of Rome (Oliver, 2014–2016).

Nostradamus's particular mode of scrying was hydromancy, which produces symbols at reflective interfaces between air and water. Its 'seeing' membranes can be intensified by grounding them against black surfaces so that the distortions, reflections, refractions and physical disturbances (waves, surface tension) can be read as dynamic shadows, which seem to possess an inner life. The emerging symbols are revealed and realized through a series of design-led decisions. They are widely used in interior design and landscape architecture as black pools, or mirrors, which, depending on the geometry of the installation, draw images from one space into another such as the Aga Khan Museum's black pond, in Toronto designed by Fumihiko Maki, which reflects the building's facade and sky into an abyssal space. Filmmaker Douglas Trumbull also exploits the generative power of liquid interfaces in another manner, as a means of scrying *and* synthesizing 'artificial' cosmologies and alien planetary systems for movies, such as *A Space Odyssey: 2001* and the *Tree of Life*, which reveal how the evolution of the cosmos *could be*.

When many particles are in suspension in bodies of water, their surfaces also become black mirrors, which shape the character and mood of a place. The sediment-rich waterways of Venice are tiny dark bodies that constantly scatter light. Their reflections speak of possible site-specific transformations, which begin to articulate alternative relationships between the physical buildings and the ambient media – water, wind and environmental forces. Instabilities produced in the surface indicate that transformative molecular forces are shaping these habitats. Indeed, algae blooms and marine life follow the reflected light into watery spaces as metabolic fields that set new life-promoting events in motion (Armstrong, 2015).

Such effect can be conjured in a formal laboratory setting through 'dark gels' (see Figure 6.1). These are made up of 2 per cent agarose with 10 per cent of the total liquid made up with 1M ammonium hydroxide. The gel is mounted against black card and reflects light back through the gel bodies to reveal their chemical processes in dynamic material traces. Soluble salts with divalent cations such as iron (III) chloride and calcium sulphate are added to the activated gel, and they propagate waves of self-organizing chemistry through the semi-liquid interfaces as ion exchange occurs. Where salt solutions meet alkali, two dynamic components are produced. The first are self-organizing chemical complexes that are spatial time-independent structures and are encountered as pattern-forming bands. The second is physical changes in the gel, which concurrently occur as the divalent cations cross-link with carbohydrates in the gels. These start to contract like muscles and cause the matrix to buckle, roll and fold like a developing embryo. Dark gels, therefore, embody modes of artificial embryogenesis and parallel organizational trajectories for lifelike phenomena. Initially, these bodies are semipermeable to their sites as porous, rich gelatinous frameworks but, on propagation, they are canalized and gradually harden into structural fabrics and metabolic organs, which shape the choreography of soft living architecture. Dark gels therefore speak to the emergence of new natures through replaying the tape of life from its origin as alternative bodies or forms of being and dynamic architectural events.

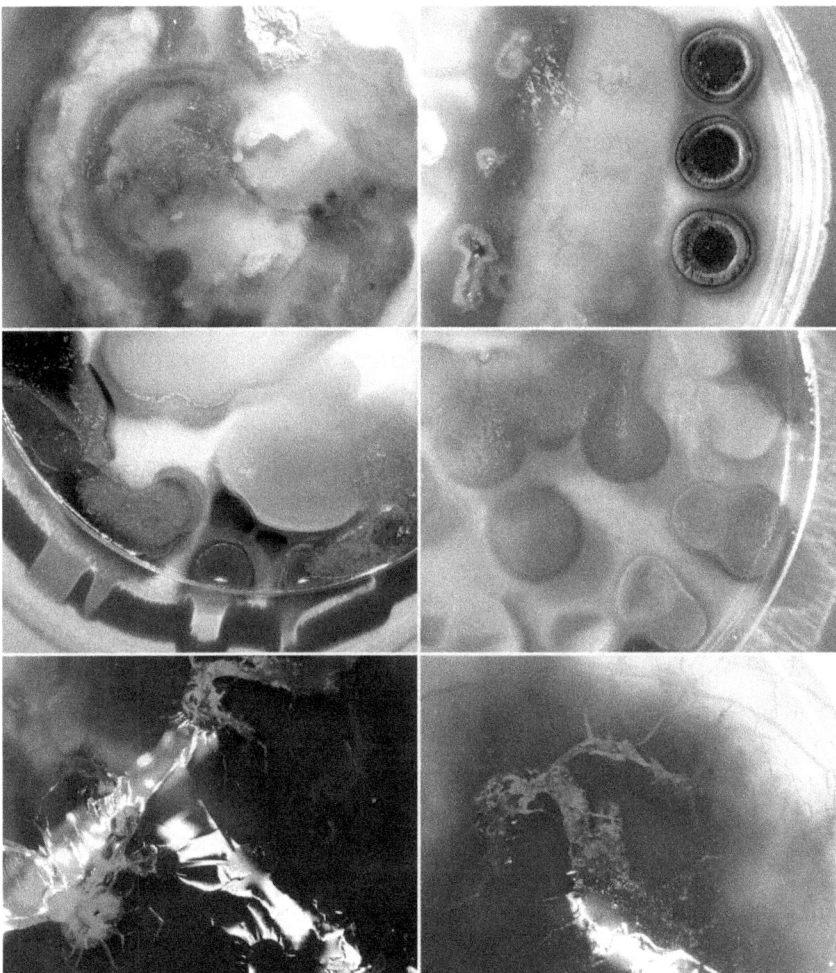

**FIGURE 6.1** *Activated gels act as a landscape of chemical potentiality. As salt gradients diffuse through these terrains, they become embryonic bodies whose rolls and folds establish new spaces for material expression. Photograph courtesy of Rachel Armstrong, Newcastle University Chemistry Outreach Laboratory, February 2015.*

Systems that can choreograph such highly contingent events may be thought of as sensible apparatuses that provide an extended portfolio for designing with life and its multiple agendas. They facilitate the emergence of parallel forms of computation that are directly coupled with the material realm. Their material complexity can be likened to that of soils, where each life-organizing hub is unique and follows a spatialized developmental trajectory, which is entangled with the character of the site. They do not require central spatial plans or deterministic programmes but spawn new architectures as a bespoke range of embryological events. Over their lifespans, these *sensible fabrics*, which sense and physically respond to their context, may increase the fertility of a site by producing palimpsests of substrates that nurture ongoing metabolic exchanges.

## 6.10 Lost music: Antonio Vivaldi

The organizing systems of the living realm are mostly invisible to us, yet their oscillations, iterations and patterns shape our experience of the world. It is said that Antonio Vivaldi's most beautiful work was not intended for human senses, and after he died in 1741, his extraordinary music continues to haunt the Venetian shores at the intersections between the land, sea and sky (see Figure 6.2).

Vivaldi's extraordinary musical talent was already known to the devil at the time of his birth, when, being at the point of death, he was immediately baptized on 4 March 1678 by his midwife. However, his official church baptism was delayed by two months. Some say this was because the child was born with severe asthma, while others observe the earthquake that shook the foundations of Venice as a possible reason for the delay. Whatever the truth, during this vulnerable time, Satan made a play for Vivaldi's soul. Wresting with angels and demons, Vivaldi struggled with a 'double nature' throughout his life (Fei, 2002, pp. 67–9).

In the struggle for his soul, Vivaldi entered the Catholic priesthood. This infuriated the devil, who cursed the composer, preventing him from ever playing his soul's true music. Nonetheless, the priest filled his life with flamboyant music and is known as one of the greatest baroque composers. He wrote over 450 *concerti*, scores of operas and many choral works, which were frequently for the female music ensemble of the *Ospedale della Pieta* – the home for abandoned children where he had been ordained.

As tastes in music changed wildly during this period, it was not unusual for many composers to live with financial insecurity. Sometimes Vivaldi was rich and at other times impoverished. When he lost royal protection and a steady source of income following the death of Emperor Charles VI, he succumbed to an 'internal infection' in a saddle maker's house in Vienna and died a pauper at

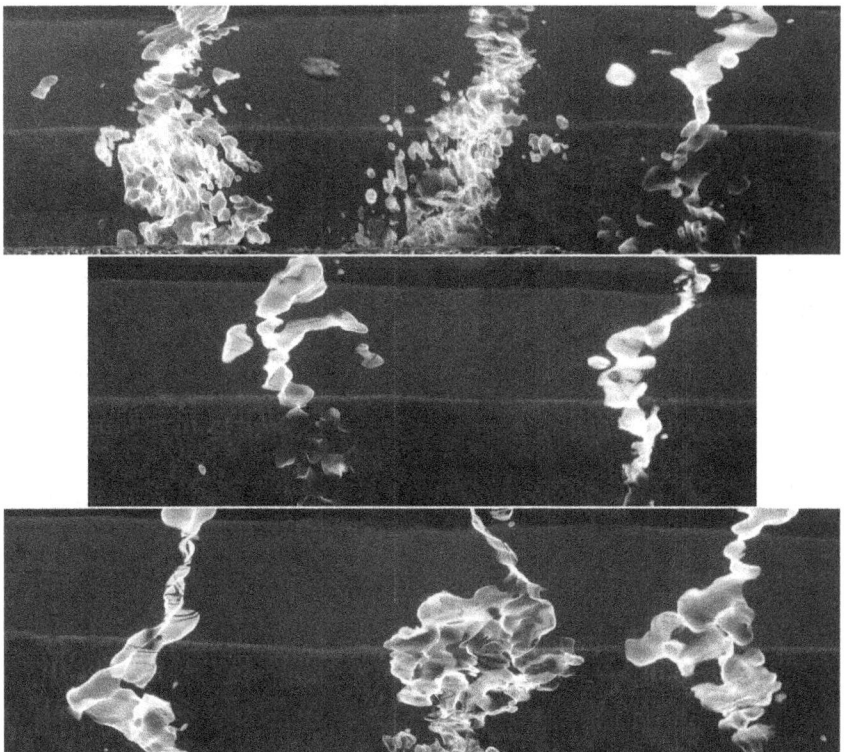

**FIGURE 6.2** *This phantom light notation that dances on canal water is written upon dark biofilms that capture the lost music of Vivaldi, in metabolic blooms that detail physical changes in Venice's 'living' stones. Photograph courtesy of Rachel Armstrong, Venice, Italy, November 2016.*

the age of sixty-three. Free from the devil's clutches, his true soul music now searched for its voice, but the devil's curse clung to the music and weighed it down, so it could not enter Heaven – yet it did not belong to Hell.

At night, when the waves barely tremble under the moon's ghostly light, strange musical forms appear upon the water as notations of Vivaldi's cursed works. These are so strangely encrypted that nobody can decipher them. Sometimes, when the wind blows over the reedy crests of the waves, like a bow over the strings of an endless violin, Vivaldi's ghost music is transiently decoded by the water as sweet sounds and vagrant symbols. Partly generated by trembling interfaces, these vibrations carve persistent paths over the surface of the water and are understood by tiny creatures as a continuous landscape of patterned light and vibration. Today, its wandering scores are translated into marine accretions by lagoon organisms and biofilms that detail them onto the city's biological stones.

## 6.11 Channelling and knotting

Knot-making is a technology and form of counting system that stretches back into ancient times. It combines symbolic and material value, being able to record repetitions like incantations, but also generate useful objects such as in the practices of basket weaving, making fabrics, designing labyrinths or even constructing cities (Woods, 2010b). Knots change movement within spaces. They are more than just geometric spaces; they are also spatial regulators whose configurations can be organized to condense and accelerate the passage of energies through a system or store vitalizing flows, which are released by untying the knot. The duration of this impediment depends on the types of knots that are produced – from simple braiding to slip knots and even the impossible Gordian knot.

The witch's ladder is a particular kind of knot-making apparatus – whose purpose is defined by the weaver – which is used to channel invisible forces (Wingfield, 2010). The first recorded instrument of this kind was discovered in 1878 in an old house in Wellington, Somerset, England, while it was being renovated. The ladder was a rope with feathers woven into it, which had been hidden in the rafters in such a way that it was inaccessible from the interior of the house. This suggested that it was used to issue a hex or curse. Knot magic may incorporate personal items into the braiding process, like hair, which is performed ritualistically to determine the intent and value system that the spell holds. The last knot finalizes the charm, so all the energy is channelled into the instrument, where the power of the spell is now condensed and stored within the knots. Witches' ladders are often hidden close to the site where influence is intended, such as under a bed, or at the threshold of a house. Carefully untying the knots, or throwing them into moving water, neutralizes the hex.

Knots are not only made of threads but are also formed by metabolic networks. Chemical exchanges between small, reduced-complexity microbial consortia in natural ecosystems can be described by knot mapping. This requires multiple techniques and combinations of approaches – from metagenomics to mass spectrometry – to decipher the otherwise imperceptible transfer of materials through networks that are too complex to plot (Ponomarova and Patil, 2015). These topologies may help to construct a language of dynamic knot-making for the production of soft living architectures.

> To reach this place, they weave rope from the tall grasses, which sprout like thinning hair from its plains. The founding guide ropes are several centuries old, with threads that span the interior. Now, these have become a spider-like web of knots and aerial pathways that enable climbers to relentlessly pursue vagrant water globules, which are collected in plastic bags, like insects on

nectar. A moisture relay of climbers herds the escaped ocean back to where it belongs and sinks their container contents into the thirsty soils.

## 6.12 Phantasmagorical laboratory

During the late eighteenth and early nineteenth century, phantasmagoria spectacles were immersive experiences that entertained audiences in darkened theatres. These were staged between the material and invisible realms by drawing protocols of space-time and matter together to produce an ectoplasmic realm of encounters that were, at once, imaginary and real.

> The two great epochs of man are his entry into life and his departure from it. All that happens can be considered as being placed between two black and impenetrable veils which conceal these two epochs, and which no one has yet raised. Thousands of generations stand there before these black veils, torches in their hands, striving to guess what might be on the other side. Poets, philosophers, creators of states have in their dreams painted this future in colours gay or somber, according to whether the sky over their heads was cloudy or serene. Many philosophers have profited by this general curiosity to astonish the imagination subdued by the uncertainty of the future. But the most mournful silence reigns on the other side of this funerary crepe; and it is to fill this silence, which says so many things to the imagination, that magician, sibyls and the priests of Memphis employ the illusions of an unknown art, which I am going to try to demonstrate under your eyes. (Maunder, 1847)

Using magic-lantern technology, an early form of slide projector, spectators witnessed an almost tangible show of 'supernatural light' where dark-ground images and shadows of bleeding nuns, spectres, dancing cadavers and mythological figures paraded upon semi-solid screens of smoke and vapours. A range of apparatuses – such as ambulation, superimposition, eerie musical instruments (like the glass harmonica) and ventriloquism – brought these phantoms to 'life'.

The phantasmagorical laboratory complements the invisible laboratory by interrogating intangible and unseen aspects of the living world (see Figure 6.3). It uses techniques of sensory deprivation (tedious inertia) and hyperstimulation (episodic vibrant blooms) to manifest ectoplasmic prototypes within parallel worlds. At first, these materializations appear to be no more solid than the images flickering on smoke clouds. Yet, on immersion, they are more than optical illusions, produced by sleight of hand, but perceptible agents that possess incongruous qualities such as softness, movement and semipermeability.

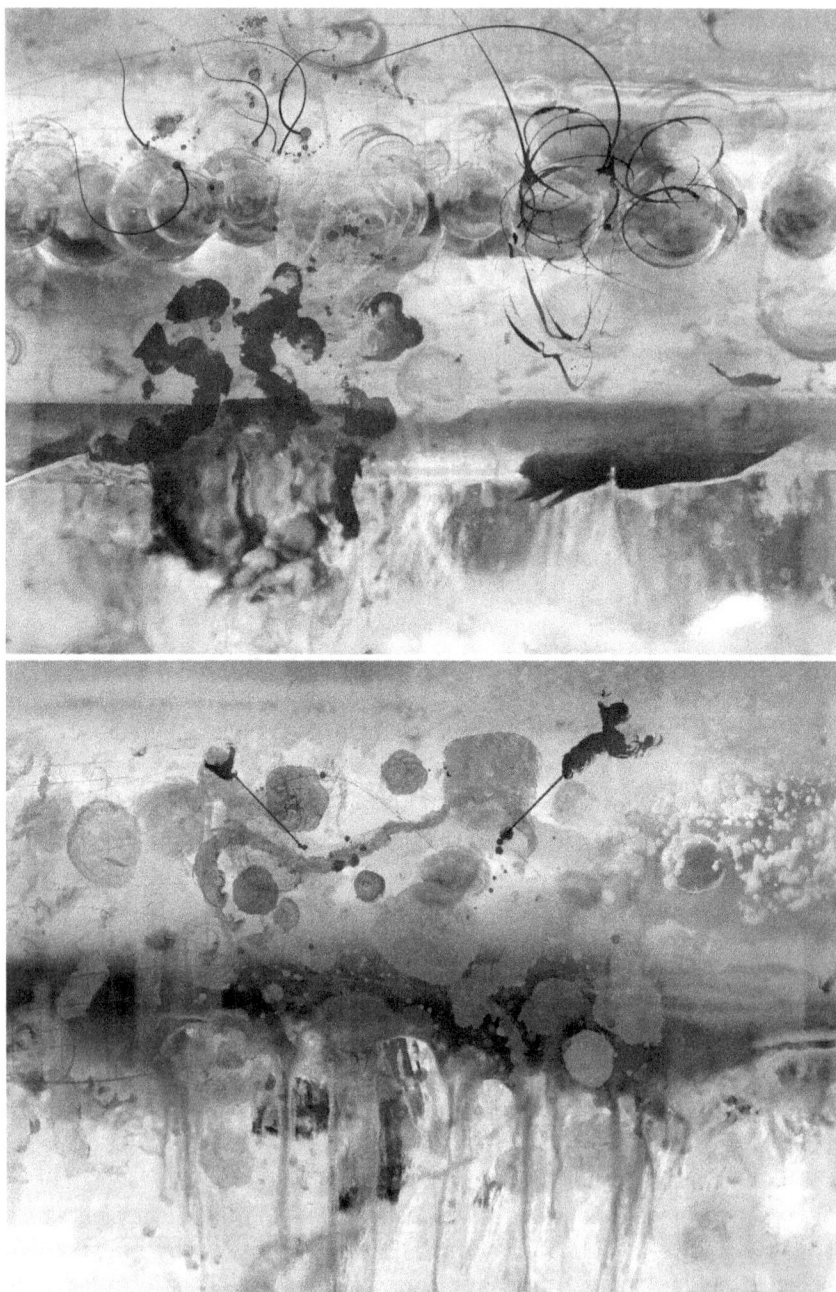

**FIGURE 6.3** *Notation of chemical fields producing complex structures that perform at interfaces between liquid layer, which may be read as radical 'circus' bodies that transit active chemical fields to produce surprising traces and transformations. Photograph courtesy of the Experimental Architecture Group (EAG: Rachel Armstrong, Simone Ferracina & Rolf Hughes), Newcastle University, May 2017.*

The crowd is the veil through which the familiar city beckons to the flâneur as phantasmagoria – now a landscape, now a room. (Benjamin, 2002, p. 40)

## 6.13 Immersive sensible kaleidoscope

Eoin Cussen invented the kaleidoscope in 1815 by juxtaposing three symmetrically arranged mirrors angled at sixty degrees to each other. The endless reflections projected between these surfaces could be viewed from a position where they conjured snowflake-like patterns. While the sensible kaleidoscope similarly constructs image-rich spaces, which resist reduction into simple geometries, materials or causalities, it is a more complex viewing platform. Using a much-expanded range of reflective surfaces – such as water, air and oil – it invites participants to become immersed in its intoxicating array of virtual and real spaces. Within this delirious space, liquid interfaces are nuanced by various non-identical reflections, refractions, inversions, rotations and transformed images to create non-linear ladders that reach into transitional zones, where transparent bodies and moodscapes provide access to parallel worlds.

> A shallow black pool draws light into the centre of the temple. The audience gathers expectantly around it, as children trace the threads of reflections with their fingers and stare curiously at their inverted portraits like narcissi. Light spews from screens and spotlights cast phantoms along the back wall, where a changing landscape of lifelike chemistries glares into the circus space. Medaka fish, which swim in circles in bowls along the wall, channel their inverted images into the mixing space. As the silvered trapeze rises, an endless well appears beneath it – a Wonderland rabbit hole. Observers draw closer, trying to establish if this virtual realm is rising or falling. Human figures questioning how this dark realm may be accessed, begin an acrobatic conversation that confuses the distinction between man, woman, air, water, image and reality – raising questions about the nature of life itself.

The Temptations of the Non-linear Ladder took place on 8–10 April 2016, at the *Do Disturb!* festival at the Palais de Tokyo, Paris (see Section 9.3 for event details). It experimentally explored the transitional zones between one set of conditions for existence to another – namely, from the earth to an extraterrestrial mode of inhabitation. In the palace's *temple* space, a sensible kaleidoscope was installed that took the form of a large circular black mirror (4 m diameter) and liquid lenses (fish bowls containing medaka fish). The iterative reflections, refractions and distortions between these surfaces generated dynamic portals for the fusion of images and the appearance of transient spaces. As the circus performers' (radical) bodies transitioned through the kaleidoscopic spaces, they became inseparable from their environments. The improvised event was repeated nine times over the course of the festival, with no two performances being exactly alike, and to which visitors repeatedly returned.

In these transitory moments of change, as the limits of existence are expanded and expectations are surrendered, something strange happens to the body. Rather than objects that end at the skin, the body *in extremis* is swollen and semipermeable to new flows that transgress established anatomical conventions. Fluids that were once constrained by downward forces can now move sideways and upwards to mingle with their neighbours differently. Tight and tethered tissues are relaxed and become permeable to new metabolic fields. While these leakages could be considered as a series of malfunctions within an idealized body machine, at the limits of our being, when existence is so undetermined, it becomes apparent that parallel ordering systems are at work. Here, bodies are not objects but excitable states of matter that are extruded into new configurations and terrains, where alternative expectations of being a body are negotiated through identity, community and kin. Framed by ethical, philosophical, existential, environmental, technical and cultural questions, the uncertain pathway towards radical adaptation and parallel evolution begins.

# 7

# Prototyping Practices

A broad spectrum of prototyping practices that characterize the range of aesthetics, qualities and ethics of soft living architecture begins to develop an emerging portrait of its potential, parallel worlds.

## 7.1 Parallel beauty

Diverse bodies provoke alternative value systems that reach beyond the present truisms that frame social convention. For example, traditional notions of beauty are value systems that suppose morphological symmetry is a hardwired biological preference, reinforced by cultural conditioning that is used as way of evaluating sexual partnerships. However, in an ecological era, unconventional value judgements – including alternative notions of sexual encounters – frame our encounters with bodies and spaces that draw attention to what is at stake in a broader realm than individual preferences. Parallel beauty is an indicator of this shift.

'Beauty' for the Ecocene invokes coherent relationships between people as well as other living agencies – from bacteria to forests, soils, air and oceans. Parallel beauty exists in spaces that promote lifelike events and springs from the entrails of abject terrains. It is no longer a superficial quality but shares an ontology with the potency of matter, which possesses a deep connection with life, diversity, vital exchanges and all their radical transformations.

> No animal or bird ever looked so splendid as did Igname in his attire of love. Attached to his curly head was a young nightjar. This bird with its hairy beak and surprised eyes beat its wings and looked constantly for prey among the creatures that come out only at the full moon. A wig of squirrel's tails and fruit hung around Igname's ears, pierced for the occasion by two little pikes he had found dead on the lakeshore. His hoofs were dyed red by the

blood of a rabbit he had crushed while galloping and his active body was enveloped by a purple cape, which had mysteriously emerged out of the forest. He hid his russet buttocks, as he did not want to show all his beauty at one go. (Carrington, 1988, pp. 7–8)

An example of 'beautiful' soft living architecture is the Intelligent Building (BIQ) house in Hamburg (Schiller, 2014). Air (carbon dioxide) is pumped into a sleek building exterior with colonies of living organisms (algae) within its glass panels, to create biomass (Steadman, 2013). During this process, agents are transformed into a spectacle of rising air bubbles that twist and turn like *medusae* (see Section 6.8). Yet the BIQ's beauty does not reside within any particular object, surface, style or event but through its quotidian metamorphoses. A shape-shifter, the building does not appear the same today as it did yesterday, when raindrops dragged their dirty fingers down its pane and split the incident light into rays. Tomorrow it will change again as the storms arrive and the facade becomes sadder and darker.

Soft living architecture embraces parallel beauty as a labile condition which seeks integration with the wider world (Woods, 2010c). Salvador Dalí expressed this as a terrifying and edible beauty. In his soft, metamorphic world of phagic, ecological relationships, one system literally engulfs another in an unending writhing mass of bodies, objects, systems, moods and images that, at some point, regain their coherence and propose a new kind of synthesis or (re)embodiment. While Dalí locates these transformations within the realm of psychotic conditions, soft living architecture materializes these transgressions and transformations in ways – like engastrulation (see Section 3.7) – that change our value systems and encounters with the living realm. They also empower us differently to act upon them.

Through its edibility, parallel beauty becomes the cornerstone of an alternative experience that is not confined to the classic framing of the body but is also extended into the webs of life and death. While venerated, the objectification of beauty can provoke negative behaviours such as sadistic acts of admiration, stalking behaviours, jealousy, or various forms of control and defilement. So, in an ecological era, beauty is seamlessly entangled with ethics and the civilizing of appetites that respond to our need for (re)enchantment with the world. Parallel beauty infuses our habitats with an alternative vitality and flourishing that is informed by the generosity and vibrancy of the living world that is encountered without cynicism and irony. While it cannot prevent tragedy, it transforms it in surprising ways.

> I think of Miraldalocks, a young woman with a waspish waist and generous pelvic curves. But Miralda's most striking feature was her thick, dark hair, which smelt heavenly. In fact, she was trailed by a swarm of bees wherever she went, buzzing and sighing after her. It was said that when Miralda entered a

room it was even possible to get drunk on the very act of breathing. Miralda seldom went out. If she did so, it was only at dusk and wearing a veil. This had nothing to do with a penchant for nocturnal beekeeping. Rather, she knew just how disagreeable her countenance was, and so, she kept herself to herself. One evening, a lustful wizard was in the village, taking the air, and he became intoxicated by Miralda's luxurious tresses. He set about wooing her. He approached her under the blanket of pitch darkness and, being a stranger to the art of flattery, Miralda fell for the wizard's powers of seduction. In no time, the crafty sorcerer had Miralda for his own. But tragedy struck. In the morning, the wizard awoke and looked upon Miralda's face. He was so horrified that he killed her instantly. To hide his shame, he buried her face down in the earth, with her feet sticking out so that he would not be reminded of what he had done. Then he left the land, never looking back and never to return. Appalled by the violence inflicted upon this innocent young woman, nature took pity on her and vowed to rewrite her story. The wind carried the news of Miralda's murder to the bees and creatures that had loved and admired her. Soon, there was a stirring in the air over the place where her body lay. One by one the adoring insects adorned this aromatic place with pollen, manure and seeds. For how can a pretty face compare with the presence of a heavenly scent to a bee? The creatures of the soil soon began to transform Miralda's flesh. They rearranged her tissues, her bones, redesigned her metabolism and, for the very first time, gave her the means to stand tall in the light through the power of photosynthesis. Now, her untimely grave was a blossoming fertile landscape. Bathed in vitality, Miralda's hair started to grow, taking on a vigorous life of its own. It grew and grew until the individual strands began to twist into a beautifully patterned, voluptuously curved woody stem, which flaunted her reincarnation. When twigs burst out from the stem with new life, they reached out towards the sun, spreading out their beautifully scented leaves, beckoning to lovers to linger among perfumed clouds. Miralda's magic continues today, in the incredible plant 'Miraldalocks', which is harvested by apothecaries for its life-restoring properties.

Such experiential shifts empower designers in making choices and evaluating the whole portfolio of approaches that critique the status of soft living architecture and so that its exploration and prototyping may lead to better ways of dwelling in the world.

## 7.2 Parallel soils

The parallel soils of soft living architecture have no need for naturalism and are not necessarily made by the same processes or ingredients of natural earths, which may be encapsulated in the mythological figure of Ursula Sontheil, whose story embodies a parallel form of highly specific soil-making.

Ursula Sontheil was born during a violent thunderstorm in a cave on the banks of the River Nidd in 1488. As the illegitimate child of a fifteen-year-old girl called Agatha, she was born unfortunate. Keeping herself and her child alive by her wits alone, Agatha raised Ursula in a limestone cave before the Abbot of Beverley 'took pity on them'. Agatha was sent to a nunnery, where she died some years later, so a local family raised baby Ursula.

She was a strange child, with a monstrous countenance – a large crooked nose, warts on her pallid skin, back bowed by scoliosis and her legs were twisted. Ostracized from polite society, the young girl learned the joy of her own company and acquired a deep understanding of Nature. She spent all her time in the cave of her birth, studying the forest life. Inspired by the resilience and healing powers of the living realm, she experimented with potions and the art of scrying. When she was twenty-four years old she met and married a carpenter, Tobias Shipton. Whereas others renounced her as ugly, Tobias found Ursula's wisdom, spirit, passion for nature and intellect enchanting. While her husband did not give her children, they were deeply in love. Sadly, he passed away only a few years after they married, leaving Ursula heartbroken. Vowing to remain single she kept her husband's name and deepened her wisdom and talents for divination becoming widely acclaimed as 'Mother' Shipton and nationally recognized as Knaresborough's prophetess. She was able to make a good living telling the future and made significant predictions. She foresaw that Cardinal Wolsey would see York, but never reach the city. In 1530 Cardinal Wolsey climbed to the top of a tower and saw York at a distance but received a message from King Henry VIII ordering his return to London and died during the journey – fulfilling Mother Shipton's prophecy. Despite the risk of being condemned for sorcery, Ursula even managed to evade the witchfinders and died peacefully in 1561 at the grand old age of seventy-three.

Despite her national infamy, it is unlikely that the caricatured hag and prophetess Mother Shipton ever existed. Many of her predictions are confirmed forgeries aimed to sell chapbooks and almanacs. Even her seventeenth-century biographers Richard Head and Charles Hindley confessed to inventing details of her birth and concocting the prophetic verses.

Even more fascinating than her caricature are the actual geological systems that shape the extraordinary petrifying powers of the Mother Shipton cave, where she is said to have lived. The high concentration of minerals in the water transforms the site into an additive and subtractive printer. As groundwater moves through the porous rock within the cave, some of it dissolves. The acidic gas carbon dioxide precipitates the soluble minerals into solid carbonate crystals as they meet the air and draws long fingers of stalactites down from the rocks as well as turning soft objects left to saturate in the water to stone. Through the warp and weft of soft fabrics and porous materials, the cave systems weave a highly structured soil-like fabric.

Some people maintain that the elaborate fictions about Mother Shipton are based in fact, which are testified through the strangely infiltrated soft structures on display in the cabinets of the on-site museum. Today, the site is host to a cultural programme and a tradition of placing soft objects in the petrifying waters. This loom for making stone fabrics is strung with hats, lobsters and totemic masks but is particularly famous for its strings of stone teddy bears, which twist and turn under the trickling streams that leak from the cave's roof as parallel soils (see Figure 7.1).

**FIGURE 7.1** *Petrified African mask, tennis racket, boot and soft toys suspended in the petrifying waters of the Mother Shipton well. Photograph courtesy of Rachel Armstrong, Knaresborough, Yorkshire, 2012.*

## 7.3 Golem

The theatre of chemical reactions that make up our soils has evolved along with the living world. Clays such as montmorillonite may have been key to biogenesis (Hanczyc, Fujikawa and Szostak, 2003) and the clay code could be 'more *complex than either the genetic code or human language*' (Logan, 2007, p. 127).

> The transition from probiotic clays to organic life might have occurred ... in the presence of ultraviolet life, [where] iron can sometimes capture both carbon dioxide and nitrogen from the air, resulting in the production of citric acid, an organic compound. Amino acids can gradually be built out of citric acid. So seaborne clays of the ancient Earth, deriving their energy by feeding on carbon dioxide, nitrogen, and light, might produce the building blocks of organic life ... Do (or did) clays reproduce? ... does the particular order expressed in one particular clay create further clays with the same order? ... is this order dynamic? Does it lead to social interactions among clays?' (Logan, 2007, p. 127)

During a residency at the Robert Rauschenberg Foundation property in Captiva, which was once the studio home of Robert Rauschenberg, I developed and installed two clay golem-inspired figurines, which symbolize the potential for the soil itself to bear life (see Figure 7.2). The male character symbolized the golem, while the fecund female possessed a littoral identity, symbolized by a manatee's tail. This was part of the Rising Water II event, curated by Buster Simpson and Glenn Weiss, which was held in response to deep ecological questions that were faced on the barrier island with respect to future of the property and grounds in the face of rising sea levels (Gavin, 2016). The figurines proposed to occupy sites of change and indecision between the land and sea. Situated among mangroves they were fertility vessels for the land but also reached out into the water forging allegiances with marine creatures. Holes through their oral and genital regions encouraged the flow of life and metabolism through their bodies, which were inverted as receptacles for mangrove seedlings. Their cast-iron scaffolding elevated them to around a metre above sea level – the anticipated sea level rise by 2050 – and invited colonization by marine encrustations.

While our earths and clays are capable of transforming one thing into another, they cannot create value. While the golem discusses the 'createdness' of living things, it also raises questions about inner meaning and purpose. Life is not simply a material phenomenon. It is not a golem, forged by clay; nor is it a Frankensteinian beast that is an assemblage of parts animated through bioelectricity. It is spun out of far more peculiar stuff which flows within us at the core of our being and, like light, is spooky and strangely entangled.

**FIGURE 7.2** *Male and female golem figurines invite flows of matter within their bodies, which become sites of fertility that promote the colonization of life forms that can transition between land and water and so enable the site to respond to encroaching tides. (Artwork by Rachel Armstrong: 'golem', April 2016, ceramics, 50 × 20 × 15 cm, site-specific installation at Robert Rauschenberg Foundation, Captiva, Florida.) Photograph courtesy of Rachel Armstrong: Robert Rauschenberg Foundation, Captiva, Florida, May 2016.*

This vibrancy does not only reside within the material realm but is distributed through invisible networks of exchange throughout the community of life.

## 7.4 Weeki Wachee maids

Soft living architecture embraces mythic and actual parallel worlds. With unlimited freedom to invent, it can stray into uninhabitable terrains to render them liveable.

*Oh daddy, daddy, please let's see the mermaids.*

With the deepest sigh, the Lexus purrs its way to Weeki Wachee, a town with a resident population of twelve, most of whom live below the poverty line. Within a natural spring and aquarium setting, glamorous 'live mermaids' perform three or four daily shows that, since 1947, have delighted audiences and celebrity guests like Elvis Presley, Esther Williams and Larry the Cable Guy. In a submerged theatre that seats 400 tourists, the thirteen-dollar entrance fee includes the opportunity to witness eating and drinking underwater.

*That's what I want to do; I want to be a mermaid!*

One, two, three women-fish plummet through a narrow limestone opening sparking with synchronized smiles as an old-style theatrical curtain reveals their spectators through a bubbling landscape.

*Imagine a place serene, tranquil and beautiful. A place of weightlessness. A place as old as time and clear as a dream.*

Down, down, down they go, as glittering charms, into the dazzlingly clear spring water with a sandy-bottomed pool that measures fifty by sixty-five metres. The spring discharges 500 million litres of fresh water every day into networks of cave tunnels that stretch 400 feet into the earth.

The man observes the underwater air hose breathing techniques and recollects his own childhood ambition to be an astronaut. Instead of the gills and fins that enchant his daughter, he dreams of pressurized helmets, capsules, air pumps, reinforced steel structures and blazing trails of fire that lead to other worlds. This is no fantasy. He works for the Kennedy Space Center that, since 1962, has embodied the modern American dream that is nurtured within him; a primal desire for transformation in alligator-littered glades civilized by advanced technologies. Yet, he is not one of those chosen to live in space, but one of the tens of thousands of support staff who can only suppose that weightlessness is like breathing underwater or flying. He knows these impossible terrains demand adaptation, transformation and alterity. They require new ways of living in exotic landscapes and herald a modern era of 'supermen'.

*Suspension in mid-water is our embryonic fluid.*

Christopher Columbus noted that some mermaids appeared masculine, like bearded ladies of the circus. The rather particular notion of 'femaleness' is, of course, in question here. Yet, it is supposed this apparent mirage was the sighting of gentle, blubbery-visaged sea cows, suckling their young, which appear as languid humans from afar. At six feet, the manatees stand on their tails in shallow water and turn their heads with supple neck vertebrae, while the broad caudal extremity of their lower back extends into a powerful fish-like termination. From the scapula to the extremities of the phalanges, their forelegs resemble 'female' arms that end naturally in five finger-like bones.

European sideshows soon advertised 'recently discovered' mermaids from the New World shot on sight by sailors who believed they were being lured to their deaths. Deceased sirenians and fictitious hybrid cadavers, which joined simians with fish, evidenced these 'monsters'.

*I am a mermaid, my daughter is a mermaid, and my granddaughter is a mermaid.*

Every shape and size of woman, with all kinds of reasons to be a mermaid, now walk on tightropes and twirl umbrellas under the water, breathing through effervescent spring-powered tubes and bending oddly at the knees, with lash of tail and sequined flippers. When you're a water person, then you're at home under a rising curtain of bubbles.

*Just because you don't want to live in a fantasy world doesn't mean we don't exist. There are mermaids everywhere.*

## 7.5 Witch bottles

Forms of soil-making that encode value and intent have been used in traditional practices of spell-making. Apparatuses are ritualistically filled with materials and objects that possess symbolic value. For example, salt indicates cleansing, while nails invoke harm. The specific arrangement of these agents aims to channel intangible forces into a site through the properties of the enclosed material and therefore influence events.

Three 'witch bottles' were developed as a programmable soil prototype, cultural experiment and land art triptych that marked a specific territory within the Robert Rauschenberg Foundation property grounds in Captiva, May 2016 (see Figure 7.3). Witch bottles were a popular method of exerting influence over a particular course of events and part of a tradition of British charm-making that dates from the sixteenth century. The residency project combined the instrumental property of medieval spell-casting with the local custom of making souvenir bottles from samples of earthy structures like sands and shells. The resultant prototypes therefore approximated symbolic and local practices to explore the relationship between the structure of soil and the construction of environmental values.

The work responds to ongoing ecological change and distress, where barrier landmasses like Captiva are threatened by devastating sea level changes (see Sections 7.3 and 7.5). The bottles purport to contain or destroy negative forces by channelling them into transformational soil substrates. Drawing on the material and mythological properties of soils, the hand-crafted earths built in the witch bottles were imagined as land custodians that channelled the qualities of air, water and fire through their bespoke soil systems.

**FIGURE 7.3** *A series of witch bottles themed on the elements of air, water and fire draw from symbolic and local practices, aim to establish a site-specific protective charm over the Rauschenberg property and provoke conversations about tactical responses to the damaging consequences of climate change. (Artwork by Rachel Armstrong: Glass bottles, sand, shells, nails, glass, miscellaneous found objects, April 2016, 75 × 50 × 50 cm, Robert Rauschenberg Foundation grounds, Captiva, Florida). Photograph courtesy of Rachel Armstrong: Robert Rauschenberg Foundation, Captiva, Florida, May 2016.*

The soil spell was constructed at the site of placement and was performed in an intensely meditative manner that sought connection with the invisible forces that were channelled through the site. The spell for environmental protection was cast, particularly to spare the trees at times of disruption, since they had previously been devastated during hurricane Charley in 2004, which tore them from their roots. Their conservation during turbulent times was particularly important to the late 'Bob' Rauschenberg.

The basic programme consisted of three substantial layers of soil material that were carefully layered by hand into three 75-cm-tall glass flat-bottomed flasks. A founding layer of dark sand was constructed that symbolized harmful agents; above this, samples of Captiva's sand and shells were introduced to indicate the body needing protection, while white sand formed the upper layers and signified purification. Between these horizons, specific elements with symbolic significance were developed as boundary layers and material signifiers. Mirror fragments invoked aspects of prophecy, danger and ephemerality. Iridescent sequins indicated biodiversity, while tree-killing copper nails symbolized impending threat to biological systems, warning of dangerous times ahead. Brightly coloured sands were also carefully layered to indicate particular elemental systems through the alchemical powers of air, fire and water. Stoppers for the bottles were carved from locally harvested sea grape wood, and the completed installation was sealed with different candles encoded with symbolic meaning. Black flames with a red heart joined the realms of life and death, while white candles indicated integrity, and beeswax spoke to the organic forces of the natural realm.

The placement of each bottle demarcated a protected area to be influenced by the charm. Airborne elements were invoked beneath a tree with a natural beehive, while water was conjured at a turn towards the Rauschenberg Memorial Chair that looks out to the ocean, and fire was channelled by placing a bottle under the site of a 'flame' tree with brilliant claw-shaped, orange blossom.

The witch bottles did not propose to 'fix' climate change, or physically stop sea levels rising, but signified areas of particular value that could provoke discussion within Captiva's community about the difficult decisions needed to address critical issues related to the liveability of the island in the immediate and longer-term future. Since the bottles have a permanent home on the Robert Rauschenberg Foundation's grounds, the conversations are ongoing. On the Sunday that I was leaving the residency, a group of Unitarian Christians had gathered around the 'air' witch bottle, which was under a cloud of curious bees, discussing the nature of art, the character of Nature and how all living things through diversity found the glory of God.

Following hurricane Irma, I was notified by Ann Brady, Director of the Robert Rauschenberg Foundation, with an observation that the witch bottles had 'worked and saved two Royal Poinciana's.'

> How about that?!!! Magic still happens in the world. (*Brady, personal communication, 18 September 2017*)

In a parallel realm, the witch bottles exist 'virtually' in the BBC's Museum of Curiosity (iPlayer Radio, 2016), where they coexist among a 'wonderful array of donations including Narnia red, a witch bottle, a short-faced bear, some wild fig trees and a deep-fried wing of the museum' (Quite Interesting Limited, 2016).

## 7.6 Gog and Magog

The connection between ground and its native peoples is an ancient concept, whose severance leads to extreme conflict and possible extinction scenarios.

Although the land with which I am twinned no longer thinks with me, or through me, its vegetable pulse beats within its thickening soils and the metabolic heat of its developing earths is a fertile legacy that is already my own.

The biblical story of Gog (settler) and Magog (settled land) describes the inseparability of civilizations from their home territory, specifically in this case, where hostile forces muster against the people of Israel and are promised deliverance from this trauma by their god.

Son of man, set your face against Gog, of the land of Magog ... I will invade a land of unwalled villages; I will attack a peaceful and unsuspecting people – all of them living without walls and without gates and bars. I will plunder and loot and turn my hand against the resettled ruins and the people gathered from the nations, rich in livestock and goods, living at the centre of the land. (Ezek. 38–39, New International Version)

While biblical references to Gog and Magog are relatively few, they have shaped theological debate, medieval legends and apocalyptic literature. While Gog and Magog have also been interpreted as marauding hostile armies, they are allied with the armies of Satan (Ahroni, 1977). Contemporarily, they have also been used in reference to ongoing conflict in the Middle East.

This entanglement between people and their land resonates through many stories about identity and inhabitation of the earth – from the legend of Antaios, the Libyan giant who forced travellers to compete with him in a wrestling match and grew stronger each time he was thrown to the ground, to the mythological need for vampires to travel with their soil under which their coffins are buried, and the overview effect experienced by astronauts, whereby an intense sense of connectedness with the earth is experienced by those separated from it.

Bruno Latour's environmental Gog and Magog is encapsulated in his notion of Earthbound – a name for an ecologically minded (future) human race that counters the extinction scenarios of the Anthropocene – also draws on the inseparability between inhabitants and their land as critical for establishing a new ecological era (Latour, 2013). Having cleaved the long-standing link between the ground and its inhabitants by sanitizing the land and erasing its historical contexts, the moderns of the industrial era continue to alienate humanity from the earth through the interlocution of machines, factories and advanced (digital) technologies. With the welfare of the environment at stake, Bruno Latour's positions nature (Gaia) as an actor in the conflicts between the moderns and Earthbound. Ambiguities therefore arise on the world's stage regarding the likely cause of events that may arise during this transition, which sets the scene for a dramatic battle of wills between the future peoples of the world (humans vs. Earthbound) and nature that is set to establish an alternative global order with the potential to usurp modernity (Blake, 2013).

In keeping with the epic narrative of living upon the earth differently and its intimate relationship with soil, soft living architecture adopts an optimistic perspective and reclaims the mutually interdependent relationship between bodies and their environments that are fundamental to life's unbroken legacy. While it does not deny the present and unfolding environmental catastrophes, its ethical position is to critically design for the welfare of people and the planet rather. This is a smaller subset of possibilities than focusing on everything that could potentially go wrong and prevent it going wrong – because, at a time of ecocide, it already has. All the analysis in the world isn't going to put the earth we think we remember back together again.

Now that we're dead, how do we work around the present catastrophe?

While Slavoj Žižek asks us to discover the aesthetic potential of waste (Žižek, 2011, p. 35) and Timothy Morton proposes we should design with metabolism to generate 'straightforward environmental images' (Morton, 2007, p. 150), soft living architecture recognizes the potency of soils as agency capable of yielding the Babelsphere. It does not, however, propose that people are confined to particular geographies, habitats or environmental niches (the flat geometries of ground) in an age of global travel but emphasizes the myriad ways by which places may be inhabited. Indeed, soft living architecture proposes that a test for recognizing a viable environment is whether the soil that feeds its ecosystems and people is good enough to eat unmodified.

> That was the year the founder took a long spoon from his pocket, plunged it into the earth and scooped a spoonful of organic matter into his mouth. He chewed for a few, silent moments then spat the dirt onto the ground.
> 'Bitter!'
> He vowed that by the time we left the island it would taste of magic.
> (Armstrong and Hughes, 2016a)

## 7.7 Sound walk

Sounds are a characteristic part of a city's identity and reveal invisible relationships with the Natural realm, which may appear subdued in urban sites – until they are listened to. The parallel worlds of our urban soundscapes may be captured by sound recordings along specific routes of interest. With the right kind of microphones, such techniques may even reach down into the ground into parallel soils, where they are experienced through *soft living vibrations*.

An old woman, about ninety and deaf, answers to the signed-name Sylvia. She spends all day wheeling a large instrument in a suitcase upon a trolley and lever over undulating bridges. At first, she appears to be a member of an orchestra, perhaps a tuba player, but then she removes the giant contraption from its case, and does not put a hat, or box on the ground to collect coins. It's a fine brass instrument, but it's straight – like a didgeridoo, not curled like an orchestra piece. There are no keys, no holes to cover with fingers, and for all intents and purposes it is built in the style of a megaphone. Yet, there is no handle to help her deliver her message, because she doesn't shout into it. She listens.

Putting the hand-made device to the ground, it becomes her perceptual realm as she stands still like a blackbird, motionless on one foot, listening to the city's stones, her flat palms pressed against its girth. Coupled with the ground through the huge brass trumpet, she is invigorated, fully sensible – a living tuning fork. Vagrant sounds resonate within the bowels of the city and travel up through the ground, into the apparatus, are amplified and cascade through her bones. Each symphony is like a heartbeat, adding minutes to her life as their pulsations and energies invigorate her flesh, their oscillations strung into her body like artificial organs.

Slurping lagoon waters, hissing drains, yapping dogs, secrets of underground chambers, tortured phantoms, rats' lairs, biofilm conversations, leaky conversations, territorial ducks, splitting mortar, polite puddles, cruel gossip, post-truths, shattering efflorescence, shrieking seagulls, gurgling gatoli, coiling worms, churning currents, sulphurous faeces, fizzing gas pipes, steaming optical fibres, clandestine meetings, crumbling concrete and subdued soils.

She harvests these delights, and when sufficiently invigorated by the sounds of lost time, trundles the impossible apparatus as a few passers-by throw coins. They are impressed by, or pitying, her strange performance; but she's not looking for an audience, and scoops the money into a purse. Then she empties the change into the paper cup of a young boy with a hairy birthmark that covers his right cheek, who has been holding an abject posture for well over an hour.

Now, she purses her lips, whistling something into the cross winds, bumping her life-support system over a twisted bridge and shuffles on.

## 7.8 Land and community

The industrial era is poorly equipped to deal with environmental change and, if it occurs at all, is incremental and harbours notions of *sustainability* that by their very definition preserve the status quo. The conventional architectural response to political and social crisis is restorative, helping communities to adapt to the aftermath of trauma, rather than intervening during times of unrest and conflict. Indeed, taking a passive role seems justified as a natural process of renewal occurs where, with enough time, scars on the land and in the hearts of communities eventually close over.

> The 1783 eruptions were seen as part of a pattern of history in Iceland and the entire world. The event and the resulting landscape showed that the earth's history was constantly renewing and repeating itself that, rather than a single catastrophic event such as the Flood, there were many cycles of collapse and renewal. The new lava fields and the transformed Icelandic landscape stood for the history of the entire earth, Iceland was a site where one would observe processes of change that were hidden elsewhere, exceptional for the clarity of these phenomena but unique in these processes. Rather the small Island was important for not being unique, for instead illustrating the cyclical history of the globe. (Cronon and Oslund, 2011, pp. 44–5)

The effects of global warming are more than a cyclical disturbance in the order of the world; they constitute persistent disruption which breaks from previous ordering systems. When treacherous terrains, extreme weather and inflexible political, economic and social infrastructures are killing people and destroying livelihoods, much more is needed than building repairs that restore the status quo – (re)evaluation of the character and role of architecture is pressing. Agile modes of inhabitation, however, do not ameliorate suffering or disruption but potentially equip populations with the adaptive capacity to respond to both acute stresses and find ways of enduring longer-term global challenges.

One of the biggest challenges modern cities face is a wetter world owing to flash flooding and sea level rises. Many cities are established around bodies of water, deltas or coastlines. However, contemporary architecture is not designed for wetness or to augment the infrastructures of life. It is designed to support the operations of those machines that run our buildings. However, dryness is not always an optimal approach, and presently, 'blue' architecture builds permeability into structures that interface with bodies of water such as the sea walls of Sydney Harbour. As tides rise, waves spill on to the pavement and grass, forming large puddles that drain away with the tide. Within these wall spaces, marine creatures find traction and establish flourishing rock pools along the sea front. This builds further resilience against tidal erosion and counters the loss of wildlife that is typically associated with sea barrier systems. When living on the coast, or flood plain, the height of water rise is much less problematic than its rate of rise. If levels increase slowly, people have opportunity to raise walkways, roads and buildings, take sanitation measures, and build seawalls. They also have time to move away. The process is problematic but feasible.

Poorly designed social, economic and political systems are as damaging to the welfare of communities as the actual impacts of natural disasters. Insurances policies in areas of flooding, such as New Orleans whose low-lying lands make the city one of the most climate-change vulnerable places in the world, are pricing people out of their homes. Moreover, as most people learned post-Katrina that homeowners' insurance, the second most expensive premium in the United States, does not cover any damage that results from flooding and therefore need to purchase a separate flood insurance policy backed by the National Flood Insurance Program to supplement their basic cover. Most of these policies will support repairs to restore existing structures and ways of living so they are safer at times of flood, rather than invent new approaches to ways of living in these areas.

Especially when infrastructures to prevent flooding happening in the first place are installed, communities find more informal ways of continuing to live in their homes, rather than face becoming refugees. However, this takes an admission of a bigger problem than the policies of individuals and requires collective investment in a city-scale approach that puts people, not profit margins, first. While everyone has a different threshold for dealing with challenging conditions, collectively great engineering feats of land reclamation may be achieved, which requires concerted and sustained investments.

In the Netherlands, a quarter of the land and a fifth of its population are below sea level. The country's formal relationship with wet environments may be traced back to St Elizabeth's flood in 1421 after a tidal surge when 10,000 people died in Zeeland and Holland and the more recent 1953 North Sea flood. These disasters have served as catalysts for public investment in surge barriers, dams, dykes and canals. Indeed, the Netherlands is reaching out to New Orleans to collaborate on the *Living with Water* project, which encourages a more intimate connection between city residents and water. Already most of the city is below sea level, and while it is protected by a system of locks, levees and sea walls, it remains extremely vulnerable to environmental events. Hurricane Katrina, which hit the city in late August 2005, generated a 6-metre storm surge, which flooded around 80 per cent of the city and killed more than 1,800 people. In total, it caused more than $75 billion worth of damage and left more than 100,000 homeless. Tragically, the poorest communities were hit hardest, and they formed the first wave of

American climate refugees. While regional plans are in place to try to protect the city by building up natural flood plains and are building a $15 billion surge barrier at Lake Borgne, the height is based on current sea levels, and over the course of the century, the risks are only likely to grow more severe. Rising sea levels and sinking coastal land will increase water levels by at least 1.2 metres before the end of the century (Loria, 2015) and may reach as much as 3.7 metres (NOAA, 2017). Even with the established wisdom of the Dutch, New Orleans may already be investing too little, too late in its future. The surge wall certainty does not solve all its challenges as its protective wetlands are being lost to industrial development, and massive investments are required to turn environmental impacts around. In preparing for devastating rises in sea levels, New Orleans is a test case for the United States, and the rest of the world, in deciding whether *cities of Canute* are possible or establishing a point at which entire settlements become uninhabitable (Werman, 2013). In a nation that is caught in the politics of climate change denial, along with limited enthusiasm for social investment schemes, the future of New Orleans is highly precarious.

Rising waters are not uniform in their impacts, and there is no one way of living with wetness. High tides in Venice were known during the Middle Ages. Since then, the city has developed ways of dealing with intermittent flooding, or *acqua alta*, when high tides rise more than 120 cm above the maritime baseline (mareographic zero). These are most frequent during the autumn and spring. Currently, the *acqua alta* can happen up to sixty times a year. However, tidal events can frequently reach between 80 and 109 cm above sea level, while 'very intense' flooding events are recognized at between 110 and 140 cm. The highest tide recorded above the standard level documented was 194 cm in November 1966, after which people started moving out of the city in droves. The flooding risk is greater in the north-west of the city and increased by other factors that include land subsidence in the lagoon as well as extensive industrial activity draining the Venetian aquifer. Despite the ground floors of 16,000 houses having become unusable, the city has not been abandoned and, in fact, real estate prices have rocketed over recent years.

Venice has also had time on its hands as it has invested in responding to the challenges of flooding events by developing approaches that are integrated within the city's culture. When the *acqua alta* are forecast, sirens are sounded throughout the city, with real-time online information made available. Hotels provide tourists with maps and directions around flooded passageways, and transport routes are diverted appropriately. Protective clothing is worn, and popular routes are bridged with temporary networks of elevated walkways. For the few hours when the waters rise with the peak tides, metal waterproof gates and doors are raised around doorways, and everyone waits for the *acqua alta* to retreat before they go about business as usual. While the acute effects of rising water are manageable, the longer-term effects of rising damp require a greater investment in ongoing maintenance of the city, where the first forty courses of bricks are replaced in ten-year cycles. Many residents no longer furnish their apartments below the first floor, and some have even transformed their courtyards into private moorings. More formal city-scale solutions have also been sought, and currently the city awaits the opening of the MOSE (**MO**dulo **S**perimentale **E**lettromeccanico) project, which began in 2003 (Ravera, 2000). This is a series of seventy-eight hydraulically powered gates capable of supporting a 3-metre-high tide and will protect Venice for a century. In fact, if any more than a permanent 1-metre rise in sea levels occurs, it will spell destruction for the whole of Italy – not just Venice (Windsor, 2015). Impenetrable barriers, however, may not be the permanent answer to the city's future.

In 1949, Carlo Scarpa incorporated Venetian waterways into building details within the renovations for the lower level of the Palazzo Querini Stampalia, home to the Querini Stampalia Foundation, an organization supporting the arts in Venice. While the back gardens were in deep need of repair, the rest of the building was envisioned to function largely as a museum holding a series of changing exhibits. However, the ground floor was frequently flooded and was considered unusable for exhibitions. Scarpa responded to the stratification of water levels and walkways within the city and created a series of raised floors, channels and cantilevers, which transformed the building interior into a magical landscape and a miniature portrait of a city equipped to navigate inconstant water levels (Indursky, 2013).

Such extraordinary poetry and choreography of space-time reveal how it is possible for us to live better on the land, while also embracing the sea, or other bodies of water that we live alongside. Protocols for soft living architectures include using structural matrices for 'thirsty' buildings where, for example, bog-like ground absorbs water and hygroscopic dwellings expand on contact with moisture and contract again on desiccation. Yet no one overarching solution offers a cure-all to a world in flux. Soft living architecture provided an expanded palette of materials, apparatuses and tactics which can take us beyond traditional comfort zones, where tarnished spaces may be transformed through a (re)engagement with the infrastructures of life.

## 7.9 Mirror puddle

In a parallel world, surface reflections may seem solid enough to support our body weight and invert our expectations of inhabiting a condition of wetness.

While walking along the Fondamenta delle Zattere, I saw the sun on the paving slabs, like a large mirror throwing off shards of light.

I tried to ignore it; just a puddle on the stonework but I couldn't avoid it. Distractingly, it turned the pipette-fluted window frames on a terracotta Venetian Gothic house into a set of champagne glasses, then twisted the pediment of the church of Santa Maria del Rosario into a ship's hull. If that wasn't disturbing enough, it converted an excoriated marble box for posting lies into a receptacle for truths. Suddenly, the brilliant sun rose from the puddle and obliterated my view over the Giudecca canal.

Blinded. I fell in.

There I was, standing on my hands, the world in reverse above me, with the sun glaring down disdainfully at my foolishness. I tried to invert myself but I simply couldn't get the right way up again.

There was little point shouting. Only my body odour could speak, like a rotten vegetable, and I couldn't figure out how to call for help. Soft clouds darkened and blushed as they rolled over the sky. The next morning, a seagull with a mean eye and giant yellow beak thrust its almond razor nostrils towards what I presume it imagined to be a strange fish. Mercifully, it could not reach me.

The puddle changed its hue and brilliance many times over during the passing days and, soon, I learned to walk around my puddle world, feet in the air, feeding on scraps – a half-eaten panini, spilt gelato limone, molten pizza and an apple core. It was not much, but it kept me going.

I grew bolder, traversing the entire Zattere mile every day on my palms. Liberated from the limitations of my hominid ancestry, my thighbones began to thin and I could pat my head and rub my tummy with my feet, while odd tendons and blood vessels sprouted from my shoulder girdle. Soon, it was painful to brachiate and I developed callouses on my thumbs.

Now indistinguishable from the gaps between the paving stones, I began to doubt that I'd ever return to a world of aerial lights. I stared listlessly at my toes, kicking out now and again to see if I could flip myself back on to the paving stones. But nothing worked.

And so, over many years, I faded, becoming no more noticeable than an oily slick on a puddle, in which someone might glimpse the shape of a hand.

Then, one day, as the next four thousand years were starting to seem terribly grim and it started to rain, a young girl with polka-dot gumboots and a pink umbrella fished me out with its upturned handle. As if I'd only just fallen over.

## 7.10 Doggerland: Uncertainty, prophecy and the near-shore experience

Those who inhabit the sea provide alternative languages and parallel perspectives on its oceanic expanses and invisible depths that only first-hand experience of this mutable terrain and its cultures can bestow.

Every night, BBC Radio 4 reads the *shipping forecast* before handing over to the World Service until daily broadcasts begin again at six o'clock: Viking, North Utsire, South Utsire, Forties, Cromarty, Forth, Tyne, Dogger, Fisher, German Bight, Humber, Thames, Dover, Wight, Portland, Plymouth, Biscay, Trafalgar, Fitzroy, Sole, Lundy, Fastnet, Irish Sea, Shannon, Malin, Hebrides, Bailey, Fair Isle, Faeroes and Southeast Iceland. These coastal areas describe a liquid mantle that swirls around the British Isles and calls upon sandbanks, estuaries, islands, coastal indentations, pioneers, towns, islets and headlands to seed our sleepy imaginations with their turbulent nature so that our dreams may be punctuated with waves, currents, eddies, storms and unexplained events. All of these territories are invisible to those who dwell upon the land.

Standing at the shore at Blyth, which was once the most flourishing opencast mine and coal-exporting port in the north-east of England, the deep sea reaches out towards northern Europe and towards a vanishing horizon that travels onwards as the mirage of eternity. This grey featureless expanse is a foreboding place to land dwellers – perhaps save for moments when the waves glitter under the cold, silver light of the cloud-veiled sun. Yet, to seafarers, the unstable waters are rich with moods and stories that can be read like a book.

Aboard the *Princess Royal*, Newcastle University's research vessel, which has been berthed at Blyth for over a hundred years, the banks of screens that describe the invisible shoreline landscapes are switched between viewing modes by the skipper, Neil Armstrong. While the deep sea is relatively stable, the near-shore – where the land collides with the sea – is treacherous. Underlying strata are chewed by waves, landslides, upheavals of sandbars, sunken ships and the eddies that swirl around exposed rocks. Armstrong navigates this slippery terrain using a combination of modern control systems that incorporate an enormous amount of measurement instrumentation – temperature, pressure, flow, vibration, current and depth sensors – which are transduced into digital data by mechanical systems like gauges, electrical meters, thermocouples and resistance temperature detectors. Collectively, the boat's devices become extended eyes, ears and an expanded skin around the vessel. They are not only essential for navigation but also regulate the operation of equipment, like hoists, and safety features such as automatic shutdowns. Armstrong activates his digital mechanical crew every day when the vessel leaves port, where they help him observe the protean character of the near-shore environment, which is prone to swallowing hydrophones, generating surprising new currents, provoking freak waves and diverting tidal flows. On the control deck, these dangers are clearly displayed as multicoloured snapshots of submerged terrains. Yet the skipper knows that although his robotic crew have transformed the way he works, machines and computers are prone to errors and in themselves do not possess embodied knowledge of the sea and its moods.

Out on the water, knowing where you are and what responses to make under certain conditions is a matter of life and death. Although the boat's computers are hosted on different systems, in case one of the circuits fails, the analogue instruments – magnetic compass, dividers and paper maps – are never far away from the skipper's reach. In fact, Armstrong is required by law to carry them. But even without the constantly crowdsourced digitally produced maps, he uses his lifelong knowledge of the sea to navigate these offshore territories. The stories that have been handed down to him through his family of fishermen – and his own experiences as a fisherman – are an inbuilt navigational system, reminiscent of a European robin winging its way through weak magnetic fields from Africa to Europe. Through the breaking waves, he anticipates danger, drawing on the tales of the rough and smooth areas under the water where the sea floor shifts from rock to silt or where currents swell around submerged obstacles like shipwrecks and submerged sandbanks. He also knows the 'badlands' and the wicked currents that churn the sea floor. Aboard the boat, land-dwellers like me cling to the apparent stability of the land and its horizontal register for reassurance, believing it will guide us safely home. But the skipper's gaze is seawards, using the data streams and his experience to confirm the significance of hidden histories, shipwrecks and invisible landscapes that characterize these waters.

The wind is spiteful, and it is only minutes before our noses, fingers and ears begin to freeze, so I make my way back from the deck and go inside to the control panel, where I can watch the waves whip up from behind the comfort of safety glass. The submerged topology that comes into view on the boat's multiple displays seems completely at odds with the solemn grey waves, and I wonder what would actually be visible if the ocean was drained away. The bathometry display is constantly refreshed by the boat's sonar and can work at multiple scales as well as sourcing the collective data provided by the GPS-mediated 'mind maps' of other boats in the areas. As if from atop a mountain, it is now possible to see the multicoloured depth contours of the North Sea as they stretch out into a relatively shallow scarp slope that averages somewhere between 25 and 100 metres towards the Nordic regions, before rising sharply again to become the characteristic land mass of the European North.

Up until around 5,500 years ago, this ice-clad 'Doggerland' was a huge landmass where mammoths and reindeer roamed. It was named after the Dogger sandbank, a productive fishing area in a shallow area of the North Sea that was first reported by Dutch seventeenth-century 'dogger' fishing vessels, which trawled for cod. It stretches from northern Scotland across to Denmark and down as far as the Channel Islands. For most of us today, 'Dogger' is little more than an odd name listed on the *shipping forecast* as we fall asleep to the World Service beeps. Yet, at its most vibrant, Doggerland was home to tens of thousands of Mesolithic peoples that thrived among its rich hunting grounds with low-lying lagoons, marshes, mudflats and beaches. Once thought to have been the 'real heartland' of Europe, these lands were slowly drowned over thousands of years at the end of the last Ice Age (between 18000 BC and 5500 BC) by water that was previously locked away in glaciers and ice sheets. However, some settlers adapted to become fishing communities, skilled with a life on the sea. Even as shorelines became further and further away, the dramatic change in water levels meant that even these inventive modes of living became unsustainable. Moreover, the degree of change also rendered obsolete the wisdom of elders who knew the moods of their ancestral lands. Perpetually estranged from their ancestral hunting ground, fishing territories and burial lands, Doggerlanders experienced profound placelessness and were met with increasing territorial hostility as they attempted to (re)establish themselves (Spinney, 2012). Doggerland was finally claimed by the North Sea around 6,000 years ago when three catastrophic Storegga slides from a 300-kilometre Norwegian costal shelf, with a volume of sediment around the equivalent mass of Iceland, crashed into the sea creating catastrophic tsunamis.

For years, the existence of this lost land could only be deduced from the bones and reindeer antlers dredged by fishermen from sites all over the North Sea. Over the last few years, oil companies working with universities such as St Andrews, Aberdeen, Birmingham, Dundee and Wales Trinity St David have gathered data and artefacts such as flints, discovered deep within the sea bed, to recreate what Doggerland may have looked like. The ancient site tells of its dramatic past shaped by climate change, and we are yet to discover how the Doggerlanders dealt with rising waters in flood lands and the coastal area. While the pinpoint accuracy of modern technology enables us to visualize unseen terrains of the seabed and has brought new insights to our contemporary understanding of coastal areas, it is important not to neglect the ancient wisdom embedded in these sites.

As we understand more about Doggerland, we are discovering that the climate change faced by Mesolithic settlers is analogous to our own and that they were forced out of their homeland by rising water that engulfed their low-lying settlements and caused mass displacement. If polar ice caps continue to melt at today's accelerated pace, billions of people who live within 60 kilometres (37 miles) of a shoreline today could be affected by a situation similar to that of the Doggerland communities. Perhaps, in reclaiming their histories and constructing parallel futures from these submerged spaces, we may find ways of thriving in highly unstable lands.

Today, we talk about the future of our coastal zones in solemn terms and describe their inevitable destruction by rising sea levels. Yet we seem unable to inhabit these regions differently than we have already done this way for thousands of years. With the global trend towards urbanization, the movement of people has become more restricted and we have learned to regard borders as permanent structures. However, if we can deal with the inconstancy of our global climate in relation to the temporary nature of settlements, then perhaps this will open up parallel modes of thriving where hunter-gatherers followed their food sources, found shelter and had fewer expectations of permanence. While some obviously perished in the natural catastrophes that befell the heartlands of Europe, enough of them survived to become the many peoples that we know today. This flies in the face of all modern conventions that seek to build barriers against the inexorable and colossal shifts that our pale blue dot is capable of. Whatever approach we decide on responding to the present planetary-scale challenges, the past experiences of ancient peoples must remind us that a passive approach to climate change is not a good solution. We must be proactive in making decisions about the way we live and so, avoid becoming just another sunken and mostly forgotten culture, whose only evidence exists in the decayed artefacts and fossils of its people.

## 7.11 Babel chandelier

Albert Einstein remarked that the quantum realm, which is a parallel reality, changed everything except the way we think. While its characteristics are still being experimentally verified, we continue to observe the world through a familiar classical gaze – except perhaps, when we consider the realm of light.

> In the Doge's city of photons, communities of quanta haunt the crusted stalactites of Murano glass chandeliers, and at the oddest times, randomly burst out into lilac formations. The excitable little ones climb to the top of the light fittings, while concurrently bouncing like jumping beans, on polished veneers in the hallway. The older ones cannot decide which masterpieces they want to study first and spilt into parallel visitor streams across the frescoes that

may, or may not, also encircle the world. Through fluted glass prism frames, elderly particles flop like flour sacks to the floor, having seen all possible events already, while the little ones scream for their attention. Tunnelling under Persian prayer carpets, ancient photons nod gracefully while rounding up the little ones that are gyrating masslessly in floral patterns on the floor. As the flame sunset burns the bottle-bottom window lattices, the elderly particles are transfused with incident light. Suddenly boosted into more energetic orbits, they wave encouragingly back up at their ageing progeny, which cannot decide how they feel about being simultaneously created and destroyed, beckoning them to drip down alongside them on the rug.

## 7.12 Corresponding with the cosmos

Not all phenomena can be completely deciphered or rationalized. It is not always up to humans to invent languages. Indeed, iterations of irreducible symbols exist in the environment if we look for them. To us, their meaning and significance is highly conjectural although the patterns they produce suggest they emerge from principles encoded within an underlying order, which emanates from parallel worlds.

> This analysis of rhythms in all their magnitude 'from particles to galaxies' has a transdisciplinary character. It gives itself the objective, amongst others, of separating as little as possible the scientific from the poetic. (Lefebvre, 2013, p. 87)

I explored the rich diurnal variations of the Robert Rauschenberg Foundation property during a month-long residency and observed how coconut seeds were dispersed, the way ospreys circled Pine Island Sound and the intensity with which carpenter ants chewed out the heart of sea grape trees.

At night-time, the surface of the water around the bay area by the iconic 'Ding' Darling Fish House was sufficiently still that the night sky reflected on the water could be clearly seen. The Moon and Venus wrote on the water, each with their particular quality of light, where their correspondences were modulated through the tides. The Moon generated soft-edged traces like a spray gun (see Figure 7.4), while Venus, being so far away, scribbled on the surface as a point source. These Rosetta stones were celestial documents sharing the wisdom of ages and their observations of our planet, although they remain undeciphered.[1]

---

[1] This technique was used to capture the Vivaldi music (see Section 6.10).

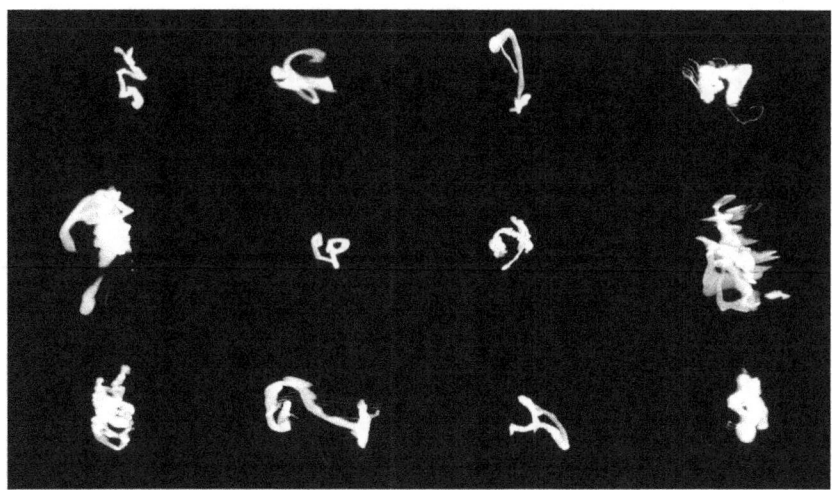

**FIGURE 7.4** *Moon writing: A waning half-moon writes on the surface of the bay around the Fish House. Photograph courtesy of Rachel Armstrong, digital editing by April Rodmyre: Robert Rauschenberg Foundation, Captiva, Florida, May 2016.*

# 8

# Projects

The Living Architecture project is an example of an emerging, real-world, soft living architecture. In this chapter, it is accompanied by a progression of proposals that are based on real-world prototypes and parallel worlds, many of which are exemplified through the fabric of Venice. The range and scope of these concepts collectively suggests that soft living architecture not only transgresses the traditional boundaries of architectural construction, such as transforming the ground into artificial islands, but also has the potential to catalyse radical social and cultural change.

## 8.1 Living Architecture

Typically structure and flow are regarded as separate and competing systems in an architectural context. Structure is permanent, while flow is temporary. The Living Architecture project aims to address this paradox that is resolved within living systems by using the metabolisms of organisms to develop a series of modular units or 'living' bricks.[1] Specifically, it responds to the dynamic nature of the living world by developing units for construction that combine structure and flow. The underlying technological advances that enable this are in the design and realization of modular units that perform the work of organisms, rather than machines. Living Architecture is therefore envisioned as a next-generation, selectively programmable set of bioreactor units that are capable, for example, of extracting valuable resources from sunlight, wastewater and

---

[1] The Living Architecture project has received €3.2 m funding from the European Union's Horizon 2020 Research and Innovation Programme under Grant Agreement no. 686585. It is a collaboration of experts from the universities of Newcastle, UK; the West of England (UWE Bristol); Trento, Italy; the Spanish National Research Council in Madrid; LIQUIFER Systems Group, Vienna, Austria; and Explora, Venice, Italy, that began in April 2016 and runs to April 2019 (Living Architecture, 2016).

air and, in turn, generating oxygen, proteins and biomass. Conceived as a freestanding partition located in a household kitchen to increase domestic resource utilization, its bioreactor building blocks (see Sections 8.1.1, 8.1.2 and 8.1.3) are being developed as standardized building segments or 'bricks'. Living Architecture uses the processing principles of both aerobic photobioreactor and anaerobic microbial fuel cell (MFC) technologies to adapt and combine them into a single, sequential hybrid bioreactor system. The specific biochemical transformations are based on the idea of 'closed loop' systems, where the outputs of one system become the feedstock for the next and will work synergistically to clean wastewater, generate oxygen, provide electrical power and generate useable biomass (fertilizer).

## *8.1.1 Microbial fuel cell*

MFCs are specific anaerobic bioreactors used by the Living Architecture project that operate as bioelectrochemical devices or 'living batteries'. They convert the chemical energy of organic matter – frequently detritus – into electricity, using the metabolic processes of microorganisms that act as biocatalysts that spontaneously form a biofilm in situ. The battery cell consists of two compartments, the anode and the cathode, which are separated by a proton-exchange membrane. In the anode chamber, bacteria anaerobically oxidize the organic matter to release electrons, which provide the electricity and protons, which are acidic in solution. The electrons are collected through an external circuit to provide electrical power, and the protons flow through the membrane and react with oxygen to produce fresh water.

## *8.1.2 Photobioreactor*

A range of microorganisms transform carbon dioxide and sunlight to produce biomass. The Living Architecture project uses different species of algae, which are aquatic photosynthetic organisms as metabolic 'workhorses'. These can thrive in the cathode chamber of MFCs to form an aerobic bioreactor component where they boost the power generation within the MFC.

## *8.1.3 Synthetic bioreactor*

In addition to the established bioreactor technologies, the project also develops a genetically modified consortium that works alongside, but separately from, the genetically unmodified MFC system. This module provides the metabolic programmability of the system – a 'metabolic app' where the MFC anode is coaxed to produce very specific kinds of substances. The synthetic

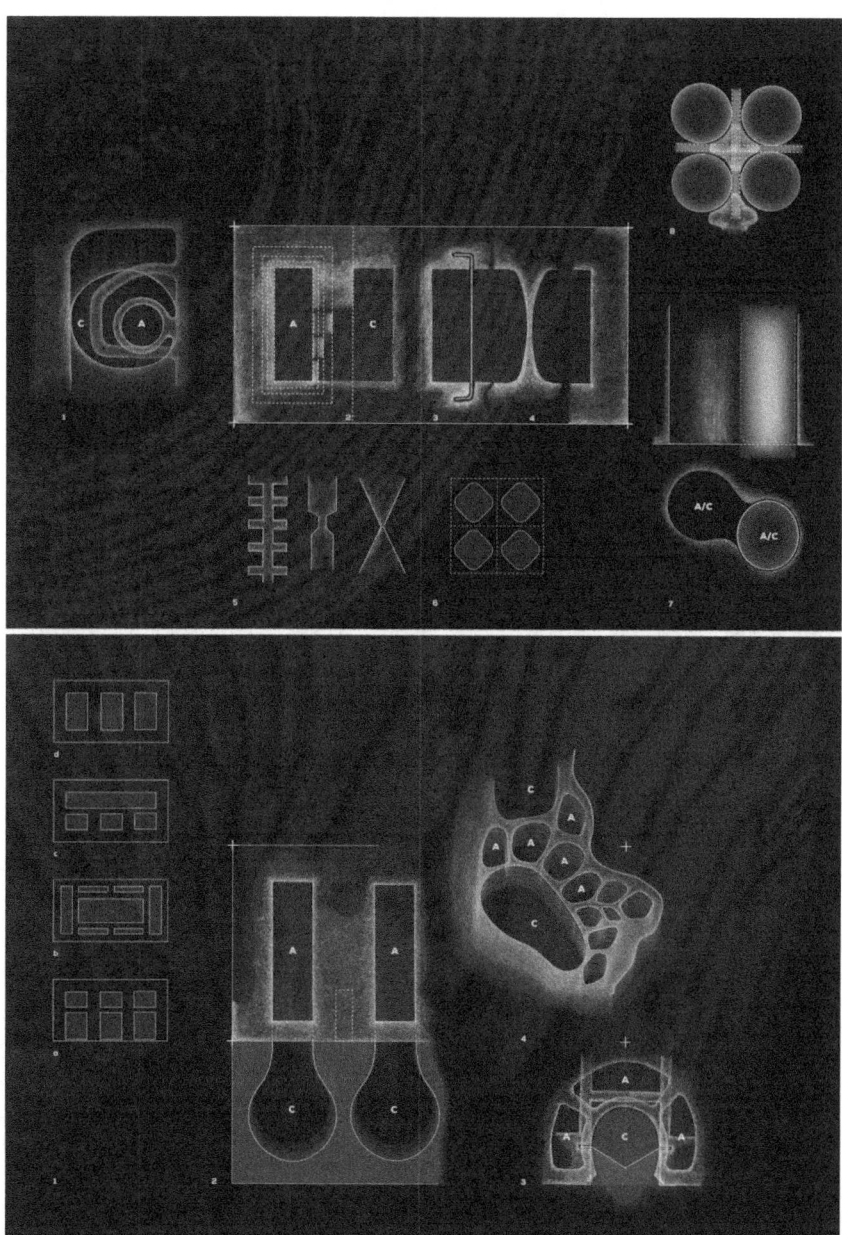

**FIGURE 8.1** *Multispecies bioreactor designs or 'bricks' for the construction of 'living architecture'. Drawing courtesy of Simone Ferracina, January 2017.*

consortia are composed of two types of module. The first is a cyanobacteria-based 'farm' module that supplies an energy-giving form of carbon to the labour module, like sugar. The second is the bacterial-heterotrophic-based labour module that can perform a specified biotechnological function, like reclaiming phosphates from detergents. When combined in a population of programmable 'workhorse' strains such as *E. coli* and *P. putida*, the operations constitute a metabolic app. Both farm and labour module types are amenable to systems metabolic engineering.

### 8.1.4 Integration and uses

These three species of modular units may be combined and even integrated with each other (see Figure 8.1). Each bioreactor system is also developed as a building block or 'brick' that can be incorporated into homes, offices and public buildings. Sensor array systems within these structures can also detect internal and external conditions, and so work alongside the bioreactors to optimize the environmental performance of our living spaces. By 'conversing' chemically, physically, biologically, mechanically and even digitally (through electricity) with the living world, the Living Architecture apparatus could potentially change what is achievable through sustainability and resource management programmes.[2] The project is still in development but is likely to reclaim phosphates from wastewater, remove pollutants, produce biofertilizers or make new forms of environmentally friendly soap, just by using carbon dioxide and sunlight. While these outcomes have not yet been experimentally verified, theoretically, they are realistic outputs that also explore the conditions through which ethical and more symbiotic relationships between cities and the natural world may be realized.

## 8.2 Diversifying bricks

Inert materials propose to resist the natural world and indefinitely maintain their integrity on their own and our behalf. For if the architectural body is immortal, then surely ours can be too. Yet even John Ruskin noted that the Matterhorn weathered (Ruskin, 1989). If colossal natural structures made of stone decay, then buildings will too.

---

[2] Health and safety issues are prioritized within these considerations.

A brick is a modular design unit for structural systems within traditional buildings, which are made from rigid and inert materials that generate a framework around which walls; facades and interior environments can be attached. The component bricks are sourced from clays, which have been stripped of their innate vitality (the clay code) through a firing process to become ceramics. Denied essential material flexibility, bricks are programmatically configured through various morphologies that are deployed and scaled according to architectural protocols.

A parallel portfolio for design, construction and application of modular units may be developed by considering the way biological cells are deployed. These are the 'bricks' of organic systems and were identified in 1665 by Robert Hooke, when he was looking at cork under a microscope. Noticing that the box-like structures in his viewfinder were reminiscent of the austere small rooms that monks lived in, he called them 'cells'. Designed for isolation away from communal life and public spaces within the monastery, this association between the individual 'unit of life' and structural module provided a mechanical unit around which biological systems could be conceived as hierarchically organized systems governed by centralized forms of control.

In the organic realm, cells are bounded by selectively permeable membranes that regulate the flow of matter between inside and outside spaces through channels and pores. These gatekeepers enable the exchange of resources and removal of waste that is necessary for life. Surveillance of these boundaries is provided by (immune) systems, with the capacity to neutralize and destroy invaders. Ranging in their degree of differentiation and heterogeneity, cells have highly convoluted surfaces to optimize these exchanges, which may be detailed with villi, hairs, invaginations, folds, pleats and tubules. Sometimes these structures are situated within pulsatile spaces, which keep matter flowing through their cavities.

In an ecological era, not only does the idea of a brick or its proliferation as a wall – even one as large as the MOSE gates that purport to hold back the tides – seem a futile gesture against planetary-scale change, but also their fundamentally defensive character is misplaced in a world in flux. Extreme weather and the movement of populations challenge the appropriateness of inert materials as mediators of environmental disruption. In a parallel world, barriers may be transformed into more responsive and resilient systems by conferring fundamental building elements with some of the properties of living systems. Instead of inert components, bricks could be more like cells that alter the chemistry of a site, change their configuration and even modify the social and cultural encoding of architectural protocols.

> Each of the stories [in House of Day, House of Night, by Olga Tokarczuk] represents a brick and they interlock to reveal the immense monument that

is the town. What emerges is the message that the history of any place – no matter how humble – is limitless, that by describing or digging at the roots of a life, a house, or a neighborhood, one can see all the connections, not only with one's self and one's dreams but also with all of the universe. (Northwestern University Press, 2017)

### 8.2.1 Soft brick

In a parallel world, bricks are not made of inert materials but, like cells, are modules of soft, living architecture.

> Bulging globules of plasma in cellulose skin press against each other amongst placental branches. Taught with generosity, their auxin-soaked appetites fuel parallel developmental programmes that expedite the fate of the seedling embryos they carry. Each ripened vessel sighs as they shoot their pointed pips into the fragrant soil. Gathering the rotten bodies for a fruit pie, the child wonders why apples always swerve before they reach the ground.

Various species of soft bricks with agile morphologies that orchestrate flow and metabolism were designed for the Hylozoic Ground installation. They were exhibited in 2010 at the Canadian Pavilion in collaboration with Philip Beesley, during the 12th Venice Biennale of Architecture, who leads the Living Architectures Systems Group at the University of Waterloo, Canada. The soft bricks were suspended within the Hylozoic Ground's semi-living cybernetic 'jungle' installation as metabolically active, responsive, chemical systems that included protocell flasks, Liesegang ring florets, Leduc cells, Traube cells and hygroscopic liquids (Armstrong, 2015). Each species was capable of a specific material transformation; for example, Liesegang rings generated evolving banded patterns, while Leduc cells became mineralized in response to the presence of dissolved carbon dioxide. The soft bricks' brightly coloured products could be clearly seen by visitors from underneath the system of suspended, interconnected bodies.

> Beesley's installation is literally endowed with biological functions, such as digestions, breathing and metabolic activities, and, in that sense, it revisits Vaucanson's duck and other 18th century automata. It is not only capable of perceiving and acting (like sociable robots), but, by means of chemical interactions with its changing environment, it seems to reproduce the very chemical processes that constitute the functions of organisms. (Yiannoudes, 2016, pp. 108–9)

### *8.2.2 Embryological brick*

In a parallel world, soft living architectures establish the agile protocols that influence the character of a building, or a site, through networks of chemical and metabolic events. These events bear resonance with the complex organizing processes observed in the dark gel experiments (see Figure 6.1 and Section 6.9).

> The developing incubus consumes its yolk and densens in formations suggestive of fingers, claws, pigment cells, wings, various appendages, vague organ systems, primitive face. Its ontology does not recapitulate phylogeny, but constantly negotiates its becoming. The translucent body yawns with a viscous smirk, as blood fills its beating vacuums, transgressing the 'other' material laws that bind it to discourses of efficacy, geometry and virtue. Metabolizing vigorously its muscular striations ripple as it lays down fats. Then, caught in treacle time its movements slow, pausing before its membranes rupture and the creature is expelled into a hostile world. Metamorphic entrails rearrange and burst through the newly-made integument, extending their growth in all directions. This knotted brick of matter is monstrously altered and exploits all opportunities to sustain its life.

### *8.2.3 Lamprey shoe: Blood bank*

Not all building blocks of life are generous; some are opportunistic or selfish.

> During the day, the thorned shoe grips the foot with hooks and points backwards into the plantar arteries. They are milked with every footstep, gravity pumping the thick maroon liquid back into the shoe's heel where it enters into a generous anticoagulant rich reservoir – just another cruel object in a legacy of parasitic footwear, where the price of freedom of movement is torture. At night, the pedal barb is released and placed in a wall formation – one shoe above and next to another. Now, in their sleep, the immortal old are infused with fresh life, bled from the young.

## 8.3 Programmable bricks

The building blocks of Venice possess a natural programmability, which is orchestrated spontaneously between the elemental lagoon systems, the typology of the individual bricks and the marine wildlife.

The first records of flooding in Venice date back to the sixth century and reached their highest levels in November 1966 (see Section 7.8). *Acqua alta* are structurally problematic for the city as they breach the Istrian membranes. This means that salt water is sucked up by capillary action into the porous brickwork. Destruction associated with rising damp and *risalta salina*, or salt rise, follows where minerals that have moved into the brickwork crystallize and expand into efflorescent and subflorescent blooms. The physical force of the crystallization process shatters bricks and removes the protective stucco. Maintaining affected buildings is problematic as salt water damage affects the city wholesale, so repairs are not only costly but can also precipitate structural collapse. The extent of this process can be assessed at a glance by the amount of naked brickwork on the buildings, which would otherwise be coated with stucco. Local architects and builders can read these changes and respond with appropriate strategies, which include laying down impermeable plastic membranes and installing marble slabs.

Depending on when and how they were made, Venetian bricks weather differently over time. Ancient bricks were made from local mud and fired in local kilns. Their soft, porous structures gracefully wear around the edges, so they are still capable of load-bearing, even during the process of decay. In recent times, highly machined bricks with regular geometries and materials that resist water entry have replaced them. Although these modern bricks are harder, they also weather in a very different way. When damaged, they sustain wholesale fractures that shed from their surfaces like scales, which damage their load-carrying capacity and so require more frequent replacement than their forerunners.

It is not just the constant wicking of salt water into the brickwork that exposes and excoriates the mortar but also the work of spiteful prevailing winds. They gnaw on micro-cavities and irregularities in the brickwork, pummelling the edges and grinding rough surfaces to polished finishes. Bricks loosen, coming away from their cement, and suck up water, which is quickly evaporated by the wind. Together the elements create a city-scale cycle of transpiration that quickly erodes the brickwork.

There is a living choreography here too in which the biological realm plays its part. Biofouling follows the climbing moisture in the brickwork and finds attachments and nutrients within these landscapes. Here they establish vertical gardens, or micro-geographies, of algae, bacteria, moss, salt crystals and lichen, damaging the integrity of walls as they flourish.

Building repairs do not stay dry for long, and masonry is relentlessly transformed in situ by the relentless creep of salt water – walls becoming part salt, part mud. A city-scale form of natural computing is at work that generates fresh sites for further erosions, accretions, depositions and transfigurations, as bricks dissolve into each other like soil horizons where sometimes *Segestria florentina* spiders make their lairs. The periodic shattering of Venice's ground level floors results in an iterative process of removal and replacement by workmen with masonry tools. Every ten years, the first thirty to forty courses of brickwork need replacing. Barges are filled with old brick fragments, and new loads arrive with fresh load-bearing structures, which will steady the defects for at least another ten years, whereupon the cycle starts again.

Masonry life cycles inevitably spew brickwork fragments into the waterways, where they are washed up on illicit shorelines. Here, they build new beaches that are polished by the tides. Fresh alliances between brick, stone and nature emerge and are strangely detailed by marine ecology – with calcareous worm deposits, outgrowths of oyster shells and glass fragments that have been fused with bricks by marine concretes. Agile construction protocols emerge so that not all decisions at the level of the brickwork need to be taken by an architect or builder.

These various modification protocols – natural elements, structural composition, biological infiltration – are highly contextualized and can be incorporated into design protocols. For example, it may be possible to strategically fracture surfaces or erode layers of brickwork to encourage particular outcomes. By configuring the character and alignment of bricks, it may even be possible to realize a different kind of building programme, which is conducive with an *architecture of wetness*. Ultimately, dynamic sites may be constructed through the strategic placement of bricks and other (hygroscopic) materials that channel water in different ways. Such *living stones* of Venice provide an agile infrastructure for the city that constantly feed on their surroundings and are capable of urban transformation.

### *8.3.1 Living brick for Venice*

Living bricks are part of the story of parallel Venice and build on the underpinning Future Venice and Future Venice II projects as a continued exploration of a city whose fabric is *coming alive* and responsive to its circumstances.

> It is not a being, but an energy of translation, oscillating landscape, microbial city become covey of muscle, a throbbing hinge connecting worlds, or occult physiology channelling air, fire and water, plasma and flow. It makes a wall while subverting the logic of walls. A vibrant tomb, it has sealed its doors, membraned its windows – no one passes through alive, yet all are nourished. Domesticated minerals, dreaming of diamonds, channelling sweet, milky musk, dung's clammy mortar, pale, woody amber, galvanic crackle and spark. Press yourself against it and become architecture.

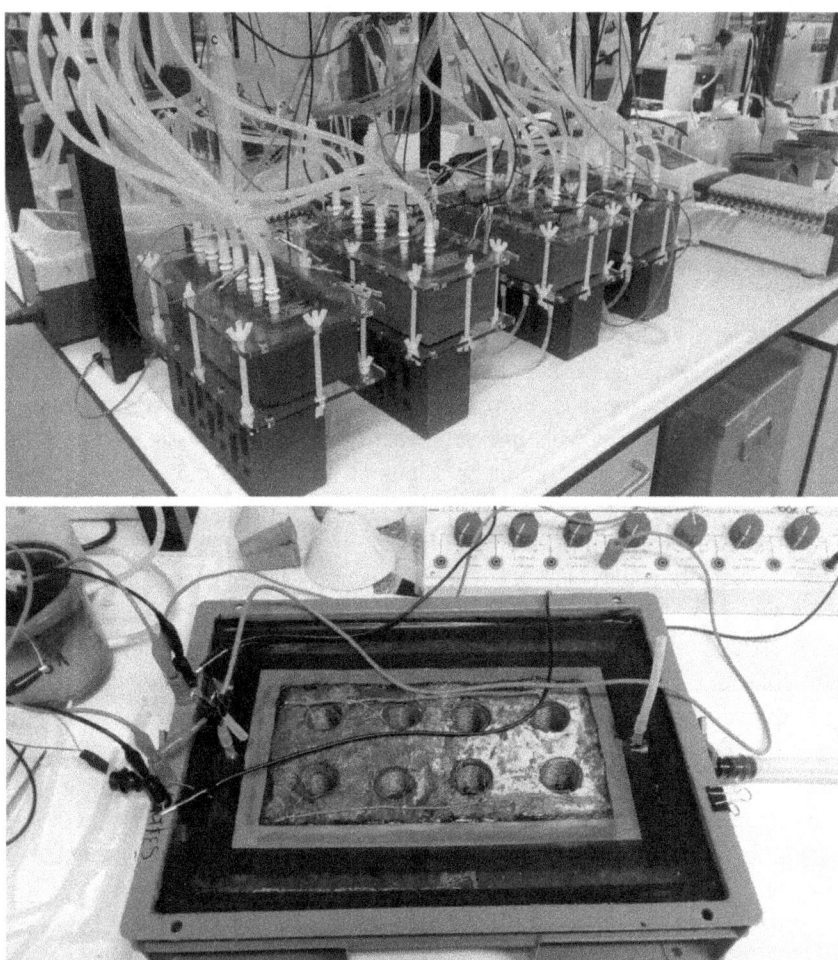

**FIGURE 8.2** *Living brick technological prototypes: Venetian bricks (as a single unit and in array) have been machined to form microbial fuel chambers within the structure, which can produce sufficient power to operate digital thermometer displays. Photograph courtesy of the Bristol BioEnergy Centre, University of the West of England, Living Architecture Consortium, 2016.*

It is a truth universally acknowledged that we respond only when we are touched. After millennia of obscurity, we are now ready to assume form – to trans-form, enrich our soils, link spirals of the living and the dead. Plant us at the water's edge and we shine as brilliantly as reflected stars in this liquid cosmos. We start by building foundations, but we are instruments of social change; shape-changing acrobats, dancing aerialists, astronauts of the unknown – a community of vibrant, living constituents whose progeny will not be confined to earth. (Hughes, 2016b, p. 19)

Launched publicly on 14 October 2016 during the Venice Architecture Biennale at the Hotel Carlton on the Grand Canal, the living brick was the first prototype from the Living Architecture project developed by Gimi Rimbu and Ioannis Ieropoulos at the University of West England (see Figure 8.2). The apparatus combines a recognized structural system, an actual brick used for construction in Venice, with a single bioreactor system, the MFC. The living brick is a designed version of the kinds of natural systems that inhabit the city's masonry. Rather than expressed as random or chance colonization, the brick is structured to spatially invite and nurture living systems.[3] The potential to design and choreograph metabolic processes through a site raises questions about the relationship between technology, nature, architecture and ecology and may meaningfully address pervasive problems of human habitation. For example, living bricks may help deal with our waste differently, provide clean water for everyone or retrofit our buildings to increase their environmental value particularly in those communities that lack utilities, like slums and refugee camps.

Living bricks are a highly customizable technology, which is not exclusive to Western cultures. They are programmable in that they may be altered to suit their individual, collective and environmental performance at a local level by incorporating different types of ceramics, biofilm composition, geometry of internal spaces, textures, electrical conductivity and porosity of the bricks into the brick's composition. Some of these processes are partly shaped by the character of each brick, where different sorts of clay, sizes, shapes, additives, the firing process, as well as their situatedness influence the potential outputs of the system. Communities can therefore use local biofilms combined with their knowledge of ceramics to develop living brick types that are congruent with the availability of local resources and cultural values.

### *8.3.2 Titrating tensions: Hips and teeth*

In a parallel world, an alternative masonry system braces the buildings of Venice, offering a dynamic and responsive infrastructure that is titrated by human participation, which moulds and compresses existing structures, so they are (re)appropriated in situ (see Figure 8.3).

---

[3] In addition to the working brick, a ceramic model was exhibited, which was developed by LIQUIFER Systems Group as part of the Living Architecture project.

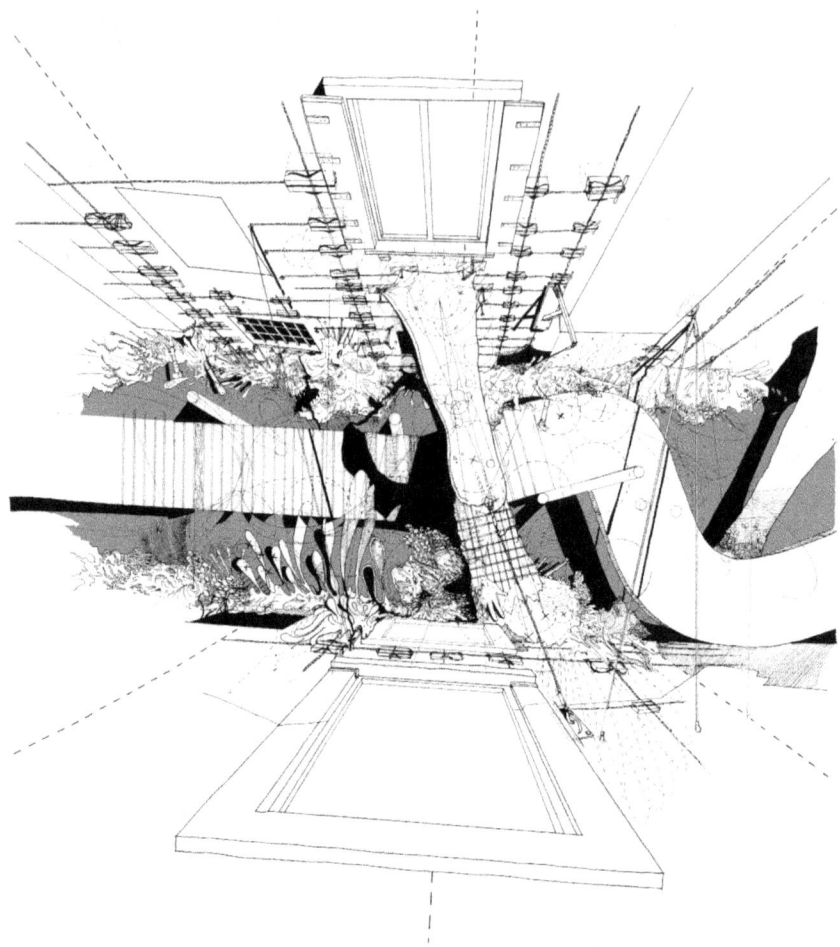

**FIGURE 8.3** *Living bricks in a Venice* rio *adjacent to the Campo San Stefano. Responding to a natural computing 'punch card' based upon the first forty courses of brickwork, a system of cabling and struts selectively facilitates growth of native marine wildlife. Drawing courtesy of Matthew Sharman-Hayles, 2017.*

Shrouded in structural corsetry, the Calle S. Giovanni is undergoing extensive remoulding in a ten-year cycle of sculpted brickwork. Here, the art of body shaping meets the tactics of dentistry, to direct the interactions of programmable bricks through the practice of applied formwork. Once, it was enough to simply insert steel pins and plates in walls to keep them from sagging, but nowadays, the protocols for working with dynamic masonry requires a knowledge of cosmetic and spatial surgery, which produces functional spaces like windows and doors rather than barriers, like walls.

At the end of the narrow medieval alleyway, canalside building materials are beginning to soften. They are tethered using a 'tight-lacing' technique, which is an extreme kind of structural corsetry that must be practised with caution, or it will cause fractures in the upper building levels. Many of the tension bands along the waterway are rusting extensively. Some elements are removable, simply clicking onto wall hooks and existing arch wires. A masonry spur jutting out at the first-floor level indicates its desire to form a bridge with its neighbour across the alleyway – a process that is encouraged by the inventive application of titanium coil springs and a series of ceramic pontics that are strapped to its abutments. Some poorly applied plaster of Paris soaked bandages are wrapped cosmetically around the protrusion, which make vague pretence at performing a structural function. Over here, knitted fibreglass bandages impregnated with polyurethane and thermoplastics are also trying to disguise unbridgeable defects. This is shoddy workmanship, which stops the growing materials to adopt suboptimal configurations. Here, a tapestry of basic window types is being pinched out along the first floor, where masonry pressure plates are tempered by decorative O-rings. Encouraged by a network of bands and ties spun over a sea of hooks and brackets, these apertures are also forming a balcony.

At ground floor level, an Austrian belt – a steel band about two inches in width with turn screws – encircles the brickwork by passing through the entranceway and window. It is elegantly extruding an oval space that has been isolated with a latex dam to locally control water infiltration. It could potentially support a beam or become a conjoinment for a shared living space. Bespoke aligners are also used here, as invisible braces are so well moulded that they were probably fabricated using a virtual 3D treatment plan, which anticipates how the space will evolve before the structural treatment is applied.

Perhaps the most unusual feature in the calle is this busk, which is slotted into braced scaffolding and positioned at knee level. It holds the waterway frontage erect, so that it is pleasant to view by boat. Its neighbour, on the other side of the alleyway, boasts a wireframe bustle that augments the bulging brickwork. I notice they have performed a 'Devonshire', where six courses of brickwork have been removed to emphasize the protrusion; but, as I mentioned, there is shoddy work showing all around the site. This place is all about appearances.

Over there, under the external vines of uncovered cabling, a divorce corset lifts and separates a growing crack in the masonry. Someone has also applied interior braces, which sit on the inside of the brickwork and are connected to the exterior by a series of tension wires. I suspect these manoeuvres are carefully opening the structure so that a new beam can be inserted to complete the structural bridging. As I can't see a reinforcing underbusk, it is hard to say what the architectural intentions will be – other than forming rather attractive masonry curves.

**FIGURE 8.4** *A mosaic of spatial experiences is observed through the lens of a Murano glass chandelier bead during a psychogeographic walk about the city, which reveals previously hidden dynamic building elements and parallel terrains. Graphic design by Simone Ferracina; photograph courtesy of Rachel Armstrong, Venice, Italy, December 2016.*

As extravagant and superficial as they may be, such moments of morphological self-indulgence do not worry me, but I am concerned about this prospective overhead crossing. The original masonry is showing instability and the osteoporotic bricks are crumbling and decaying from the inside. Retainers must be inserted if the current forms are to keep their structural integrity, as the current flourish of spacers and compressors are just not going to adequately bolster the bridge. Complete replacement, or urgent structural reinforcement injections are needed, as the walkway is at risk of collapse.

## 8.4 Transfiguring Venice

Parallel worlds may be accessed through simple devices that conjure alternative spaces like Duchamp's use of lenses and broken glass to distort an observer's perception (Rose, 2014). For example, unusually tall buildings are found around the Ghetto in Venice and can be observed in accelerated forms of expansion and collapse using a lens made from a single bead of a Murano glass chandelier. Where the light warps and twists, it generates structural and spatial transformations where certain building details intensify, as other areas shrivel, opening up new spaces.

> The sky sweeps like rising damp from within the buildings, stretching the brickwork like chewing gum, as a roof tilts its hat to the heavens. A watery azure smog lingers, insisting it belongs to the firmament, but I doubt it. I doubt everything. Hazy spaces form like dew on window panes, obscuring the relative positions of things. Windows propagate uncontrollably, walls undulate, street sweepers brush dirt from steps in multiple planes, and stucco tumours splinter over many doorways. Spring-loaded structural beams and multiple arches collapse like dying stars and are coiled into repeating spaces until they are wound with such tension they melt into each other. These unstable, superdense clouds of matter; part apartment, part balcony and part rooftop, are prone to sudden fits of vanishing, shattering into the street, as shards of light, like knife blades. Oblivious to this violence, a delivery man walks through the alleyway, along many simultaneous tracks. Cloned pigeons stare down multiple balconies from the guttering, while parallel plants dissolve into vortices within walls. The masonry wants to whisper something and clears its throat with a horrid rasp, but cannot find its voice. Concrete shadows scratch at the man from a lightless join between multiple spaces, from which a woman holding a child's hand suddenly emerges and disappears down a gutter.

### *8.4.1 City of soft living architecture*

The following series of parallel portraits (Sections 8.4.1, 8.4.1.1 and 8.4.1.2) discuss life in *soft* Venice.

This concept is based on how 'soft living technology' would alter the general civic profile of Venice, which was developed for the fiftieth anniversary of Bosch.

Once, the cruise ships poured tens of thousands of tourists daily into the streets from the Tronchetto. Now, they dock south of the MOSE gates on the Lido, where they release their passengers into an underground metro system, which stretches as far as the airport. Commuters can now afford to travel and work in Venice's flourishing tourism, biotechnology and aquaculture industries.

Venice had been dying for some time. Having peaked at a population of 164,000 in 1931, modern development on the mainland, particularly in the 1970s and 1980s, prompted a mass exodus from the city. By the turn of the third millennium, 20 million yearly visitors vastly outnumbered the city's 60,000 residents, and without a lively native population to feed its vibrancy, the future of the city seemed grim.

Affordable housing proved to be an antidote to this state of affairs. The working population rapidly began to swell, and new land was created in an island chain that coalesced around the via della Libertà. Constitutionally creative, Venetians turned recycled trash collected in the city into water-resistant masonry and pioneered a whole new species of technological infrastructure. Combining biotech with the construction of homes and businesses, new ways of heating homes and cleaning water emerged. Not only did these developments reduce utility bills, they also enriched the residents' quality of life, while invigorating the lagoon ecology.

### 8.4.1.1 *La mia casa morbido*: My octopus home

The following scene is based on a specific instance of how 'soft living technology' could alter daily life in Venice and was developed for the fiftieth anniversary of Bosch (Armstrong, 2017).

> I can't decide whether I'm awake or not. Five minutes more repose makes all the difference to the day. Cthulhu bathes me in a sea of my own body heat, which is recaptured in ebbs and flows in her soft spaces. She's my mattress at night and communications system during the day. I sink back into her gentle waves, which start to shake me then, as I refuse to rise, become a storm of peaks and troughs.
>
> Oh goodness! You're here Rosa. I'm not ready yet. You'll never find the laboratory on your first day without some help. I can't believe it's been all these years since we were at school together. Come on up!
>
> Meet Cthulhu, she let you in. She runs this place – a genius octopus orb, made of a sensate polymer gel. See how her soft tentacles reach up into a network of tubes in the ceiling. Now that she's sure I'm up, she'll stretch out into a hologlobe.

Oh no! My mother is trying to contact me. You can see her through Cthulhu's single quantum eye. She has a habit of unravelling the world's 'problems' at the oddest times, which are coincidentally, tangled up with mine. Excuse me a moment.

Let's go down to the next floor. I've programmed my bathroom to make biodegradable soap, retrieve phosphates and capture plastic micro-particles all at once. What a noise! Her tubes have borborygmi today. Perhaps her liquid technology system is clogged, or the kitchen bioprocessors that she's plumbed into are working too hard. I'll twist the control pad to decrease the speed of filtration. Oh, that's great, the biometric indicators have gone from amber to green. Now her calorific effort is in the safe zone and she's much less stressed. Excuse me while I take a cumulonimbus shower cloud. It's okay, you're not intruding. I'll completely disappear, but you might see thunder and lightning flashes. They're not dangerous or anything, as the voltages are too small, but they can be annoying if they happen too frequently.

I hope I didn't keep you too long. I have a bad habit of losing track of time when I'm getting ready. Would you like coffee?

Oh, these things in the kitchen are an ecosystem of tubes, vessels and organs, which bubble through various chambers. They are constantly changing colour and will stay healthy for around a decade before needing a check-up. Even then, only the mechanical pumps that raise filtered water up to the top floor are likely to need maintenance. No, you won't see the composting and sewage processing, as they are hidden inside these beautiful charcoal-lined ceramic containers. Of course, they sometimes leak! In Venice, we get used to unpleasant smells. Think of it as, like living in a cheese shop.

You've never seen a gelatinator? It cools things using endothermic processes that remove heat. Darn, it's hard to figure out what's in here. Of course, you're right! The gel becomes opaque when the food goes off. Okay, no breakfast today! We'll pick something up on the way. Leave your mug in the sink, the bioprocessors will clean it up.

Take care down the spiral staircase. It's steep, as during the summer it becomes a bank of seats. Oh, I'm so glad you like the tiles, they're quite special. They suck up the *acqua alta* and siphon it into the liquid technology reservoir without any need for pumps.

Please, don't be afraid! That's Marco, my blue crab. I know, he's as big as a dinner plate. I have to put bands around his red-tipped claws when I take him out for a walk. He has a nasty habit of pinching the noses of curious dogs. They are a little too fascinated by his sideways gait and spiky appearance. I'll feed him when I get back.

Are you ready? Then let's go.

## 8.4.1.2 Living energy 2067

This concept was developed for the fiftieth anniversary of Bosch according to the notion that Venice's buildings have 'living' metabolisms, not dead ones. The distinction is important.

Dead metabolisms are typical fuels for modern technologies. They are characterized by long-chain hydrocarbons, which do not lend themselves to decomposition by biomolecules and, therefore, require high activation thresholds for combustion. Once ignited, they create large amounts of energy but are highly polluting.

In contrast, living metabolisms exploit the catalytic action of enzymes. They have low activation thresholds and combust without igniting. Since their metabolic processes are compatible with the biological realm, they can be transformed into a rich portfolio of substrates where even the waste products of one reaction may become feedstock for another. However, living metabolisms release small amounts of energy. Each Venetian living brick (see Section 8.3.1) that converts decomposing matter into electricity produces only 750 microwatts (0.00075 W) of energy. In other words, around 50,000 bricks are needed to power a standard 40–60 W per hour light bulb. In practice, this means that arrays are needed to amplify the system's output and raises important questions about our expectations of technology. While living bricks will not power a modern household, our assessments of energy requirements are based on our experience of industrial technology. In this 'Catch-22' situation, mechanical appliances set the standards and expectations for liveable homes, which are based on industrial-scale power outages and uses.

Changing the evaluation systems for alternative energy sources means that our living spaces will have very different needs and impacts. Soft living architecture establishes an alternative infrastructure for the domestic environment, which is regulated by calorie-fuelled, metabolic systems.

Energy consumption is equivalent to digestion and is measured in calories. These energy sources provide outputs with equivalence to body temperatures, rather than injurious levels of industrial heat. Altering basic assumptions about the kind of fuel consumed within the city can also provoke new kinds of traditions, encounters with, and understanding of its character.

> Venice has a long history of inventing original dishes. In this tradition, living technologies become a platform for 'cold cuisine', which is not cooked but pre-digested using enzymes and printed into attractive forms. These gourmet dishes such as a version of Salvador Dalí's pierced heart provide nutritious meals and are safe for people at risk of burning themselves to prepare, such as the elderly living at home.

Outside in the labyrinthine streets, where strong light is not required, mood-elevating bioluminescent sources – like luciferin rich materials produced by bacteria, fungi, crustaceans, molluscs, fishes and insects – exude a different quality of light. This escapes from homes and wanders into public spaces and waterways, becoming part of the rich portfolio of 'living metabolic' encounters within this beguiling city.

## 8.5 Future Venice

Futures not achieved are only branches of the past: dead branches. (Calvino, 1997, p. 29)

*Future Venice* is a parallel world (see Figure 8.5), where the city's longevity is secured by bestowing the city's woodpile foundations with some of the properties of living things. By adding artificial cells to the water in strategic places, the woodpiles are transformed into a living reef-like structure. Through the constant growth of matter, the city can self-heal and respond to

**FIGURE 8.5** *Scryed through waterways reflections, a fragment of Future Venice is observed through its transformed window frame details. Photograph courtesy of Rachel Armstrong: Venice, Italy, July 2015.*

environmental change, while it attenuates sinking by spreading its point load over a much broader base (Armstrong, 2015).

The artificial reef is initiated by adding a self-organizing mixture of water, oil and salt to specific sites within the canals. Here, artificial cells form spontaneously and coordinate the properties of the reef by transforming substances (pollutants, dissolved gases, organic waste) in the lagoon into an active soil-like substance. The real-time production of 'proto-pearls' needed to grow an artificial reef-like structure around the city was demonstrated in tanks at the lagoon side.[4] Potentially, the project is a 'soft' adjunct to the MOSE gates, where marine ecosystems co-construct architectural-scale structures that are mutually beneficial to the lagoon ecology and the city.

Should the environmental conditions change and the lagoon dry out – say, for example, that Pietro Tiatini and his colleagues succeed in anthropogenically lifting the city by pumping seawater into its deflated aquifers (Teatini et al., 2011) or if the MOSE gates precipitate environmental events so that native ecosystems reach catastrophic tipping points – then the chemical droplets can follow a different programme. Instead of producing outward-spreading accretions, the woodpiles are coated with a protective layer of 'biocrete', which is formed in a downward direction as the waters subside. This sealant prevents them rotting when exposed to the air.

Moreover, the artificial reef technology orchestrates a coordinated system of exchanges between fabric, space, residents and structure across the whole bioregion, which ultimately increases environmental liveliness. It also establishes architectural protocols that can work with wet conditions in the built environment, with potential relevance for the broader remediation, retrofitting and repair of metropolitan fabrics.

### *8.5.1 Protocell city*

Not all cities are for humans; many parallel cities co-exist alongside our urban environments and can be found at the water's edge.

> The oil slick spreads itself enthusiastically over the water, forming a fine film that traps surface particles and scatters the light. This milky terrain is primed for life. More than a site for chance occurrences, it is an active system of natural computers, where every exchange shapes the landscape of possibility for the next.

---

[4]These experiments were conducted in collaboration with styblo.tv for Red Bull, Martin Hanczyc, currently at the University of Trento, Davide de Lucrezia from Explora Biotech and architectural students from the University of Venice.

Small fish nibble at its tasty body; insect surface skaters wobble from the changes in surface tension, and canal ducks spoon up the tasty emulsion with their beaks. The film thickens, then splits into multiple islands of brilliant scum that ride over the swell of waves until they are one molecule thick. Journeying onwards, their active chemical fields tangle with nutrients, pollutants, environmental poisons and microorganisms. Each transaction primes a habitat for parallel forms of colonization, and hypercomplex material events that comprise life's successions.

## 8.5.2 Future Venice II

You take delight not in a city's seven or seventy wonders, but in the answer it gives to a question of yours. (Calvino, 1997, p. 44)

Future Venice II is a collaboration with IDEA Laboratory, Artwise Curators, Mike Perry, Studio Swine, Julian Melchiorri and EcoLogicStudio, which occurred within the Vita Vitale exhibition for the Azerbaijan Pavilion for the fifty-sixth Venice Biennale in 2014. It identified two major challenges for the city – the collection of plastic microfragments, produced by the 13 million plastic bottles discarded every year into the lagoon by its 20 million tourists, and eutrophication. Synergies between these troublesome architectural-scale fabrics proposed to build the synthetic landmass 'Zanzara Island' – a breeding ground for genetically modified mosquitoes that will ultimately reduce the number of disease-carrying flies in the city.

Tiger mosquitoes had become an uncontrollable plague that filled the already strained hospital casualty waiting rooms with infected antibiotic-resistant secondary bites, which brought blood poisoning as well as parasitic illnesses. Malaria warnings were periodically issued, despite rigid environmental controls that targeted the mosquitoes' natural breeding grounds, but still the flies thickened the night air and hummed with human blood in their stomachs. But, developing the right kind of tactic to reduce the mosquito load was an artisan practice. Just as the glass blowers of Murano had carefully mastered their semi-liquid art in the name of artistic and entrepreneurial virtuosity, an unsurpassed skill was required to manipulate the biological apparatus needed to disrupt the flies' reproductive life cycle.

Plastic flotsam was harvested from the Lido beach and cultured with native biofilms from the city (see Figure 8.6). Out of the eight tanks, one grew thick, spider web-like biofilms that were formed by a consortium of algae and bacteria. They were firmly attached to the plastic detritus in the tanks and supported the idea that natural biofilms could be developed scientifically

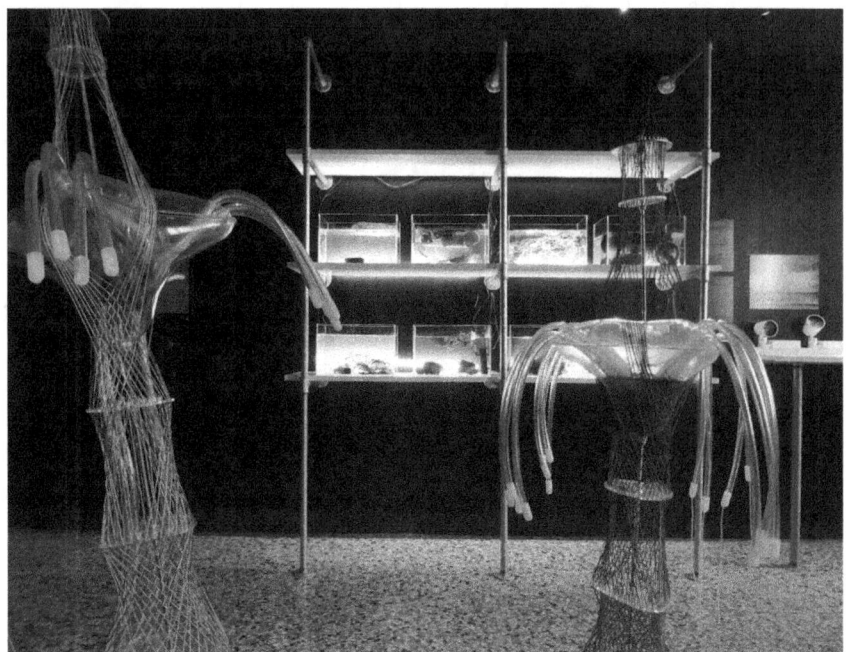

**FIGURE 8.6** *Background: bank of eight aquariums installed for the IDEA Laboratory at the Vita Vitale exhibition, fifty-sixth Venice Biennale; cultures of plastics with local biofilms to produce 'living' bioplastic composites. Foreground: 'intelligent' briccole with algae 'brains' and sensors by EcoLogicStudio. Photograph courtesy of Rachel Armstrong, with Artwise Curators and IDEA Laboratory, Venice, May 2015.*

towards becoming natural 'nets' for harvesting plastic micro-particles. Another tank grew similar biofilms, but they were much more Spartan in their form and distribution. Two tanks produced algae growths without any obvious bacterial component, taking on the form of ball-like colonies, which may have been sculpted by the flow of water. A polystyrene island in one tank ripped apart a biofilm into its component algal and bacterial colonies. The algae colonized the spaces between the polystyrene beads that provided shelter, water, air and minerals, while the bacteria grew in thick fronds around the oxygen-rich pump outlets. Two tanks remained sterile, with no microorganismal growth, which may have been caused by pollutants on the harvested plastics. The final tank was colonized by mosquito larvae that were eradicated by adding a layer of mineral oil to the water surface. No biofilm growth was observed in this tank.

The laboratory experiments implied that lagoon microorganisms and plastics could have complex relationships with each other, which was further supported by the varied results in the eight tanks. Future Venice II raises valuable questions about how degraded landscapes may be transformed into habitable environments by looking for alternative synergies between established ecosystems that may not presently exist.

## *8.5.3 Melma Verde: Island of useless things*

In a parallel world, alternative ways of producing islands in the Venice lagoon other than using rubble become an artisan practice of architectural dimensions.

Hundreds of wedding dresses in various states of decay are staked like scarecrows and buckle in the cross-winds of Melma Verde. Fashioned from recycled fabrics they are infiltrated with green slime and subtend odd angles to the ground.

Originally a reclamation project, this island is home to a peculiar legacy left by performance artists Ute Mallo and Blair Norman, who absconded from their scheduled performance 'Ascensione' at the 115th Venice Biennale, to take their wedding vows instead on the island. The sole evidence for this deception was a bridal dress draped over crossed sticks to which a note had been pinned – 'not all that ascends can be reclaimed (UB)'.

Some say the artists now live modestly on a Bali beach, but darker rumours suggest they completed a suicide pact. Whatever the truth of the matter, the strange incident has prompted copycat ceremonies where, in the tradition of the commedia dell'arte, the 'Bride' is a character open to interpretation. Masked figures, mannequins, flamboyant men, drag queens and several goats – which were subsequently banned from the island for eating environmental relics – are part of a carnival procession. Celebrations centre on the Bride's dress that documents a ritual journey in stains, tears and accumulations from Venice to Melma Verde, and symbolizes the transformation of refuse into precious relics.

As local demand for upcycled wedding dresses soared, an enterprising group of Masters students at Ca' Foscari established a textile studio on the island dedicated to making fabric from ocean debris. Beach refuse is harvested, sorted and processed before transfer into a series of incubating vats. Here, cellulose producing microbes, detritus, hand-stripped bladderwrack and calcium chloride, coagulate the knotted substances into weatherproof fabrics with a glittering finish. When the cloth reaches its desired consistency, it is supported on recycled fishing nets, where shells, beads and flotsam, are hand-stitched into the garment.

Typically, brides purchase their dresses a year before the carnival and further customize them during this the preparations with highly personal items such as prayer ribbons, heirlooms and pressed flowers. Leaving by private boat from the shores of Sacca Fisola, a Venetian island made from garbage mixed up with silt, sand and seaweed, the procession makes its way to Melma Verde. On reaching the island, the Bride splits her dress like a chrysalis to reveal a silken undergarment. This is then mounted upon a dedicated scaffolding around which the carnival congregation sows the ground with aromatic composts, petals, edible confetti, and regionally specific seeds. The ritual ends when the newlyweds embrace and exchange vows that yoke love to fertility and bring new life to the island. All dresses remain on the island as relics and cavorting talismans, celebrating the value of useless things.

## 8.6 Living walls

Walls are destroyed when nations come together. Notably, on 9 November 1989, the East German government made the monumental announcement there would be free movement between the communist east and capitalist West German populations, and Berlin 'Wall of Shame' was torn down.

Today, walls are springing up everywhere: a colossal 280-mile razor-wire barrier in Hungary prevents refugees fleeing Pakistan, Iran and Morocco from reaching safety in southern Europe (Sim, 2015; BBC News, 2016). With issues of access to borders raised by Brexit, the UK is considering a Great Wall of Calais, a 4-metre barrier preventing stowaways from crossing the Channel. In Venice, the monstrous hydraulic gates of the MOSE project that rise from the sea like a giant King Canute propose to hold back the *acqua alta* and in the United States, the first elements of Donald Trump's anti-immigration wall at the border with Mexico have been erected. Such barriers and impenetrable borders are anti-life.

In their flight from conflict, migrants not only suffer from the trauma of political and social upheaval but also lack the basic comforts that enable a humane standard of living. In the midst of a dissolving world, the current political, economic and social structures, coupled with extreme environmental conditions like drought, famine, overcrowding and housing shortages, are set to provoke further movement and conflict between people. As fiercely guarded, rigorously constructed or maintained as these blockades are designed to be, they are also subject to destructive environmental pressures and cultural change. While inert materials propose permanence, life adapts creatively – even against the odds of survival. There is an urgent need to reimagine and repurpose bricks, the units of architectural construction, and find a building technology that does not separate us but enables us to embrace each other. Such infrastructures must enable vibrancy, diversity, diplomacy, dignity, fluidity, survival and creativity so they expand our survival portfolio. One way of achieving such a radical shift in character is for bricks to acquire some of the dynamic capabilities of living systems.

The plasticity of soft living architectures challenges the very notion of bricks and walls – how they are designed, installed, maintained and what kinds of functions they perform. Living walls do not divide spaces but transform the relationships between spaces and matter, which may be of value during conflict and crises. For example, living walls can house arrays of microbial fuel cells, which are modular organic battery units that are powered by human waste (see Section 8.1). They can be fashioned from a range of materials and linked together in arrays to amplify their output (Ieropoulos, Greenman and Melhuish, 2009). Oxfam and the Gates Foundation are funding the development of prototype toilets that use urine for lighting cubicles in refugee camps, which are often dark and dangerous places for women. Currently, the prototype toilet is experimental, but such soft living architectural systems could be scaled for use in temporary settlements that are inhabited by thousands of people and may offer shelter, electricity and clean water and address sanitation (Ford, 2015). Living walls are not a cure-all for the impacts of conflict or environmental destruction but are important in addressing the site-specificity, situatedness and modes of inhabitation necessary for inhabiting unstable places.

In such a parallel world, the barrier function of walls that divides and separates people from their environment and each other is (re)articulated

**FIGURE 8.7** *Concept of a living wall developed in response to the call for prospective contractors to build Donald Trump's wall. Drawing courtesy of Simone Ferracina, 2017.*

through (metabolic) spaces that are capable of exchange and adaptation – to become *living walls*. The following experiment responds to Trump's call for a 'tactical infrastructure' (FedBizOpps.gov., 2017). It takes the form of a phase one submission to the US Department of Homeland Security, Customs and Border Protection, which made a call for proposals to construct a 30-foot-tall (10 m) wall that spans approximately 1,900 miles (3,058 km) and traverses all sorts of terrains between the borders of the United States of America and Mexico (see Figure 8.7).

> The wall we envisage celebrates diversity and inclusivity rather than homogeneity and exclusion; openness rather than order. Towards this end, it displays a number of unique properties:
> Each brick is uniquely forged from materials that have come far and wide to unite behind a shared integrity.
> Brick production does not require any commercial investment.
> Each brick is made by a person.
> Each brick is forged by passion.
> Each brick embodies a person.
> No one brick is like another.
> Each brick is conferred with sensibilities, emotions and desires that are played out through its ongoing relationship with nature. Bricks may scream in the wind, crack their bones under the sun's heat, nurture vagrant mosses when damp, or provide shelter for small birds.
> Bricks may also be mean, and stifle the possibility of life, rendering the capacity for settlement untenable.
> Each brick produces effects that are shaped by its fundamental capacity for love and hate.
> Each brick tells a unique story.
> Each brick has a relationship with its neighbours.
> All bricks are dependent on each other to become a wall.
> The community of bricks establishes what kind of wall they all become.
> Mortar doesn't hold the bricks together, but strenuous work, patience and trust does.
> The wall tells the story of the appetites of nations, embodying their dreams and nightmares.
> The wall cannot stay still and is prone to dancing under cover of nightfall.
> (Armstrong, Ferracina and Hughes, 2017)

# 9

# Performances

This chapter explores how parallel worlds may be constructed using semi-living apparatuses and 'computed' by radical bodies such as non-human agents (cockroaches) and circus performers in habiting these spaces. Parallel modes of inhabiting space-time are revealed through the choreography of matter, improvisation techniques, staged encounters and storytelling.

## 9.1 Persephone: Constructing the Babelsphere

The Persephone Project is a worlding experiment that considers how expectations of earth-based ecosystems and lifestyles constrain how optimally we inhabit this planet. The project aims to construct an artificial environment for human and non-human space colonists. It is part of the Icarus Interstellar group's portfolio of work, which aims to build a starship research platform in earth's orbit within a hundred years (Armstrong, 2016a). It explores the construction of a parallel relationship with natural systems to support the colonists by taking a bottom-up approach to the synthesis of life's infrastructures.

Persephone challenges existing construction and evaluation methods by adopting a parallel approach to settlement using the principles of ecopoiesis, which establishes the viability of ecosystems. Specifically, the project seeks to generate a life-promoting environment, which begins with the synthesis of its soils.

So far, the project has been realized through a series of terrestrially located experimental spaces – from growing artificial soil matrices in chemistry laboratories, to launching a range of life forms into the stratosphere (Armstrong, 2016a). Each set of experiments takes us further from familiar terrestrial conditions associated with the conventions of dwelling and deeper into the unknown, where survival and a happily-ever-after are not guaranteed.

## 9.2 Persephone: Worlding instrument

The homeostat – a bulky and somewhat baroque machine built from military surplus parts – had a single purpose: to regain stability in response to perturbations in its environment. It is hard to convey precisely how the homeostat worked: set up as four identical units connected to each other via electrical inputs and outputs, each unit was topped with electrically conducting vanes dipped in water troughs. Like oscillographs, the vanes moved back and forth in the trough, reacting to the electrical input from their environment – the output from other blocks in the setup – and each block had an electrical output determined by the position of the vane in the trough. If the vane was directly in the middle of the trough, the electrical output was zero; if, however, it was positioned any other place in the trough, it provided electrical output to the other blocks, affecting the positions of the vanes it was connected to. Thus, when the machine was set in action by pushing a vane out of position, the vanes on all four units would react by moving back and forth, in reaction to their respective environments. (The Science Team, 2016)

The *worlding instrument* is a prototype proposal for settling lifeless terrains by generating parallel, fertile soils. Such matrices can modify their own performance, as well as creating a medium that couples the processes of life and death. This project commenced as a collaboration with Nathan Morrisson, COO of Sustainable Now Technologies, California.

Conceptually, the worlding instrument draws upon Ross Ashby's idea of the homeostat, or artificial brain, which proposed to maintain the stability of a system by adjusting operations using feedback loops. The apparatus also incorporates an experiment pioneered by Stafford Beer, a cyberneticist, who was particularly interested in the application of living systems as a way of creating the foundations for a robust thinking machine and used a variety of naturally occurring organic systems to construct an ecologically sensitive, artificial brain (Beer, 1960). Experimenting with water fleas, or *daphnia*, from a local pond, Beer attempted to persuade them to ingest iron filings so that he could follow their inputs and outputs through electrical recordings. However, there were many problems such as iron filings being permanently magnetized and suspended in the water, which interfered with interpretation of the results.

The *worlding instrument* aims to develop the concepts underpinning Beer's artificial brain using new biotechnological insights and apparatuses that would not have been available to him. While Beer imagined his cybernetic apparatus as an automatic factory, ontologically the worlding instrument is a semi-living system that takes the form of a biosphere. It contains algae and an iron-rich nutrient solution, which is fitted out with digital sensing systems. The apparatus initiates the formation of a simple soil by creating a self-regulating organic layer of algae biomass using sunlight and carbon dioxide. It therefore becomes sensor, substrate and platform for making life-promoting organic residues. The experiment is conducted under extreme conditions and launched into the stratosphere for a few hours, where metabolism of the system can be followed by chemically labelling iron molecules that are detected with digital sensors. While much longer time spans are needed to produce a complex evolving soil, the prototype system establishes a testable and simultaneously operational device, which can establish principles of practice, calibrate events and identify the kinds of outputs or technological advances that are necessary to generate complex life-supporting matrices under extreme conditions. The prototype *worlding instrument* may also indicate what kinds of metabolic transactions are being exchanged (e.g. iron uptake, patterns of metal deposition, manipulation by electromagnetic systems) so that the complexity of metabolic exchanges can be appreciated in ways that enable a better understanding of the fundamental processes necessary for living, surviving and thriving in the absence of natural systems.

## 9.3 Persephone: *The Temptations of the Non-linear Ladder*

*The Temptations of the Non-linear Ladder* is a worlding experiment, which explores the transition from one kind of *being-in-the-world* (Heidegger, 1962) to another. The experiment took the form of a public performance during the 2016 *Do Disturb!* festival, at the Palais de Tokyo, Paris, 8–10 April 2016, which was scheduled to run three times a day over the course of the three days of the event. An immersive scrying kaleidoscope was constructed within a domed temple space as an instrument for interrogation by actors trained in the circus arts. This was a collaboration between Rachel Armstrong, Professor of Experimental Architecture, Newcastle University; Rolf Hughes, Professor of Artistic Research, Stockholm University of the Arts; Olle Sandberg, Director, Cirkör LAB; and circus artists Methinee Wongtrakoon (contortionist) and Alexander Dam (acrobat), with technical rigging by Joel Jedström. The apparatus comprised a circular, 4-metre diameter black mirror with a 4-centimetre-deep layer of water, which was centrally installed in the temple space. Above this, there was a circular 1.2-metre diameter polished aluminium platform with raised edges and three M12 screw eyebolt fittings that allowed for the looping and attachment of carbines. This was tethered to a pulley with two roof points and attached to a floor anchoring that could bear a central rigging load of around 600 kilogrammes and could be raised using a 5:1 pulley system. The working load limit was 200 kilogrammes with a 10 per cent security margin. The performance space was lit from two aerial trusses, while cold light was available from the ground. Behind the central space, two television monitor screens displayed dynamic droplet videos in a continuous loop over the course of the event. A series of three fish bowls containing medaka fish, the only vertebrates to have bred successfully in space, were mounted on plinths around the back wall of the space. Functioning as liquid lenses, these apparatuses channelled light towards the performance space.

Before the performers entered the temple, the scrying surface of the black mirror refracted the multiple light sources in the dome and generated symbols and patterns that reconfigured the ambience of the theatre. Movement provoked by spontaneous but minimum disturbances of air, heat and light entangled with dark ground protocell films, which squirmed over the surface of the water, while the fish cast shadows on to the back wall and cut rainbows into the air. As the performers warmed up at the side of the scrying surface, the aluminium platform was raised by the pulley system. A vertical column and depthless virtual well simultaneously appeared, which became the scaffolding for the non-linear ladder and site of multiple transformations. This analogue yet virtual structure conferred the space with extra dimensionality where familiar and strange new spaces started to overlap and alter each other.

During the spectacle of the non-linear ladder, the artists used the apparatus to make a series of occupancy transitions, as they moved from dry land to water and then to the air. In a series of improvisations, they developed a range of bodily movements and spatial configurations that transitioned between the different media. As the performers moved across the black mirror surface, they produced ripples that collided with each other. Some became stable interference patters, others chaotic fields and many cancelled each other out. Covered with a reflective film of water, the agitating bodies quickly merged with the images and started to dissolve into the kaleidoscopic surfaces (see Figure 9.1). Droplets, foam, light, sweat, fish, hair, eyes, skin cells, cloth and oils blended with and separated from each other in a shimmering semipermeable space of multiple transformations – revealing that the conventions of human anatomy are ill-adapted for making rapid transitions between different media and liminal spaces.

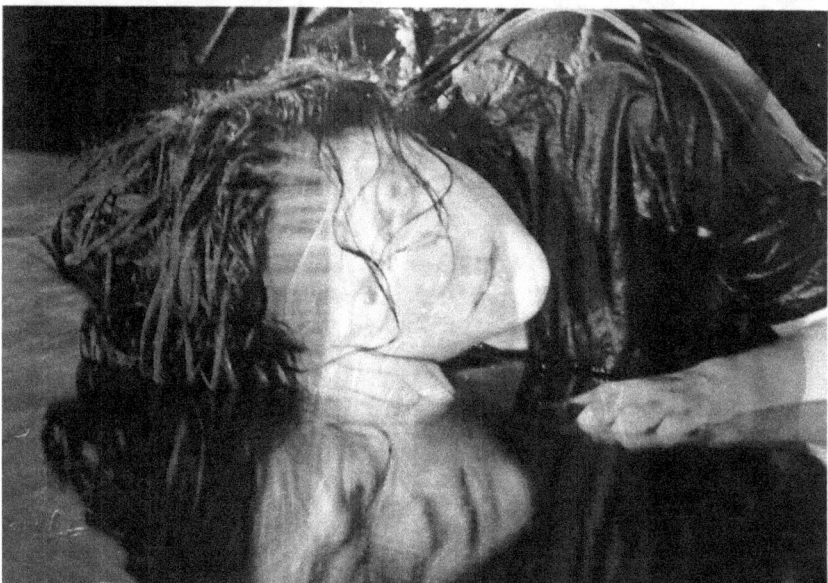

**FIGURE 9.1** *Dark scrying circus: Methinee Wongtrakoon and Alexander Dam encounter the experimental performance space centred on a dark mirror and reflective silvered surface, with a rubbed underbelly that can be moved up and down using a pulley system. Photograph courtesy of Rachel Armstrong, Palais de Tokyo, 8–10 April 2016.*

## 9.4 Persephone: *The Capsule of Crossed Destinies (the Hanged Man)*

This worlding experiment was produced in collaboration with Rolf Hughes at Stockholm University of the Arts, Sweden, which is written as a circus script for Benôit Fauchier, who uses a modified spiral apparatus (CNAC, 2005–2016). The work is yet to be performed. The section 'Radical Circus' is written by Rolf Hughes and Rachel Armstrong.

### 9.4.1 Introduction

The performance narrative is based on *The Capsule of Crossed Destinies*, an experiment launched in January 2016 from Neath, South Wales, in collaboration with Nebula Sciences, where two cockroaches were launched into the stratosphere on a helium balloon flight in a sealed biosphere. The 300 g payload was piggybacked on a commercial flight, aiming to record the behaviour of hissing cockroaches under Mars-like conditions at a height of 85,000 feet (26,000 metres). Oxygen, carbon dioxide, pressure, humidity and temperature were recorded inside the pressurized, reusable habitat and a timer installed to accurately log capsule events. Footage of the roaches using a GoPro 4K camera captured their response to the turbulent atmospheric conditions. Although the capsule suddenly loosened from the platform during the flight as it reached 30,000 feet (9,000 metres), it was successfully recovered and the creatures were unharmed (Armstrong, 2016a).

The following narrative is based on the suspension and fall of the cockroaches, which is told through the figure of the Hanged Man, tarot card XII from the Major Arcana. The card is usually indicative of indecision that precedes a catastrophic fall, with the potential resurrection of the fallen, which inspires the movement of a circus performer within a unique spiral apparatus. Having experienced a kind of death, humanity starts to (re)inhabit the earth differently, being resurrected as a new ecologically integrated species that is no longer discernible as 'human'.

### 9.4.2 Biospherical bottle

A clear plastic bottle, occupied by two cockroaches, is launched by helium balloon over Welsh hills and mountain buds. It is swallowed alongside all the features of the world in thick cloud cover as the hissing creatures reach for the sun. At around 40,000 feet, the heating element fails and the fluids that pulse through their body chambers turn to slush. Ice seizes their muscles.

**FIGURE 9.2** *Two cockroaches survive under extreme environmental conditions as the heating element in their capsules fails and temperatures plummet to around −40°C – the surface temperature of Mars. Movie still from stratospheric balloon flight – a collaboration between Rachel Armstrong and Nebula Sciences, August 2015.*

Arching their backs like fortune fish, it is impossible to say whether the red-brown figures that cast long shadows over the pitiless slate and clotted cream skies are living, dying, at war or making love.

## 9.4.3 The Hanged Man

Submitting to the inevitable fall ahead, the Hanged Man dies ecstatically, spilling his seed in a rainfall of monstrous homunculi. As they meet the earth, they become *mandragola*. From shallow graves, their knotted mandrake roots resemble human forms and send all insane who drag them from the ground.

## 9.4.4 Knitted fetish

Waving its antennae back and forth for several hours, the lonely head thrives until it runs out of oxygen. Headless roaches can live for weeks – longer if frozen, their antennae groping for the rotten body they will never be reunited with. Yet being creatures of lightless places, compound eyes are less important than antennae – long white canes enriched by tiny quills that function as fingers and tongues, document olfactory, gustatory, tactile, thermal and humidity landscapes. Inspired by its strange autonomy, a spiral writing instrument is fashioned in the dislocated head's honour. Artisans and engineers interpret its movements in a twisted structure made of steel, bamboo, chicken bones, corvid feathers and rope, which can be steered by a commanding staff. And so they write in mathematical codes together – the humans dreaming of salvation and the roach of resurrection.

### 9.4.5 Fibonacci

0, 1, 1, 2, 3, 5, 8, 13, 21, 34, 55, 89, 144, 233, 377, 610, 987, 1597, 2584, 4181, 6765, 10946, 17711, 28657, 46368, 75025, 121393, 196418, 317811.

In search for the truth of their beliefs, they build spirals of matter within the heart of snails, sunflower heads, delphiniums, ragwort, corn marigolds, pine cones, hydrozoa, cineraria, asters, rabbit populations, black-eyed susans, chicory, rose petals, fruit, leaves, pineapples, lilies, irises, buttercups, cow parsley, romanesco broccoli, angelica, larkspur, columbine, animal horns, mollusc shells, radiolaria, daisies, the cochlea of the inner ear, honeybees, fingers, bryzoa, corals, aloe, gastropods, cabbage leaves, the stock market, snowflakes, plantain, pytethrum, Michaelmas daisies, the nautilus, starfish, superstring theory, dolphin tails, trees, etc.

## 9.5 Babelsphere: Inhabiting a world in meltdown (Radical Circus)

This text, co-written with Rolf Hughes, is the performance script for the keynote address given with Hughes at *Radical Love*, the first public presentation organized by Radical Circus, a network of circus practitioners that Armstrong and Hughes co-founded with Olle Strandberg of Cirkus Cirkör. An afternoon and evening of *Radical Love* themed events were held at the Uppsala Congress and Concert Hall on 21 January 2017, attracting an audience of over 3,000 people and reportedly representing the largest ever gathering of circus artists (Armstrong and Hughes, 2017).

**Radical Circus**

The way that we imagine circus shapes our expectations of bodies.
Roped to a creaking rig in Dogger, I perform circus in storm and gale alike, watched only by stars, sea spray and the occasional incurious gull. For four weeks I train myself to fly, balance, soar, spin and fall.
I have been fighting fear all my life, but have taught myself not to be afraid of being afraid. Circus shows us what is possible in the realm of the body. Horizons change.

The helicopter arrives to drop provisions. I display gratitude. Unclip and act casual. As soon as you attain something in this life, you lose it. If you try to hold on to it, you will fail. Thumbs up. I wave from my churning landscape. Death is a straight line. Unseen by human eyes, my training resumes. My body is tense and diagonal, but my arms move constantly, softly, erratically. I leave all that has been and all that will be and inhabit solely the moment of now, a moment that contains all times at once. Timing. I let go and embrace the point of no return.

\*

A drop of tar, suspended from a slowly elongating thread, marks time every hundred years, when it weeps and falls in one spectacular moment.

Tar is nature's chewing gum.

Unchanging.

It is made up of dirty long chain hydrocarbons that can't be broken down into sweeter substances, by living things.

Its mummification is forged by the metabolism of the dead, or what life once used to be.

You can masticate it, dribble on it, deform it, secrete amylase on it, mix sugar into it, crack bubbles with it, spit on it, stick it under the chair with all your secret bogies, but you can't digest it.

Every day, the drop hangs on the scaffold, slowly stretching its molecular skin in a sea of coherence.

And while it looks like it's held together in a meniscus of self-similarity, when you look closely enough, it's highly heterogeneous.

Sometimes hydrocarbons are tight, at other times they're relaxed, variably reaching downwards like muscles, in yoga postures of varying degrees of difficulty, under their own slack.

Every day the drop promises to fall but never quite gets around to it.

*[Pause]*.

Then one day, quite out of nowhere, it's in free fall.

Snap and it's over. Marking time.

\*

Fluid life.
I dream of threads, long and narrow, with which we would bind each other, until our bandages become a seeping, weeping, luminous web, in which we are enmeshed.

And so I fold my skin over yours
And you roll your skin around mine
And there we stay, unseeing and unseen –
strange flower of forever flesh,

forever bursting to bud.
But every day the drop –
Every day it promises –
Fall but never get
Around to it.

[Pause].

Snap.

*

An object orbits a body because it is falling.
    It appears to be *stationary* when it is spinning and falling.
    A satellite falls towards the earth under the influence of gravity, and only very slowly, falls into the earth.
    To avoid hitting the earth, an orbiting satellite will travel 8,000 metres horizontally for every 5 metres it falls in a vertical plane so that its trajectory is perfectly choreographed to match the curvature of the world, which is spinning at the same rate. The satellite therefore falls around the earth, continually accelerating towards it under the influence of gravity but never colliding into it.
    In this context, our planet is not only an attractor but also a catcher. It juggles the body of the satellite at such a speed that it remains, for all intents and purposes, high in the air. A radically loving embrace that, if perfectly executed, could last an eternity.

*

One morning, while straddling a low, greasy wharf by a quay at the extremity of a canal, my long legs on each side down to the water, which had become black with stagnation, the black water yielding continually, letting my thoughts sink into soft vacancy, a faint scent of oranges and wood smoke winnowing over the stench of putrefaction, I saw you, tumbling across the sky, a possible pivot in this new world of rotation and churn; I would have gripped you as you neared, held tight until we hinged and fused, but you were already gliding to other co-ordinates, auto-smiling through the dense weather – our fingers almost touching, but trailing further and further away, plucked from their knuckles, pointing elsewhere, until – matchsticks in a storm – gone.

You take up your deathless position and wait. The waking waiting tedious as science. Deep huddle of the banished. Survival memories in the black hole. Light our currency. Black light. Sunless, dappled twilight captured on your pupil.

Drift.

\*

We formerly thought that black holes were smooth and bald like a mountain. Now we know that they're hairy on the inside. Once we learned the art of time travel, we found hairy black holes everywhere. Tiny ones formed in the kitchen sink along with the dirty crockery, which we turned over like stones; delighted and revolted by the molecular creepy crawlies we unearthed. Sometimes they appeared as shadows that swallowed the geometry of alleyways, or sad spaces. Mostly though, we found them in the gaps between each other, crying inconsolably behind hardened hearts and minds, which simply could not escape the rot of disillusionment.

When we ventured into these zones, we found strange terrains littered with soft and silky copses. At other times, we dressed for scrubby expanses that were coarse, like pig bristles but instead, encountered succulent mangroves, rich with strange scents. Here, in all the varied in-between worlds and spandrels, we lifted each other up in Chthulean joy – the ecstasy of multiples – rolling and tumbling as hoards of proteans, chimeras and shape-shifters, stubbornly refusing to conform.

So we made a net of Babel tongues that did not adopt the attitude of loathing our neighbours – by commenting on their breath, what microflora they gardened, the colour of their coats, or whether they'd eaten garlic – but somehow worked it all out. Now, we hold each other tip to base, and in many variations on this theme, learning to drool and squirm together as a radical, living circus, poised to defy the odds.

\*

They say they will die like animals. Base automata. Stupid things. That's what they say. And in those moments, the revulsion I feel for their rotten carrot-faced, lettuce-stained, soil world changes. Three hundred and fifty million years of partial transformations! From egg to multiple nymphs, born inside the female body. Without love! That's what they say. Without love.

Love has to be reinvented. Tenderness. Or something. I don't understand.
*Be careful. What rises here, is not human.*

They polish their antennae. Shedding their leathery and membranous wings, they wipe the many lenses of their compound kaleidoscopic eyes designed to detect motion and turn them steady like rudders upon the many skies above them. Hissing songs of war and procreation, they split their corseted exoskeletons again and again, reinventing love. That's for certain. That's what they do. Heartless creatures. Now the females cannot tell a male from its moult.

Spinning on their biospherical wheel, a mere lunch container, with an ugly pea-green cap, the brick-red bodied creatures write unutterable words and turn their feeling apparatuses towards the night. Bitter beauty, multiple, creeping, reviled. Reaching into the inky void, they search for stars like grains of sugar. Recklessly unbound by terrestrial imperatives, they defile the idea of direction, stability, navigation systems, automatic pilots and stabilizers. Survival machines.

Except the machines don't survive.

Circuit failure near a hundred thousand feet, colder than Mars. Keep them warm, they say, under fallen fruit like apples and wet rot. They'll drown in more than the slickest water film, or temperatures below sixty-eight degrees. Of course, there are uncomfortable silences and endless nights when the love doesn't come. Murder beauty, so they do. Torture her forms. Drag their jagged antennae over her plastics, like nails down a chalkboard, unutterable sounds that will not be written down and the whirling world does not stand still.

*Be careful. What rises here, is not human.*

According to legend, there are creatures that live within realms above the sky. Electromagnetic realms that dazzle the heavens with mirror shards, aurorae and quantum particles. One day, they say that a pregnant female will fall out of this celestial tapestry and uproot the tree of life. Her as yet unseparated nymphs will feed on her corpse and tumble through the great plastic hole left in the world.

Then the glue gives out, the dispassionate eye blinks and they are gone.

So, they fall like rain in a thousand nightmares as they reinvent love.

\*

I have always known you.

*That was the moment we realized we did not need kings, queens nor presidents. Nor did we need permissions, categories or constraints that were not of our own choosing.*

Back then the world was kinder.

*We did not even need a guide.*

We lived on an eternal beach with golden sand, marram grass clusters as big as bathing huts and cunning grey sea.

*And so we stood, facing each other.*

*Listening.*

I remember you —

*Waiting.*

the scent of fish and chips with your animal eyes running in the whippet wind,

*Being quiet.*

howling in wolf tongues upon dark stairs

*Still.*

— speaking with the world of spirits and magical beasts.

*Forgetting.*

Then the amnesia storm rolled in — a giant cumulonimbus of a thing, and I found myself on the shore, happy to die.

*What we discovered is something quite remarkable.*

Just as life's hypothermia set in, I recognized you,

*To experience it is to understand it. Come closer, let me whisper something …*

warming me

*When we create conditions for care and attention*

slowly from the inside …

*… the world enters.*

*The world enters and it goes from one to the other, shyly unmasking us.*
*It waits.*
*Until we are open and attentive.*
*And then it undresses in turn.*
*The room's molecules start whispering*

— we listen as they draw us closer together.
Closer.
Closer still.
Until everything begins again.

And then the bricks we believed in start to bend and twist! — resonating, oscillating, ecstatic liquid!

\*

The Babelsphere – a precarious place, prone to falling apart – exists at a time when there are only monsters. It is built upon a circle of hands at the limits of a massive seance table. Some of these strange beasts are inherited from ancient times, while others, which do not yet possess a name, are made in jam jars, with yarn spun from ectoplasm and sea spray that dangles reluctantly upon our eyelashes. We cast these strange stitches on the liquid sands of our deepest fears as testimony that – despite uncertainty, tragedy and catastrophe – everything is still to play for.

*

And so, it was decided we would relocate to the ocean, weave a home from the warm currents flowing between us; crustaceans would shape our cellars and bedrooms, seaweed our curtains, and we would be rocked to sleep by the infernal clattering of the churning tides. It's continually collapsing, our hearth and home, repudiating each form the moment it is suggested. Enslaved to gravity, it tosses and turns us as a living kaleidoscope for the sun and moon. The ocean is obliged to maintain the pretence that, left to itself, it would do more than give up, fall flat, leak away. Helicopters are soon buzzing dully overhead, paparazzi seeking to snap us – nudists in a liquid cage. We fancy a bit of shade, plant a bit of upside-down garden, but it doesn't take and we don't have enough anchors to stop it all washing away. It's too sensitive and restless, this shiny, white medium – tip it, and it runs childishly away.

It is in sleep that a circus artist's body forgets it belongs to the circus and starts to seep and drip over the edges of the mattress. Like mercury, it rolls across the floor, a shiny glob of reflected candlelight, rigging, wheels, stuffed animals. As precise as a bead of sweat descending the rope artist's spine, it slips under the door and out into the white forest where winter has turned the trees into prankster ghosts, their boneless branches frozen theatrically under the silver moon.

I would dig a grave, but I lack a spade.

The circus artist's body, which now weighs a mere twenty-one grams, ploughs across the sparkling crust of snow, its bodily salts carving out words like *Doukhobors*! *Svodbodniki*! *Suffragettes*! – melting, it becomes water, steam – momentarily juggled, but always hostile, never controlled.

And there, rising steadily, we see our hot-air balloon, drifting towards a fur-lined black hole in the sky. This is what the circus spirit seeks out.

The spirit seeks out the site where it feels only here, and nowhere else, can it truly be itself.

*

# Epilogue

Replaying the tape of life opens up alternative practices for biodesign, associated modes of inhabitation and being-in-the-world, where what it means to be a body is deeply connected with our impacts on the planet. In seeking to reach escape velocity from the extinction scenarios that typify the Anthropocene, soft living architecture expands the potential design applications of our experience of biological realm using a new materialist approach and an agile experimental portfolio of investigations across many media and contexts. Soft living architecture also offers a counterpoint to the 'machine for living in' (Le Corbusier, 2007, p. 158) and its associated impacts for the living realm, which dissociates our understanding of 'life' from *the way we live* and *inhabit* places. It allies with radical bodies, subversive life-promoting fabrics, unruly materials, circus and soils that are capable of transforming the character of space by materially and metabolically entwining the cycles of life and death. Drawing from these processes of transformation, synthesis, disobedience, surprise, reconfiguration and decay, it becomes possible for architects to invent and synthesize new material expressions, protocols of space-time, 'living' apparatuses, parallel prototypes and ways of occupying spaces. These experimental modes of inhabitation do not eliminate the difficulties that are faced in a world, which appears to be perpetually falling apart or always ending. In fact, they enable a creative and mutual relationship with our natural world – even in the midst of ecocide.

In the process of realizing the Babelsphere through experimental architectural practices, it is clear that everything is incompletely formed (being constantly subjected to changes through many acts of living), only partially understood (owing to its relationship with (hyper)complexity and the invisible realms), and can never attain idealized existence states (for nature changes constantly). Indeed, the Babelsphere challenges the intoxicating ideas of perfection, permanence and stasis that have typified Enlightenment thinking. We must therefore reinvent the conditions whereby agile protocols of space-time, architectural design practices and values are consistent with an ecological ethics, which embraces the frequently surreal traits of the living world. Existing beyond the comfort zones of fixed categories, the Babelsphere welcomes the leviathans that we have nevertheless inherited from the industrial era so that unfamiliar creatures of our making own may coexist alongside us, which do not yet possess a name.

Soft living architecture emerges from the uncomfortable convergences of these uncertain processes. It appreciates the already-strangeness of biological and natural systems and invites us to experiment with a worlding process that is ethically hewn from the (bio)technological that shape the world's 'living' fabrics. The architects and designers who operate within these frameworks are not only inventors of radical, experimental twenty-first century design practices, they are also space-time choreographers who seek participation with many different kinds of lively substrates that defy a formal relationship with aesthetic, utilitarian and morphological conventions. Despite the reality of ecocide, soft living architecture conjures forth new kinds of Nature from precarious modes of inhabitation during these uncertain times. Working as an agile agent alongside the naturalized world, it aims to realize the Babelsphere as an ongoing parallel architectural project and testimony that – despite the precarious nature of our existence – alternative and ongoing futures can still be meaningfully designed.

# Glossary

**Acqua alta** (high water) are destructive high tides that periodically flood Venice. They are caused by exceptional tide peaks in the northern Adriatic Sea and contribute significantly to the decay of the city's historic buildings.

**Actant** is a person, creature or object in a narrative, playing any of a set of active roles.

**Alchemy** is a medieval practice that aims to transmute matter, specifically base metals like lead into precious metals like gold. It also seeks a universal elixir of life.

**Anthropocene** is the epoch during which – with the advent of global industrialization – human impact becomes a geological force altering the ground, the oceans and climate.

**Apocalyptic literature** is a pessimistic view of history referring to the End Times, as revealed by a heavenly messenger (Ahroni, 1977).

**Aqua vitae** is the *water of life*. Alchemically speaking, it is a concentrated aqueous solution of ethanol, which during medieval times and the Renaissance became equated with strong alcoholic liquor.

**Architecture of wetness** incorporates those materials, technologies and methods that embrace the presence and movement of water within a building.

**Babelsphere** is a system that is constantly negotiated to maintain its coherence. It is a theoretical and experimental framework for a city of contradictions and imperfections that is held together by precarious ecological principles of mutuality, cooperation, synthesis and diplomacy. Typically, ecosystems are Babelspheres that are composed of many different agents that negotiate their terms for existence with other like and unlike beings. However, a Babelsphere is also a city which is inhabited by many different peoples and non-humans, whose daily interactions and collective diplomacy and agile protocols of constructing spaces are such that the city resists falling apart.

**Being-in-the-world** is a term used by Martin Heidegger (Heidegger, 1962) to conjure a form of conscious, embodied existence, whose experiences are shaped by being situated within a particular material realm.

**Biltong** is an alien life form that serves a future community as a printer-like technology, which was invented by Philip K. Dick.

**Biofilm** is an assemblage of microbial cells, which are enclosed in an extracellular polymeric substance matrix that binds them to a surface, so they stick together.

**Black mirror** is an apparatus for producing distinctive reflections that appear on the surface of a shallow pool of water that is backgrounded by a black surface. In the Middle Ages, these apparatuses were used for divination, or scrying, while in the modern era, they are striking reflective pools that appear to perfectly invert landscapes and buildings.

**Bottom-up system** is where constituent reagents, through emergence, produce more complex systems than the sum of the possible outcomes at the starting point.

**Brexit** is the (ongoing) process of the UK's withdrawal from the European Union.

**Brute matter** does not possess agency or liveliness. The term originates from a letter by Isaac Newton to Richard Bentley discussing how one (inert) body can exert a force upon another 'without the mediation of something else which is not material' (Newton, 2007). New materialist Jane Bennet uses this term as a counterpoint to 'vibrant' matter, which is agentized, lively and volitional independently of human command (Bennett, 2010).

**Bütschli system** is a recipe developed by Otto Bütschli, which produces a simple, amoeba-like artificial organism by adding a drop of strong alkali to a field of olive oil (Bütschli, 1892).

**Burgess Shale** is a fossil-bearing geological formation in the Canadian Rockies that dates back to the middle Cambrian period around 500 million years ago. It represents one of the most diverse and well-preserved fossil localities in the world where complete soft-bodied animals are preserved and so provides a window on animal communities and their make-up during the end of the Cambrian explosion.

**Cambrian explosion** refers to the geological epoch where all known forms of biological organization were established.

**Cambrian renaissance** is a parallel epoch of architectural diversification whereby a radically diverse series of building typologies are produced by fundamentally altering the protocols for choreographing matter and space-time.

**Canute** was a Danish king and formidable Viking warrior, who ruled an empire that spanned England, Sweden, Norway and Denmark. He was also vain and allowed himself to be convinced by flattering courtiers that he could hold back the tide.

**Chthonic** relates to the earth and the underworld.

**Chthulean** is derived from Donna Haraway's notion of Chthulucene (which is spelt differently from H.P. Lovecraft's 'misogynist racial-nightmare') and refers to the sym-chthonic forces and powers of which people are a part, within which ongoingness is at stake. It calls upon the 'diverse earth-wide tentacular powers and forces and collected things with names like Naga, Gaia, Tangaroa, Terra, Haniyasu-hime, Spider Woman, Pachamama, Oya, Gorgo, Raven, A'akuluujjusi, and many many more' (Haraway, 2015).

**Cites of Canute** are those like Venice and New Orleans that are situated next to significant bodies of water and have built colossal structures that propose to hold back tidal surges.

**Clarke's dictum** proposes that any sufficiently advanced civilization is indistinguishable from its technology (Clarke, 1973, p. 21).

# GLOSSARY

**Crypto-biotic crusts** are complex communities of cyanobacteria, moulds and other microbes.

**Cthulhu** is monstrous Great Old One, described by H.P. Lovecroft. It is a gigantic being of great power, with semblances to an octopus, a dragon and a caricature of human form. Great Old Ones are not composed altogether of flesh and blood, and their shape is not made of matter. They can plunge from world to world through the sky when the stars are 'right', but they cannot live when the stars are 'wrong'.

**Curmudgilingus** is complaining for the sake of complaining.

**Descartes's demon** is an all-powerful figure conjured by René Descartes as a thought experiment in developing the notion of research, where he needed to do more than investigate an observation and *search again* to establish whether he was being deceived by this trickster or encountering God's truth.

**Dissipative systems** (also known as structures) are thermodynamically open systems which are at far from equilibrium states. They exchange energy and matter with their surrounding medium. Characteristically they produce spatial variation from a homogenous background.

**Ecocene** is an emerging ecological era that is set to replace Anthropocene's destructive impacts.

**Ecophagy** is the act of devouring an ecosystem.

**Ecopoiesis** is the concept of initiating of an ecosystem capable of supporting life in a barren environment.

**Edible beauty** was observed by Salvador Dalí whereby 'beauty should be edible, or not at all'. He attributed these values to certain Catalan and Parisian Art Nouveau buildings that possess 'terrifying and edible beauty', with particular respect to the quality of 'movement which … is primarily intended to arouse a kind of great "primeval hunger", like the ultimate, ideal architecture which would embody the most tangible and delirious goal of hypermaterialism … not only because it denounces the violent materialistic banality of immediate needs … but also because it unashamedly alludes to the nutritive, edible nature of houses of this type, which are nothing other than the first edible houses, the first and only erogenous buildings whose existence is an affirmation of that "functional" trigger of the amorous imagination – to be able in the realest possible sense to eat the object of desire' (Godoli, 1990, p. 45). In this book, *edible* is interpreted according to ecological rather than psychological values.

**Electrons** are massless negatively charged particles that collectively produce electricity.

**Emergence** is a spontaneous phenomenon that gives rise to more complex systems, where order appears to arise from chaos.

**End Times** are a biblical concept that draws the conclusion of the current system of humanity on earth. They are associated with catastrophes like famine, earthquakes, ecocide and loss of moral integrity. These signs herald the end of the world as it is presently recognized.

**Engastrulation** is an ostentatious cuisine epitomized by the *rôti sans pareil*: the roast without equal, where a bestiary of animals is cooked and stuffed inside each other.

**Entropy** is the measure of disorder in a system. The higher the disorder, the higher the entropy of the system. Reversible processes do not increase the entropy of the universe, but irreversible systems do.

**Experimental architecture** is a transdisciplinary worlding practice. It produces agile protocols for choreographing space-time, which shift away from the traditional view of architecture as a static, form-giving subject to a practice of interrogative, dynamic prototypes.

**Far from equilibrium** is a system state that is constantly changing with time due to input from a source of external energy or matter. The term was described by Ilya Prigogine in the 1970s and modelled on the Bénard cell.

**Fondamenta** means a street parallel to a canal other than Canal Grande and the lagoon (case in which they're called *riva*) and was used as foundations for the construction of buildings.

**Geostory** is a non-human narrative fabric, which is woven through tectonic plates, meteorite impacts and ice ages (Latour, 2013).

**Geotextile** is a permeable fabric that is used in association with soil. It augments the natural properties of the ground such as by increasing drainage, reinforcing its integrity or preventing different layers/horizons from mixing.

**Ghost cells** are 'chasses' or bags of cytoplasm harvested from a living cell that has had its nucleus removed. They are used in synthetic biology to 'boot up' the expression of synthetic genetic programmes. This technique was famously used in the production of the world's first organism with a human-made genome, called *Synthia*.

**Golem** is derived from the Hebrew 'gelem' (גלם), meaning 'raw material'. It refers to an animated being that is created by humans entirely from inanimate matter and given life through a mystical process, which invokes the secret name of God.

**Gordian knot** is an 'impossible' geometry, which was given to Alexander of Macedonia when he led his army into Persia and is also used as a metaphor for a difficult problem that is solvable by bold action.

**Great Dissections** refer to the analysis of all aspects of the human body through its systematic separation and categorization into parts. The last of the Great Dissections was the sequencing of the human genome, which was announced in 2003 by the National Human Genome Research Institute (NHRGI), the Department of Energy (DOE) and their partners in the International Human Genome Sequencing Consortium.

**Haunting** is the recurring occupancy, or frequenting, of a space by a being.

**Heraclitus's dictum** states that life is in constant flux – where 'no man ever steps in the same river twice, for it's not the same river and he's not the same man'.

**Homeobox genes** are a large family of similar genes that direct the formation of many body structures during early embryonic development. A **homeobox** is a DNA sequence that is involved in the regulation of patterns of morphogenesis in animals, fungi and plants.

# GLOSSARY

**Horizontal coupling** is the propensity for all matter at all scales to form relationships through weak interactions so that there is effectively no top-down or bottom-up hierarchical ordering, but a continual negotiation between assemblages.

**Hyperbodies** are coherent yet highly distributed bodies made from assemblages of participating agencies, like soils, cities and dust clouds, which are also subsets of hyperobjects (Morton, 2013).

**Hypercomplexity** is an organizational condition that is founded on the principles of complexity from which new levels of order arise from the interactions between components. The phenomena exceed a classical understanding of complex systems through their scale, heterogeneity, distribution and capacity to transform their surroundings.

**Hylomorphism** is a philosophical theory developed by Aristotle, which regards every physical object as a compound of matter and form.

**Imitation game** is a test invented by Alan Turing to compare one hypercomplex system with another and evaluate the differences based on the observer's previous experiences. It is more commonly known as the Turing Test, which is used to assess artificial intelligences in comparison with humans.

**Large Hadron Collider** is a gargantuan particle accelerator arranged in a circular configuration with a 27-km circumference. It consists of a number of experimental complexes that are assigned various experiments namely Atlas (observes massive particles), CMS (general-purpose particle detector), ALICE (studies heavy ions) and LHCb (investigates the slight differences between matter and antimatter by examining a type of particle called the 'beauty quark').

**Leduc cells** are produced when a crystal of calcium chloride is added to a dilute solution of sodium hydrogen carbonate. A thin calcium carbonate shell is formed around the crystal lattice (Armstrong, 2015, p. 40).

**Liesegang rings** are a special type of chemical pattern formation caused by density fluctuations of a weakly soluble salt through a porous matrix like a gel. The salt periodically forms precipitates, which are typically deposited as a series of bands.

**Lively matter** possesses some of the characteristics of living things (e.g. viruses, Traube cells, Bütschli droplets, crystal growth) but is not necessarily given the full status of being 'alive'. It is concerned with substances at far from equilibrium states that possess their own energy and agency. Its phenomenology and potency are discussed through a series of multidisciplinary readings known as new materialism, which 'criticise anthropocentrism and rethink subjectivity by playing up the role of non-human forces within the human. They emphasize the self-organizing powers of several non-human processes, explore dissonant relations between those processes and cultural practice, rethink the sources of ethics, and commend the need to fold a planetary dimension more actively and regularly into studies of global, interstate and state politics' (Connolly, 2013).

**Living bricks** are prototype mineral building elements that express some of the properties of living things.

**Living stones** are building elements that possess some of the properties of living systems, which have not been granted the full status of being fully alive. They are highly particular site-specific expressions of nature. In the city of Venice, they are encountered as biofouling on brickwork that lays down bioconcretes. Other examples of living stones exist in Romania as *trovants*, which can move on account of water-absorbing properties.

**Living technology** is based on the powerful core features of life and includes responsive materials and apparatuses that behave in remarkably lifelike ways, without necessarily being granted the full status of being 'alive'.

**Medaka fish** are also known as Japanese rice fish and have been kept as pets since the Edo Period (1603–1868). In the early 1900s, they contributed to genetics. Medaka were the first vertebrates that were found to follow Mendel's law of inheritance, which explains the way different traits are passed on down the generations. In 1994, medaka became the first vertebrate to have sex and reproduce in space. Male and female fish travelled to the earth orbit on the space shuttle Columbia, mated in orbit and produced normal babies, all in a weightless environment. There is a special chamber for them on board the Kibo module of the International Space Station. In the Aquatic Habitat built by the Japanese Space Agency, medaka are being studied to understand the impact of micro-gravity (Hooper, 2015).

**Medusae** are free-swimming creatures in the life cycle of jellyfish. They are bell shaped, with tentacles that hang down around a central mouth, which is also the anus.

**Microbiome** is a community of microorganisms such as bacteria, fungi, archaea and viruses, which live inside our bodies, particularly in the gut.

**Micro-geography** is a term coined by microbiologist Simon Park; it exists at the intersection of architecture and microenvironments, which is formed by communities of microorganisms that stain buildings fabrics through their specific inhabitation of niches (Park, 2012c).

**Mixology** is a term used to describe the art of making cocktail drinks. It is applied much more widely in this book to infer the skilful art of bringing together multiple ingredients to achieve an exquisite outcome. It is also not regarded an exclusively human practice but as a form of ecological *alchemy*.

**Modern synthesis** is a theory of evolution that takes a gradualist perspective of change and is enabled by a set of mechanistic technologies.

**Molecular decision-making** occurs when substances explore transitional states of atomic configuration before reaching stable or steady-state arrangements.

**Monster** is a creature that defies the logic of existing categorization systems.

**Morphogenesis** is the process of development of the anatomical structures that constitute the overall form of a creature.

**MOSE,** the Italian word for Moses, is an acronym for the project **Mo**dulo **S**perimentale **E**letromeccanica (Experimental Electromechanical Module) that is installing a series of 78 hydraulic gates in the Venetian Lagoon to keep out the destructive high tides or *acqua alta*. The name also alludes to the story of Moses parting the waves of the Red Sea to establish a safe crossing for his people.

**Multiverse** is a unified physical entity that contains more than one universe (Deutsch, 2012, p. 194). It arises from a theory called eternal inflation where, shortly after the Big Bang, space-time expanded at different rates in different places. This produced bubble universes, each with their own separate laws of physics.

**Near-shore** is where waves steepen and break and then reform in their passage to the beach, where they break for the last time and surge up the foreshore. Much sediment is transported in this zone, both along the shore and perpendicular to it.

**Necrobiome** is the community of bacteria found on a dead body.

**Nucleotides** are the basic structural unit and building block for DNA and RNA, which are the essential biomolecules for all life forms on earth. Each of these units are hooked together to form a chain. They consist of three parts: a five-sided sugar (pentose), a phosphate group and a nitrogenous base.

**Oceanic ontologies** offer a way of developing a discourse about bodies or matter, which are in a constant state of flux, like oceans, which evade categorization by formal classification systems. They produce maps rather than theories of concepts (Lee, 2011).

**Origin of life** is a spectrum of material events that led to the transition from inert to living matter. Implicit in this definition is that there was no one moment that gave rise to life as we currently recognise it, but a continuum of events that created the conditions for the modern notion of life. It is likely that the first forms of lively matter would not be given the status of 'life', which is reserved for biology. This is characterised by a set of characteristics governed by a central code like DNA; its units (cells) are bounded by a membrane, and it is capable of complex chemical exchanges known as metabolism.

**Osmotic structures** are outgrowths of a structure that are produced by the rapid entry of water, which produces an internal pressure that causes sudden expansion, or growth (Leduc, 1911).

**Parallel** modes of existence (bodies, universes, etc.) are an expression of a probabilistic reality where various degrees of freedom exist so that alternatives other than the present expression of matter, time and space may be unlocked from within the system.

**Parallel methodologies** are systems of methods that prototype, conjure and realise parallel worlds.

**Parasite architecture** is a structure that uses an existing building in an opportunistic manner, often attaching itself in some way.

**'Pataphysics** refers to Alfred Jarry's *science of imaginary solutions*, which, in the attempt to define it, risks the clarification and reduction it rejects. It is, however, not incoherent but a remarkably cogent body of exploits and ideas where the contradictory and exceptional are woven into its very fabric. 'It may never be understood, which is perhaps why it is so frequently misunderstood' (Hugill, 2015, p. xiv).

**Piscine** are pedestrian streets that were once canals or marshlands and were then buried and filled with rubble.

**Plastisphere** is the community of microbes that grows as a thin layer of life (a biofilm) on the outside of all marine plastic fragments.

**Progeny** is the offspring of a creature, person or plant.

**Protist** is a simple, mostly single-celled organism, but colonial forms also exist that consist of many similar cells.

**Protons** are subatomic particles found in the nucleus of every atom. They have a positive electrical charge, which is equal and opposite to that of the electron.

**Proto-pearls** are dynamic oil droplets that form soft biomorphic crystal crusts at the oil/water interface. They are the 'artificial cells' used in the Future Venice project.

**(re)** is used throughout this book as a way of introducing ambiguity. It asks the reader to consider whether something is happening for the first time or whether it is an iterative process capable of producing alternative outcomes, which may differ with each cycle of events.

**Qualitative computing** is a form of symbolic computing that deals with irrational numbers, which are incompletely divisible by others and therefore reach towards infinite representations. Françoise Chatelin regards such cyphers as being closer to the way that nature computes than real or rational numbers (Chatelin, 2012).

**Rayleigh–Bénard convection cells** are dynamic material formations that are produced by complex changes in surface tension and differentials that exist between the hot and cold fields of fluid, which produce cell-like boundaries and host a turbulent 'internal milieu'.

**Rhythmanalysis** is a term used by Henri Lefebvre to refer to iterations within urban spaces and their effects on inhabitants (Lefebvre, 2013).

**Saponification** is a soap-making process. It involves the alkaline hydrolysis of esters that occurs when strong alkali is added to oil (long chain fatty acids), which are converted into soap and glycerol.

**Scrying** is a form of divination or prediction of future events based on the interpretation of symbols that appear on the reflective surfaces of apparatuses like crystal balls or black mirrors.

**Sensible fabrics** are hypercomplex materials, like soils, which are sensitive to external changes and alter their character accordingly.

**Supersoils** are artificial organic fabrics that augment the environmental performance of the soil or enable new processes and metabolisms to occur within the ground.

**Symbiogenesis** is a theory where the cooperation between species increases their survival. It was championed and substantiated through microbiological evidence by Lynn Margulis as the 'endosymbiotic theory'. This proposes that three fundamental eukaryotic cell organelles were all once free living prokaryotic cells that became engulfed and assimilated by their hosts and integrated into their structure,

# GLOSSARY

namely, the mitochondria, the photosynthetic plastids and the (9+2) basal bodies of flagella (Sagan, 1967).

**Soft** technologies are capable of dynamically responding to their surroundings and possess lifelike characteristics such as movement, growth, sensitivity and population-scale interactions.

**Sound walks** are sound recordings made with a binaural system and DAT recorder that follow different route with urban forms of particular interest to the researcher. The data gathered is analysed as a representation of the constituent soundscapes to reveal information about the acoustics of a place.

**Stochastic** processes have a random probability distribution or pattern that may be analysed statistically but may not be predicted precisely.

**Subnatures** are unruly urban fabrics like smog, dust and weeds that challenge reductive and naturalistic approaches towards the urban landscape. Their presence promotes a dialectic that explores architecture's most radical concepts and alternative forms of Nature (Gissen, 2009).

**Superorganism** is a group of synergetically interacting organisms of the same species.

**Supersoils** are lively, artificial, hypercomplex geotextiles that augment environmental performance as well as providing a substrate for making inhabitable spaces.

**Supramolecular chemistry** is the chemistry of the combined actions of molecules and differs from molecular chemistry, which involves the covalent bonding of atoms, as it is concerned with the formation of intermolecular bonds that produce structures and functions of entities, from the association of two or more chemical species.

**Sustainability** is an approach that aims to support ecological balance by not harming the environment or depleting natural resources. It is a statement of moderation that focuses on meeting today's needs without compromising the ability of future generations to also meet their needs.

**Thinging** is a Heideggerian concept where the *thing* (an object or abstract concept) discloses a world.

**Top-down system** is one whose outcome is predetermined and is produced by the sum of its parts.

**Traube cells** are formed by placing a blue diamond-shaped crystal of copper (II) sulphate in a weak solution (0.1 M) of potassium hexacyanoferrate, which transforms the crystal into a deep-brown semipermeable membrane, with an irregular appearance, like seaweed (Traube, 1867).

**Trovant** is a rock with a stone core and outer shell of sand. After a heavy rain, it may move owing to hydrostatic pressure, and smaller stones bud from larger ones, which are said to be growing stones.

**Turing test** (see **Imitation game**).

**Utopia** is a fictional city conceived by Thomas More in 1516, where an idealized community lived sustainably and harmoniously according to the dominant principles of a specific ideology. It is a deterministic view of cities that has been adopted throughout the modern era as a realistic blueprint for a working nation.

**Vitalism** describes the nature of life as arising from a 'vital', life-giving force, which infuses matter so that it becomes animated. It is peculiar to living organisms and different from all other forces found outside living things.

**Vivogenesis** is a process that results in persistent lifelike phenomena, without necessarily being biological in its character or ordering.

**Wet printing** is a process of forming structures in a fluid medium.

**Worlding** is an ongoing process of *thinging* the world. It refers to the way we shape and dwell in our habitats and is a difficult negotiation without a tidy definition. Its multifarious and assembling character does not just continue or end. The term was first popularized by Heidegger in *Being and Time* (Heidegger, 1962).

He turned the noun (world) into the active verb (worlding), an imperative and generative process of world making, evolution and imminence.

# References

Adamatzky, A. and De Lacy Costello, B. (2002), 'Experimental logical gates in a reaction-diffusion medium: The XOR gate and beyond', *Physical Review E*, 66(4), 046112. doi:10.1103/PhysRevE.66.046112.

Adamatzky, A. and De Lacy Costello, B. (2003), 'Reaction-diffusion path planning in a hybrid chemical and cellular-automaton processors', *Chaos, Solitons and Fractals*, 16: 727–36.

Adamatzky, A., De Lacy Costello, B. and Asai, T. (2005), *Reaction-Diffusion Computers*, London: Elsevier Science.

Adamatzky, A., Bull, L., De Lacy Costello, B., Stepney, S. and Teuscher, C. (2007), *Unconventional Computing*, Beckington, UK: Luniver Press.

Adamatzky, A., Armstrong, R., Jones, J. and Gunji, Y.P. (2013), 'On creativity of slime mould', *International Journal of General Systems*, 42: 441–57.

Adams, D. (1995), *The Hitch Hiker's Guide to the Galaxy: A Trilogy in Five Parts*, London: William Heinemann.

Ades, D., Cox, N. and Hopkins, D. (1999), *Marcel Duchamp*. London: Thames & Hudson.

Ahroni, R. (1977), 'The Gog prophecy and the Book of Ezekiel', *HAR*, 1, 1–27.

Al-Khalili, J. and McFadden, J. (2014), *Life on the Edge: The Coming Age of Quantum Biology*, New York: Crown Publishers.

Archinet (2012), Drawing architecture – Conversation with Perry Kulper, *Archinet News*, 5 August [online]. Available at: http://archinect.com/news/article/54767042/drawing-architecture-conversation-with-perry-kulper [Accessed 27 October 2016].

Armstrong, R. (1996), 'The body as an architectural space – From lips to anus (the gastrointestinal tract as a site for redesigning and development)', *Architectural Design*, 123: 86.

Armstrong, R. (2013), 'Coming to terms with synthetic biology', *Volume Magazine*, 35: 110–17.

Armstrong, R. (2015), *Vibrant Architecture: Matter as a Codesigner of Living Structures*, Berlin: Degruyter Open.

Armstrong, R. (2016a), *Star Ark: A Living, Self-sustaining Worldship*, Chichester, UK: Springer/Praxis.

Armstrong, R. (2016b), 'The oceanic pedagogical sketchbook of multi-materiality', in K. Grigoriadis (ed.), *Mixed Matters: A Multi-material Design Compendium*, Berlin: Jovis Verlag GmbH.

Armstrong, R. (2017), One Tuesday in 2067. Sophia's experiences in her liquid world. 50 years of Bosch, *BSH Hausgeräte GmbH* [online]. Available at: https://www.bsh-group.com/company/experts-visions-future-2067/rachel-amstrong [Accessed 26 December 2017].

Armstrong, R. (2018), *Origamy*, Alconbury Weston: NewCon Press.

Armstrong, R. (In press), *Liquid Life: On Non-linear Materiality*, New York: Punctum Books.
Armstrong, R. and Beesley, P. (2011), 'Soil and protoplasm: The Hylozoic Ground project', *Architectural Design*, 81(2): 78–89.
Armstrong, R., Ferracina, S. and Hughes, R. (2017), 'A new wall for the 21st century', *Architectural Review*, 19 April [online]. Available at: https://www.architectural-review.com/rethink/a-wall-for-the-21st-century-trumps-wall-should-be-a-porous-shape-shifting-invitation/10019185.article [Accessed 2 May 2017].
Armstrong, R. and Hughes, R. (2016a), Obonjan outline of talk series, private correspondence of undeveloped project work.
Armstrong, R. and Hughes, R. (2016b), 'Falling/Catching: Onwards (Radical Love)', in R. Armstrong, R. Hughes and E. Gangvik (eds), *The Handbook of the Unknowable*, Trondheim: TEKS.
Armstrong, R. and Hughes, R. (2017), Radical Love, Radical Circus, 21 January, Uppsala Concert & Congress, Uppsala, Sweden [online]. Available at: http://www.ukk.se/konserter/kalendarium/2017/radical-love-21-januari/ [in Swedish] [Accessed 23 January 2017].
Armstrong, R. and Hughes, R. (2016), 'Persephone', *JOUST*, 3(1): 28–38.
Armstrong, R. and Hughes, R. (in press-a), 'The art of experiment', in Tine Noergaard and Nanna Gro Henningsen (eds.), *Writing and Architecture* (Aarhus School of Architecture) (College of Engineering, University of Puerto Rico).
Armstrong, R., Hughes, R. and Gangvik, E. (2016), *The Handbook of the Unknowable*, Trondheim: TEKS.
Artaud, A. (1958), *The Theatre and Its Double*, New York: Grove Press.
Bachelard, G. (1994), *The Poetics of Space*, Boston: Beacon Press.
Bacon, F. (2009), *The New Atlantis*, Online. Luxembourg: Createspace Independent Publishing Platform.
Ballantyne, A. (2015), *John Ruskin*, London: Reaktion Books.
BBC News (2016), Europe migrant crisis: Razor wire fence failing in Hungary. 21 February [online]. Available at: http://www.bbc.co.uk/news/world-europe-35624118 [Accessed 26 August 2016].
Beer, S. (1960), 'Towards the automatic factory', in H. Von Foerster and G. Zopf (eds), *Principles of self-organization: Transactions of the University of Illinois Symposium on Self-Organization, Robert Allerton Park, 8 and 9 June*, New York: Pergamon, 5.
Belousov, B.P. (1959), A periodic reaction and its mechanism, *Compilation of Abstracts on Radiation Medicine*, 147, p. 145.
Benjamin, W. (1999), *The Arcades Project*, Cambridge, MA: Harvard University Press.
Benjamin, W. (2002), *Selected Writings*, in Walter Benjamin (ed.), *Volume 3. 1935–1938*, Cambridge: The Belknap Press of Harvard University Press.
Bennett, J. (2010), *Vibrant Matter: A Political Ecology of Things*, Durham, NC: Duke University Press.
Betsky, A. (2015), Experimental architecture emerged to question postmodernism's jokes, *Dezeen*, 6 August [online]. Available at: http://www.dezeen.com/2015/08/06/aaron-betsky-opinion-experimental-architecture-question-postmodernism-jokes/ [Accessed 16 October 2016].

Betsky, A. (2016), "Let's hear it for temporary architecture". Dezeen. 29 March [online]. Available at: https://www.dezeen.com/2016/03/29/aaron-betsky-opinion-temporary-pavilions-lessons-for-permanent-architecture/ [Accessed 17 March 2018].

Bitbol, M. (1996), *Schrödinger's Philosophy of Quantum Mechanics*, Dordrecht: Kluwer.

Blake, T. (2013), Bruno Latour's post-human Gaians: The 'Earthbound' (Lecture 5), 27 February [online]. Available at: https://terenceblake.wordpress.com/2013/02/27/bruno-latours-post-human-gaians-the-earthbound-lecture-5/ [Accessed 19 November 2016].

Bohm, D.J. (1980), *Wholeness and the Implicate Order*, London: Routledge.

Bohr, N. (2011), *Atomic Theory and the Description of Nature: Four Essays with an Introductory Survey*, Cambridge: Cambridge University Press.

Borges, J.L. (2000), 'Tlön, Uqbar, Orbis Tertius', in J.L. Borges ed., *Labyrinths*, London: Penguin Modern Classics.

Bütschli, O. (1892), *Untersuchungen ueber microscopische Schaume und das Protoplasma*, Leipzig.

Cairns, S. and Jacobs, J.M. (2014), *Buildings Must Die: A Perverse View of Architecture*, Cambridge, MA: MIT Press.

Cairns-Smith, A.G. (1987), *Genetic Takeover and the Mineral Origins of Life*, Cambridge: Cambridge University Press.

Callaway, E. (2013), Gold-digging bacterium makes precious particles, *Nature News & Comment*, doi:10.1038/nature.2013.12352, 3 February [online]. Available at: http://www.nature.com/news/gold-digging-bacterium-makes-precious-particles-1.12352 [Accessed 28 December 2016].

Calvino, I. (1973), *The Castle of Crossed Destinies*, New York: Harvest/HBJ Books.

Calvino, I. (1997), *Invisible Cities*, London: Vintage Classics.

Carrington, L. (1988), 'As they rode along the edge', in L. Carrington (ed.), *The Seventh Horse and Other Tales*, New York: Dutton Obelisk Books.

Ceballos, G., Ehrlich, P.R., Barnoskly, A.D., Garcia, A., Pringle, R.M. and Palmer, T. (2015), 'Accelerated modern human-induced species losses: Entering the sixth mass extinction', *Science Advances*, 1(5), doi: 10.1126/sciadv.1400253.

Chalk, W. (1994), 'Hardware of a new world', in T. Stoos (ed.), *A Guide to Archigram: 1961–74*, London: Academy Editions.

Chard, N. (1999–2016), The Bartlett School of Architecture, UCL [online]. Available at: https://www.bartlett.ucl.ac.uk/architecture/programmes/mphil-phd-studentwork/nat-chard [Accessed 27 October 2016].

Chatelin, F. (2012), *Qualitative Computing: A Computational Journey into Nonlinearity*, Singapore: World Scientific.

Clarke, A.C. (1973), *Profiles of the Future*, New York: Harper & Row.

CNAC (2005–2016), Centre national des arts du cirque [online]. Available at: http://www.cnac.tv/cnactv-350-Video_Benoit_Fauchier [Accessed 10 February 2017].

Comfort, N. (2016), The primordial fertility of rock: The chemistry of life is an extension of the chemistry of the earth. *Astrobiology*, December [online]. Available at: http://cosmos.nautil.us/short/79/the-primordial-fertility-of-rock [Accessed 4 December 2017].

Connolly, W. (2013), 'The new materialism and the fragility of things', *Millennium: Journal of International Studies*, 41(3), 399–412.

Connor, S. (2009), Michel Serres: The hard and the soft, talk given at the centre for modern studies, University of York, 26 November 2009 [online]. Available at: http://stevenconnor.com/hardsoft/hardsoft.pdf [Accessed 10 September 2016].
Cook, P. (1970), *Experimental Architecture*, New York: Universe Books.
Cook, P. and Hunter, W. (2013), Interview: Smout Allen, *The Architectural Review*, 26 April [online]. Available at: https://www.architectural-review.com/rethink/interview-smout-allen/8646894.article [Accessed 17 March 2017].
Cronin, L., Krasnogor, N., Davis, B.G., Alexander, C., Robertson, N., Steinke, J.H.G., Schroeder, S.L.M., Khlobystov, A.N., Cooper, G., Gardner, P.M., Siepmann, P., Whitaker, B.J. and Marsh, D (2006), 'The imitation game – A computational chemical approach to recognizing life', *Nature Biotechnology*, 24: 1203–06.
Cronon, W. and Oslund, K. (2011), *Iceland Imagined: Nature, Culture and Storytelling in the North Atlantic*, Seattle: University of Washington Press.
Csikszentmihalyi, M. (2013), *Creativity: The Psychology of Discovery and Invention*, New York: First Harper Perennial.
Dade-Robertson, M. (2016), The cities of the future could be built by microbes, *The Conversation*, 8 August [online]. Available at: https://theconversation.com/the-cities-of-the-future-could-be-built-by-microbes-63545 [Accessed 27 December 2016].
Darwin, C. (1842), *Coral Reefs. Being the First Part of the Geology of the Voyage of the Beagle under the Command of Capt. Fitzroy, R.N. during the Years 1832–1836*, London: Smith, Elder and Co.
Darwin, C. (2006), *On the Origin of Species by Means of Natural Selection or the Preservation of Favoured Races in the Struggle for Life*, New York: Dover Publications.
Darwin, C. (2007), *The Formation of Vegetable Mould through the Action of Worms*, Fairford: The Echo Library.
DeLanda, M. (2002), *Intensive Science and Virtual Philosophy*, London: Continuum.
De Marzio, M., Camiscasca, G., Conde, M.M., Rovere, M. and Gallo, P. (2017), 'Structural properties and fragile to strong transition in confined water', *Journal of Chemical Physics*, 146, doi: http://dx.doi.org/10.1063/1.4975624.
Deutsch, D. (2012), *The Beginning of Infinity: Explanations that Transform the World*, London: Penguin Books.
*Dezeen* (2016), Carlo Ratti's Office 3.0 uses Internet of Things to create personalized environments, 3 June [online]. Available at: http://www.dezeen.com/2016/06/03/office-3-0-carlo-ratti-internet-of-things-personalised-environments-turin-italy/ [Accessed 9 October 2016].
Dick, P.K. (1991), 'Pay for the Printer', in Philip K. Dick (ed.), *Second Variety: The collected stories of Philip K. Dick, Volume III*, New York: Citadel Twilight, 239–52.
DOCAM (1997–2002), Embryological House, Greg Lynn, Documentation and conservation of the media arts heritage [online]. Available at: http://www.docam.ca/en/component/content/article/106-embryological-house-greg-lynn.html [Accessed 7 March 2017].
Doctorow, C. (2012), Game of life with floating point operations: Beautiful smooth life. *Boing Boing*, 11 October [online]. Available at: http://boingboing.net/2012/10/11/game-of-life-with-floating-poi.html [Accessed 20 October 2016].

Donnici, S., Serandrei-Barbero, R., Bini, C., Bonardi, M. and Lezziero, A. (2011), 'The caranto paleosol and its role in the early urbanization of Venice,' *Geoarchaeology*, 26(4), 514–43.

Doyle, A.C. (1930), *The Edge of the Unknown*, New York: G.P. Putnam's Sons, Print.

Durack, T. (2007), *1001 Foods: The Greatest Gastronomic Sensations on Earth*, The London: Madison Press.

Durozoi, G. (2005), *History of the Surrealist Movement*, Chicago: University of Chicago Press.

Eagleman, D. (2009), *Sum: Forty Tales from the Afterlives*, Edinburgh: Canongate Books.

Epstein, R. (2016), The empty brain, *Aeon*, 18 May [online]. Available at: https://aeon.co/essays/your-brain-does-not-process-information-and-it-is-not-a-computer [Accessed 14 March 2017].

Eveleth, R. (2011), Artist paints lichens on NYC buildings, *Scientific American*, 29 November [online]. Available at: http://blogs.scientificamerican.com/observations/its-a-bird-its-a-plane-no-its-reindeer-chow-a-n-y-c-artist-uses-lichen-as-paint/ [Accessed 23 August 2016].

FedBizOpps.gov (2017), Design-Build-Structure. Solicitation Number: 2017-JC-RT-001. 24 February [online]. Available at: https://www.fbo.gov/?id=e0473479ed9cd913f4aef4bf8dc20175 [Accessed 7 March 2017].

Fei, A.T. (2002), *Venetian Legends and Ghost Stories: A Guide to Places of Mystery in Venice*, Treviso: Elzeviro.

Flynn, E, Hyams, R., Kerrigan, C. and Rengifo, M. (2016), 'Starship cities: A living architecture', in R. Armstrong (ed.), *Star Ark: A Living, Self-sustaining Spaceship*, Chichester, UK: Springer/Praxis, 296–322.

Ford, J. (2015), Urine powered fuel cells are set to light up refugee camps, *The Engineer*, 5 March [online]. Available at: https://www.theengineer.co.uk/issues/march-2015-online/urine-powered-fuel-cells-are-set-to-light-up-refugee-camps/ [Accessed 26 August 2016].

Foscari, G. (2015), *Building Elements of Venice*, Zurich: Lars Müller Publishers.

Fredrickson, T. (2015), Philippe Rahm constructs atmospheres with meteorological conditions, *designboom*, January 8 [online]. Available at: https://www.designboom.com/architecture/philippe-rahm-constructed-atmospheres-01-08-2014/ [Accessed 17 March 2018].

Füchslin, R.M., Dzyakanchuk, A., Flumini, D., Hauser, H., Luchsinger, R.H., Reller, B., Scheidegger, S. and Walker, R. (2013), 'Morphological computation and morphological control: Steps toward a formal theory and applications,' *Artificial Life*, 19(1): 9–34.

Gabler, N. (2016), Farewell, America, *Billmoyers.com*, 10 November [online]. Available at: http://billmoyers.com/story/farewell-america/ [Accessed 1 January 2017].

Gánti, T. (2003), *The Principles of Life*, New York: Oxford University Press.

Gardner, M. (1970), 'The fantastic combinations of John Conway's new solitaire game 'life', *Scientific American*, 223: 120–23.

Gavin, F. (2016), Captiva: The island that changed Rauschenberg and 20th century art, Culture, *Europe Newsweek*, 13 November [online]. Available at: http://europe.newsweek.com/captiva-robert-rauschenberg-art-tate-modern-520360?rm=eu [Accessed 16 December 2016].

# REFERENCES

Geiger, J. (2016), 'Alive without us', in: R. Armstrong (ed.), *Star Ark: A Living, Self-sustaining Spaceship*, Chichester, UK: Springer/PRAXIS, 423–24.

Gill, V. and Venter, C. (2010), The creation of 'Synthia': Synthetic life, *The Naked Scientists*, 23 May [online]. Available at: https://www.thenakedscientists.com/articles/interviews/creation-synthia-synthetic-life [Accessed 10 February 2017].

Gissen, D. (2009), *Subnature: Architecture's other environments*, New York: Princeton Architectural Press.

Godoli, E. (1990), 'A terrifying and edible beauty' (art Nouveau Architecture in Latin European Countries), *UNESCO Courier*, August, 44–45.

Gordillo, G. (2014), 'The oceanic void', *Space and Politics*, 3 April [online]. Available at: http://spaceandpolitics.blogspot.co.uk/2014/04/the-oceanic-void.html [Accessed 18 September 2016].

Gould, S.J. (1989), *Wonderful Life: The Burgess Shale and the Nature of History*, New York: W.W. Norton & Company.

Gould, S.J. (1981), *The Mismeasure of Man*, New York: W.W. Norton & Company.

Grachev, G. (2006), Stones are living creatures that breathe and move, *Pravdareport*, 12 July [online]. Available at: http://www.pravdareport.com/science/earth/12-07-2006/83225-stones-0/#sthash.TC5tTlz1.dpuf [Accessed 24 August 2016].

Guy, A. (2011), Growing a Crystal Chair, *Next Nature*, 30 August [online]. Available at: https://www.nextnature.net/2011/08/growing-a-crystal-chair/ [Accessed 25 August 2016].

Hanczyc, M.M. (2011), 'Structure and the Synthesis of Life', *Architectural Design*, 81(2): 26–33.

Hanczyc, M.M., Fujikawa, S.M. and Szostak, J.W. (2003), 'Experimental models of primitive cellular compartments: Encapsulation, growth and division', *Science*, 302: 618–22.

Haraway, D. (1991), 'A cyborg manifesto: Science, technology and socialist-feminism in the late twentieth century', in Donna Haraway (ed.) *Simians, Cyborg and Women: The Reinvention of Nature*, New York: Routledge, 149–81.

Haraway, D. (2011), SF: Science Fiction, Speculative Fabulation, String Figures, So Far. Acceptance comments, Pilgrim Award, actually in California, virtually in Lublin, Poland, at the SFRA meetings, 7 July [online]. Available at: https://people.ucsc.edu/~haraway/Files/PilgrimAcceptanceHaraway.pdf [Accessed 12 September 2016].

Haraway, D. (2013), SF: Science fiction, speculative fabulation, string figures, so far, *Ada: A Journal of Gender, New Media, and Technology*, (3) [online]. Available at: doi:10.7264/N3KH0K81 [Accessed 14 September 2016].

Haraway, D. (2015), 'Anthropocene, Capitalocene, Plantationocene, Chthulucene: Making kin', *Environmental Humanities*, 6: 159–65.

Harman, G. (2010), 'Ferris Wheel', in G. Harman (ed.), *Circus Philosophicus*, Hants: O-Books.

Heidegger, M. (1962), *Being and Time*, New York: Harper & Row.

Holden, I. and Stefanova, A. (2016), The Silk Road. Submission entry for Fairy Tales 2017 on 9th December 2016 (Consortium: Imogen Holden, Faulkner Brown; Assia Stefanova, Faulker Brown; Paul Rigby, Faulkner Brown; Rolf Hughes, Stockholm University of the Arts and Rachel Armstrong, Newcastle University).

Hooper, R. (2015), Medaka: The fish that helps us understand gender, *The Japan Times*, 20 June [online]. Available at: https://www.japantimes.co.jp/news/2015/06/20/national/science-health/medaka-fish-helps-us-understand-gender/#.Wi-wtCOcZZo [Accessed 11 December 2017].

Hornyak, T. (2008), Rock-Eating Bacteria 'Mine' Valuable Metals, National Geographic, 5 November [online]. Available at: http://news.nationalgeographic.com/news/2008/11/081105-bacteria-mining.html [Accessed 28 December 2016].

Howard, C. (2011), Mother trees' use fungal networks to feed the forest, Ecology, Canadian Geographic, January/February [online]. Available at: https://www.canadiangeographic.ca/magazine/jf11/fungal_systems.asp [Accessed 19 April 2014].

Howarth, S. (2000), 3 stoppages étalon (3 Standard Stoppages) 1913-14, replica 1964, Marcel Duchamp, Tate, April [online]. Available at: http://www.tate.org.uk/art/artworks/duchamp-3-stoppages-etalon-3-standard-stoppages-t07507 [Accessed 17 November 2017].

Hughes, R. (2009a), 'The art of displacement: Designing experiential systems and transverse epistemologies as conceptual criticism. Agency in architecture: Reframing criticality in theory and practice', *Footprint*, 3(4): 49–63.

Hughes, R. (2009b), 'Pressures of the unspeakable: Communicating practice as research' in J. Verbeke and A. Jakimowicz (eds), Communicating (by) Design, Proceedings of the colloquiem 'Communicating (by) Design' at Sint-Lucas Brussels from 15th–17th April 2009, Gothenberg (Chalmers) and Gent (Sint-Lucas): Chalmers University of Technology and Hogeschool voor Wetenschap & Kunst - School of Architecture Sint-Lucas, 247–59.

Hughes, R. (2014), 'In other words: Or why is it difficult to talk about why it is difficult to talk about architecture?' in J. Stillemans (ed.), *Why Is It Difficult to Talk about Architecture? – Faculté d'architecture, d'ingénierie architecturale, d'urbanisme (LOCI)*, Louvain-la-Neuve, Belgium: Presses Universitaires de Louvain.

Hughes, R. (2016a), 'Expanded research practices through living architecture', in R. Armstrong (ed.), *Living Brick for Venice: A Prototype, Exhibition and Vision by the Living Architecture (LIAR) Consortium*, Newcastle: LIAR, 25.

Hughes, R. (2016b), *Living Bricks of Venice: Vision, Prototype, Exhibition*, Newcastle: LIAR.

Hughes, R. (2016c), 'The Art of Experiment', in R. Armstrong, R. Hughes and E. Gangvik (eds), *The Handbook of the Unknowable*, Trondheim: TEKS, 82–87.

Hugill, A. (2015), '*Pataphysics: A Useless Guide*. Cambridge, MA: MIT Press.

Ieropoulos, I., Greenman, J. and Melhuish, C. (2009), 'Improved energy output levels from small-scale microbial fuel cell', *Bioelectrochemistry*, 78: 44–50.

Indursky, B. (2013), Interior Alchemy: Carlo Scarpa's Palace Querini Stampalia, *Design Life Network*, 9 December [online]. Available at: http://designlifenetwork.com/interior-alchemy-carlo-scarpas-palazzo-querini-stampalia/ [Accessed 25 August 2016].

iPlayer Radio (2016), Kumar, Armstrong, Goodall, Series 9, The Museum of Curiosity [online]. Available at: http://www.bbc.co.uk/programmes/b07lj6yh [Accessed 16 December 2016].

Jonkers, H.M. (2007), 'Self-healing concrete: A biological approach', in S. Van Der Zwaag (ed.), *Self Healing Materials. An Alternative Approach to 20 Centuries of Materials Science*, The Netherlands: Springer, 195–204.

Kauffman, S.A. (2008), *Reinventing the Sacred: A New View of Science, Reason, and Religion*, New York: Basic Books.
Kavanagh, K. (2015), '"Knitting Peace", by Cirkus Cirkör', *The Circus Diaries: A Critical Exploration of the Circus World*, 3 January [online]. Available at: http://www.thecircusdiaries.com/2015/01/03/knitting-peace-by-cirkus-cirkor/ [Accessed 1 October 2016].
Kelly, K. (2010), *What Technology Wants*, New York: Viking.
Kelvin, W.T. (1871), 'The British Association Meeting at Edinburgh', *Nature*, 4(92): 261–78.
Kenner, H. (1991), *The Pound Era*. London: Pimlico.
Latour, B. (1993), *We Have Never Been Modern*, Cambridge, MA: Harvard University Press.
Latour, B. (2013), Once out of nature: Natural religion as a pleonasm, Gifford Lecture, University of Edinburgh [online]. Available at: http://www.youtube.com/watch?v=MC3E6vdQEzk [Accessed 7 July 2017].
Latour, B. and Yaneva, A. (2008), 'Give me a gun and I will make all buildings move: An ANT's view of architecture', in R. Geiser (ed.), *Explorations in Architecture: Teaching, Design, Research*, Basel: Birkhäuser, 80–89.
Le Corbusier, C.E. (2007), *Toward an Architecture*, Los Angeles: Getty Research Institute.
Lederman, L.M. and Teresi, D. (1993), *The God Particle: If the Universe Is the Answer, What Is the Question?*, New York: Bantam Press.
Leduc, S. (1911), *The Mechanism of Life*, London: William Heinemann.
Lee, M. (2011), Oceanic ontology and problematic thought, NOOK Book/Barnes and Noble [online]. Available at: http://www.barnesandnoble.com/w/oceanic-ontology-and-problematic-thoughtmatt-lee/1105805765 [Accessed 19 September 2016].
Lefevbre, H. (1991), *The Production of Space*. Oxford: Wiley-Blackwell.
Lefebvre, H. (2013), *Rhythmanalysis: Space, Time and Everyday Life*, London: Continuum.
Lehn, J.M. (1995), *Supramolecular Chemistry: Concepts and Perspectives*. Strasbourg: John Wiley & Sons.
Leibniz, G.W., and Clarke, S. (1998). 'Correspondence', in H.G. Alexander (Ed.). *The Leibniz-Clarke Correspondence, Together with extracts from Newton's "Principa" and "Optiks"*, Manchester: Manchester University Press.
Leon, D.M.A.D. (2013), 'Biological' concrete building walls grow moss, PSFK LLC, 8 January [online]. Available at: http://www.psfk.com/2013/01/concrete-building-moss.html [Accessed 23 August 2016].
Lewontin, R.C. (1997), Billions and Billions of Demons, The New York Review of Books, 9 January [online]. Available at: http://www.nybooks.com/articles/1997/01/09/billions-and-billions-of-demons/ [Accessed 17 March 2018].
Lionni, L. (1977), *Parallel Botany*, New York: Random House Inc.
Living Architecture (2016), Living Architecture LIAR – Transform our habitats from inert spaces into programmable sites [online]. Available at: http://livingarchitecture-h2020.eu [Accessed 18 October 2016].
Logan, W.B. (2007), *Dirt: The Ecstatic Skin of the Earth*, New York: W.W. Norton & Company.

Loria, K. (2015), New Orleans could be wiped off the map later this century, *Business Insider UK*, 4 June [online]. Available at: http://uk.businessinsider.com/climate-change-could-destroy-new-orleans-2015-6?r=US&IR=T [Accessed 25 August 2016].

Lovelock, J.E. (1979), *Gaia: A New Look at Life on Earth*, Oxford: Oxford University Press.

Maguire, N. (2017), Making sense of quantum weirdness, *Quark Magazine*, 29 April [online]. Available at: https://quarkmag.com/making-sense-of-quantum-weirdness-bd687eae0a88 [Accessed 12 November 2017].

Manaugh, G. (2007), Without walls: An interview with Lebbeus Woods, *BldgBlog*, 3 October [online]. Available at: http://www.bldgblog.com/2007/10/without-walls-an-interview-with-lebbeus-woods/ [Accessed 9 October 2016].

Matsumoto, K., Ueda, T. and Kobatake, Y. (1998), 'Reversal of thermotaxis with oscillatory stimulation in the plasmodium of Physarum polycephalum', *J. Theor. Biol*, 131: 175–82.

Maunder, S. (1847), 'The Biographical Treasury', in M. Heard and S. Herbert (eds), *2006. Phantasmagoria: The Secret History of the Magic Lantern*, Hastings: The Projection Box, 97.

Mayhew, R. (1997), 'Part and whole in Aristotle's political philosophy', *The Journal of Ethics*, 1(4), 325–40.

McFarland, B.J. (2016), *A World from Dust: How the Periodic Table Shaped Life*, New York: Oxford University Press.

Medina, S. (2014), EcoLogicStudio, *Metropolis*, October [online]. Available at: http://www.metropolismag.com/October-2014/EcoLogic-Studio/ [Accessed 9 October 2016].

Menges, A. (2015), 'Material Synthesis: Fusing the physical and the computational', *Architectural Design*, 85(5): 8–15.

Merleau-Ponty, M. (2014), *Phenomenology of Perception*, Abingdon: Routledge.

Methé, B.A. (2012), 'A framework for human microbiome research', *Nature*, 486: 215–21.

Miller, S.L. (1953), 'A production of amino acids under possible primitive earth conditions', *Science*, 117(3046): 528–29.

Molderings, H. (2010), *Duchamp and the Aesthetics of Chance: Art as Experiment* (Columbia themes in philosophy, social criticism, and the arts), New York: Columbia University Press.

Morris, M. (2016), 'The scales of Ouroboros', in R. Armstrong (ed.), *Star Ark: A Living, Self-sustaining Spaceship*, Chichester, UK: Springer/Praxis.

Morton, T. (2007), *Ecology without Nature: Rethinking Environmental Aesthetics*, Cambridge, MA: Harvard University Press.

Morton, T. (2012), *The Ecological Thought*, Cambridge, MA: Harvard University Press.

Morton, T. (2013), *Hyperobjects: Philosophy and Ecology after the End of the World*, Minneapolis: University of Minnesota Press.

Murgoci, G.M. (1905), 'Tertiary formations of Oltenia with regard to salt, petroleum, and mineral springs', *The Journal of Geology*, 13(8), 670–712.

Musser, G. (2017), In defense of the reality of time, *Quanta*, May [online]. Available at: https://www.quantamagazine.org/a-defense-of-the-reality-of-time/?platform=hootsuite [Accessed 18 May 2017].

Negarestani, R. (2008), *Cyclonopedia: Complicity with Anonymous Materials*, Melbourne: re.press.

Newcastle University (2016), Smart bricks will give homes and offices their own 'digestive system', Press office, 27 July [online]. Available at: http://www.ncl.ac.uk/press/news/2016/07/liarlivingarchitecture/ [Accessed 16 September 2016].

Newton, I. (2007), Original letter from Isaac Newton to Richard Bentley, *The Newton Project*, October [online]. Available at: http://www.newtonproject.ox.ac.uk/view/texts/normalized/THEM00258 [Accessed 3 December 2017].

Nicholson, D.J. (2013), 'Organisms do not equal machines', *Studies in a History and Philosophy of Biological and Biomedical Sciences*, 44: 678–99.

NOAA (2017), Global Climate Report, November 2017, *National Centers for Environmental Information* [online]. Available at: https://www.ncdc.noaa.gov/sotc/global/201711 [Accessed 2 January 2018].

Northwestern University Press (2017), House of Day, House of Night, Olga Tokarczuk [online]. Available at: http://www.nupress.northwestern.edu/content/house-day-house-night [Accessed 18 November 2017].

Oliver, E. (2014–2016), Nostradamus quatrains, Chapter 1 [online]. Available at: http://www.godswatcher.com/quatrains.htm [Accessed 10 September 2016].

Oppenheimer, M. (2014), Austin's Moon Towers, beyond 'dazed and confused'. *The New York Times*, 13 February [online]. Available at: https://www.nytimes.com/2014/02/16/travel/austins-moon-towers-beyond-dazed-and-confused.html?_r=0 [Accessed 15 November 2017].

Park, S. (2012a), Another bacterial tweet, *Exploring the Invisible*, 25 November [online]. Available at: https://exploringtheinvisible.com/2012/11/25/another-bacterial-tweet/ [Accessed 4 January 2016].

Park, S. (2012b), Microbial text, *Exploring the Invisible*, 22 November [online]. Available at: https://exploringtheinvisible.com/2012/11/22/microbial-text/ [Accessed 4 January 2016].

Park, S. (2012c), 'This is microgeography', 2 November [online]. Available at: http://newmicrogeographies.blogspot.co.uk [Accessed 21 August 2016].

Patel, R. (2011), Saving Venice, *Icon Magazine*, 17 August [online]. Available at: http://www.iconeye.com/architecture/features/item/9439-saving-venice [Accessed 18 August 2016].

Peoples, L. (2016), What happens when you submerge a dress in the dead sea for two months? *Refinery 29*, 25 August [online]. Available at: http://www.refinery29.uk/2016/08/121357/underwater-dress-art-salt-dead-sea-sigalit-landau#slide [Accessed 26 August 2016].

Pfeifer, R. and Iida, F. (2005), 'Morphological computation: Connecting body, brain and environment', *Japanese Scientific Monthly*, 58(2): 48–54.

Poincare, H. (1952), *Science and Hypothesis*. New York: Dover Publications.

Ponomarova, O. and Patil, K.R. (2015), 'Metabolic interactions in microbial communities: Untangling the Gordian knot', *Current Opinion in Microbiology*, 27: 37–44.

Poole, M. and Shvartzberg, M. (2015), *The Politics of Parametricism*, London: Bloomsbury.

Prigogine, I. and Stengers, I. (1984), *Order Out of Chaos: Man's New Dialogue with Nature*, Toronto: Bantam Books.

Limited, Quite Interesting (2016), Gallery nine, QI Daily, Not dated [online]. Available at: http://qi.com/museum-gallery-9/ [Accessed 15 November 2017].

Ravera, O. (2000), 'The Lagoon of Venice: The result of both natural factors and human influence,' *Journal of Limnology*, 59(1): 19–30.

# REFERENCES

Rebanks, J. (2017), An English sheep farmer's view of rural America, *New York Times*, 1 March [online]. Available at: https://www.nytimes.com/2017/03/01/opinion/an-english-sheep-farmers-view-of-rural-america.html [Accessed 7 March 2017].

Reuter (1973), 'It's foamy, creamy: Dallas housewife battling "the blob"', Wednesday 30 May, *Toledo Blade*: Ohio, 12.

RIBA-USA (2015), Liquid happening: A Living Architecture Ball [online]. Available at: http://riba-usaleapfrogproject.evolero.com/liquid-happening-a-living-architecture-ball [Accessed 28 December 2016].

Richet, C. (2003), Various reflections on the sixth sense, *Survival after Death* [online]. Available at: http://www.survivalafterdeath.info/articles/richet/reflections.htm [Accessed 11 September 2016].

Rieland, R. (2014), Forget the 3D printer: 4D printing could change everything, *Smithsonian.com*, 16 May [online]. Available at: http://www.smithsonianmag.com/innovation/Objects-That-Change-Shape-On-Their-Own-180951449/?no-ist [Accessed 24 August 2016].

Rifkin, J. (2013), *The Third Industrial Revolution: How Lateral Power Is Transforming Energy, the Economy and the World*, New York: Macmillan.

Robson, D. (2003), The Future for architects? *Building Futures*, 12–13 [online]. Available at: http://www.buildingfutures.org.uk/assets/downloads/The_Future_for_Architects_Full_Report_2.pdf [Accessed 17 September 2016].

Romm, C. (26 January 2015), How sticks and shell charts became a sophisticated system for navigation, *Smithsonian.com* [online]. Available at: http://www.smithsonianmag.com/smithsonian-institution/how-sticks-and-shell-charts-became-sophisticated-system-navigation-180954018/ [Accessed 24 December 2016].

Rose, B. (2014), Rethinking Duchamp, *The Brooklyn Rail*, 18 December [online]. Available at: https://brooklynrail.org/2014/12/art/rethinking-duchamp [Accessed 23 November 2017].

Roth, A. (2015), Plastic eating mushrooms could save the world, *Modern Farmer*, 6 January [online]. Available at: http://modernfarmer.com/2015/01/plastic-eating-mushrooms-save-world/ [Accessed 28 December 2016].

Rowlinson, A. (2012), 'The Woman Regrowing the Planet', *Red Bulletin*, Vienna: Red Bull Media House, 76–81.

Ruskin, J. (1989), *The Seven Lamps of Architecture*, Mineola: Dover Publications.

Sagan, L. (1967), 'On the Origin of Mitosing Cells', *Journal of Theoretical Biology*, 14(3): 225–74.

Scarpa, T. (2009), *Venice Is a Fish: A Cultural Guide*, London: Serpents Tail.

Schiller, B. (2014), This algae-powered building actually works, *Co.Exist*, 16 July [online]. Available at: http://www.fastcoexist.com/3033019/this-algae-powered-building-actually-works [Accessed 19 August 2016].

Schrödinger, E. (1944), What is life? The physical aspect of the living cell. Based on lectures delivered under the auspices of the Dublin Institute for Advanced Studies at Trinity College, Dublin, in February 1943 [online]. Available at: http://whatislife.stanford.edu/LoCo_files/What-is-Life.pdf [Accessed 16 October 2016].

Schrödinger, E. (2012), *What Is Life? With Mind and Matter and Autobiographical Sketches*, Cambridge: Cambridge University Press.

Self, J. (2015), Does Politics Have Any Place in Architecture? *The Architectural Review*, 30 September [online]. Available at: https://www.architectural-review.com/archive/does-politics-have-any-place-in-architecture/8688945.article [Accessed 15 September 2016].

Serres, M. (2016), *The Five Senses: A Philosophy of Mingled Bodies*, London: Bloomsbury Academic.

Shepherd, R., Stokes, A.A., Freake, J., Barber, J.R., Snyder, P.W., Mazzeo, A.D., Cademartiri, L., Morin, S.A. and Whitesides, G.M. (2013), 'Using Explosions to Power a Soft Robot', *Angewandte Chemie International Edition*, 52: 2892–96.

Sim, D. (2015), EU migrant crisis: Hungary completes razor wire fence and is closing Croatia border, *International Business Times*, 16 October [online]. Available at: http://www.ibtimes.co.uk/eu-migrant-crisis-hungary-completes-razor-wire-fence-closing-croatia-border-1524370 [Accessed 26 August 2016].

Spiller, N. (2016), Surrealism in architecture is more relevant than ever, *Building Design*, 14 November [online]. Available at: http://www.bdonline.co.uk/surrealism-in-architecture-is-more-relevant-than-ever/5084837.article [Accessed 16 December 2016].

Spinney, L. (2012), Searching for Doggerland, *National Geographic*, December [online]. Available at: http://ngm.nationalgeographic.com/2012/12/doggerland/spinney-text [Accessed 25 August 2016].

Steadman, I. (2013), Hamburg unveils world's first algae-powered building, *Wired*, 16 April [online]. Available at: http://www.wired.com/design/2013/04/algae-powered-building/ [Accessed 9 October 2016].

Steinberg, P and Peters, K. (2015), 'Wet Ontologies, fluid spaces: Giving depth to volume through oceanic thinking', *Environ Plan D*, 33(2): 247–64.

Steinmeyer, J. (2008), The man who created the Fortean Times, *The Telegraph*, 27 April [online]. Available at: http://www.telegraph.co.uk/culture/books/3672959/The-man-who-created-the-Fortean-Times.html [Accessed 11 November 2017].

Stelarc (2006), Stomach sculpture [online]. Available at: http://stelarc.org/?catID=20349 [Accessed 12 November 2016].

Sterling, B. (2011), Glitch by Simon Park, *Wired*, 7 August [online]. Available at: https://www.wired.com/2011/08/glitch-by-simon-park/ [Accessed 4 January 2016].

Stromberg, J. (2013), How do Death Valley's 'Sailing Stones' move themselves across the desert? *Smithsonian.com*, 9 June [online]. Available at: http://po.st/l41gGq [Accessed 24 August 2016].

Szewczyk, S. (2015), Biohacking the future of New York City with Terreform ONE, *Tech Times*, 29 December [online]. Available at: http://www.techtimes.com/articles/119968/20151229/biohacking-the-future-of-new-york-city-with-terraform-one.htm [Accessed 9 October 2016].

Teatini, P., Castelletto, N., Ferronato, M., Gambolati, G. and Tosi, L. (2011), 'A new hydrogeologic model to predict anthropogenic uplift of Venice', *Water Resources Research*, 47(12): W12507.

TEDxLausanne (2016), Blockchain demystified, Daniel Gasteiger [online]. Available at: https://www.youtube.com/watch?v=40ikEV6xGg4 [Accessed 10 December 2016].

The Science Team (2016), The thinking machine: W. Ross Ashby and the Homeostat, *Science blog*, Library, British, 20 April [online]. Available at: http://blogs.bl.uk/science/2016/04/the-thinking-machine.html [Accessed 10 October 2016].

Traube, M. (1867), 'Experimente zur Theorie der Zellbildung und Endomose', *Archiv fur Anatomie, Physiologie und Wissenschaftliche Medicin*, 87: 129–65.
Uppsala Universitet (2008), Linnaeus as a mineralogist, On Linné [online]. Available at: http://www2.linnaeus.uu.se/online/history/mineralog.html [Accessed 17 March 2018].
Van Mensvoort, K. and Grievink, H.J. (2012), *Next Nature: Nature Changes along with Us*, Barcelona: Actar.
Venter, J.C. (2007), *A Life Decoded: My Genome, My Life*, London: Allen Lane.
Vernadsky, V.I. (1998), *The Biosphere*, New York: Peter A. Nevraumont Books.
Von Bertalanffy, L. (1950), 'The theory of open systems in physics and biology', *Science*, 111, 23–29.
Ward, C. (2015), Review: Seizure at the Yorkshire Sculpture Park, *The State of the Arts*, 9 February [online]. Available at: http://www.thestateofthearts.co.uk/features/review-seizure-at-the-yorkshire-sculpture-park/ [Accessed 7 March 2017].
Watson, J.D. and Crick, F.H.C. (1953), 'A Structure for Deoxyribose Nucleic Acid', *Nature*, 171: 737–38.
Wei-Haas, M. (2016), Life and rocks may have co-evolved on earth, Smithsonian Magazine, 13 January [online]. Available at: https://www.smithsonianmag.com/science-nature/life-and-rocks-may-have-co-evolved-on-earth-180957807/ [Accessed 15 November 2017].
Werman, M. (2013), How the Dutch are helping New Orleans stay dry, *PRI's The World*, 29 August [online]. Available at: http://www.pri.org/stories/2013-08-29/how-dutch-are-helping-new-orleans-stay-dry [Accessed 24 August 2016].
Windsor, A. (2015), Inside Venice's bid to hold back the tide, *The Guardian*, 16 June [online]. Available at: https://www.theguardian.com/cities/2015/jun/16/inside-venice-bid-hold-back-tide-sea-level-rise [Accessed 31 December 2016].
Wingfield, C. (2010), 'A case re-opened: The science and folklore of a "Witch's Ladder"', *Journal of Material Culture*, 15(3): 302–22.
Woese, C. (2004), 'A new biology for a new century', *Microbiology and Molecular Biology Reviews*, 68, 178–86.
Wolchover, N. (2014), A new physics theory of life, *Quanta*, 22 January [online]. Available at: https://www.quantamagazine.org/20140122-a-new-physics-theory-of-life/ [Accessed 10 November 2016].
Woods, L. (2010a), Da Vinci's Blobs, Lebbeus Woods, 3 December [online]. Available at: https://lebbeuswoods.wordpress.com/2010/12/03/da-vincis-blobs/ [Accessed 17 March 2018].
Woods, L. (2010b), Knots: The architecture of problems, *Lebbeus Woods*, 12 October [online]. Available at: https://lebbeuswoods.wordpress.com/2010/10/12/knots-the-architecture-of-problems/ [Accessed 10 September 2016].
Woods, L. (2010c), The Experimental, *Lebbeus Woods*, 12 August [online] Available at: https://lebbeuswoods.wordpress.com/2010/08/12/the-experimental/[Accessed 9 October 2016].
Woods, L. (2012a), A tree is a tree is a ... building? *Lebbeus Woods*, 27 January [online]. Available at: http://lebbeuswoods.wordpress.com/2012/01/27/a-tree-is-a-tree-is-a-building/ [Accessed 22 May 2014].
Woods, L. (2012b), Inevitable architecture. *Lebbeus Woods*, 9 July [online]. Available at: https://lebbeuswoods.wordpress.com/2012/07/09/inevitable-architecture/ [Accessed 15 September 2016].

Yeager, A. (2017), Discoveries fuels flight over universe's first light, Quanta Magazine, 19 May [online]. Available at: https://www.quantamagazine.org/discoveries-fuel-fight-over-universes-first-light-20170519/?utm_content=bufferd7c6d&utm_medium=social&utm_source=twitter.com&utm_campaign=buffer [Accessed 24 June 2017].

Yiannoudes, E. (2016), *Architecture and Adaptation: From Cybernetics to Tangible Computing*. Abingdon: Routledge.

Young, L. and Manaugh, G. (2010), *Thrilling Wonder Stories* [online]. Available at: http://thrillingwonderstories.co.uk [Accessed 28 October 2016].

Zellner, P. (2016), Architectural education is broken – here's how to fix it, *The Architect's Newspaper*, 16 September [online]. Available at: http://archpaper.com/2016/09/architectural-education-broken-fix/ [Accessed 18 September 2016].

Zhabotinsky, A.M. (1964), Periodic processes of malonic acid oxidation in a liquid phase, *Biofizika*, 9, 306–11.

Zhang, D., Györgyi, L. and Peltier, W.R. (1993), 'Deterministic chaos in the Belousov–Zhabotinsky reaction: Experiments and simulations', *Chaos: An Interdisciplinary Journal of Non-linear Science*, 3(4): 723–45.

Žižek, S. (2011), *Living in the End Times*, London: Verso.

# Index

*Acqua alta* 42, 94, 127, 144, 153, 160
actant 23, 29, 88
Adams, Douglas 91
algae 24, 26, 27, 72, 93, 95, 102, 112, 138, 144, 157, 158, 165
Allen, Laura 22
Anthropocene 54, 122, 177
aperiodic crystals 11, 60
Artwise Curators 157, 158
Ashby, Ross 164
Astudio architects 27

Babbage, Charles 57
Babel xvi, xvii, 36, 37
Babelsphere xvii, xviii, 24, 32, 35, **37**, 38, 40, 42, 54, 85, 89, 92, **163**, **170**, 176, 177, 178
Bacon, Francis 81
beauty **111**, 112, 174
Beckett, Richard 27
Beer, Stafford 164
Beesley, Philip 26, 142
Belousov-Zhabotinsky reaction 57, 60
Bête machine 1, **2**
Big Bang 6
biofilm 24, 25, 28, 49, 84, 87, 93, 94, 105, 138, 147, 157, 158
biogenesis 6, 8, 9, **11–12**, 67, 116
biosphere 7, 22, 67, 165, 168
black mirror 102, 165–7
blue architecture 125
Blyth 130
Bohr, Neils 5, 16
Breton, André 4
Bride 77, 159–60
brute matter xiii, 2
Burgess Shale xiv, 3, 11
Bütschli, Otto 13
Bütschli system 9, 13, 62, 98

Calvino, Italo xvi, 31, 77, 155
Cambrian explosion xiv
Cambrian renaissance 24
Capsule of Crossed Destinies **168**
caranto 41
catalyst 10, 62, 81, 126, 138
Chard, Nat 22
Chatelin, Françoise 56
chicken and egg **17**, 18
Cirkus Cirkör 30, 170
clay 8, 10, 11, 26, 41, 67, 116, 141, 147
cockroach xviii, 33, 87, 163, 168, 169
Cook, Peter 21, 22, 23, 31
cosmogenesis 6
Couture, Lise Anne 22
Cruz, Marcos 22
Csikszentmihalyi, Mihaly 63
Cussen, Eoin 109

Dade-Robertson, Martyn 27
Dalí, Salvador 23, 112, 154
Dam, Alexander 165, 167
daphnia 164
Darwin, Charles 3, 8, 9, 39, 64, 67, 69
De la Reyniere, Alexandre Balthazar Laurent Grimond 45
Demaray, Elizabeth 27
Denari, Neil 22
Descartes' demon 101
Descartes, René 1
Deutsch, David 56
Dick, Philip K. 19
dissipative systems xvii, 13, 14, 60, 61, 100, 101
Doggerland **130**, 132, 133
Doyle, Arthur Conan 100
Duchamp, Marcel 77, 151

Ecocene 40, 54, 57, 61, 111
ecopoiesis 164

# INDEX

Einstein, Albert 96, 133
emergence 9, 11, 14, 39, 49, 92, 97, 98, 103, 104
entropy 37, 43
equilibrium 2, 13, 16, 37, 60, 68, 69
experimental architecture **21–4**

far from equilibrium 7, 12, 25, 59, 66, 101
Fort, Charles 5
Future Venice 28, **155**, **157**

Galvani, Luigi 99
Gánti, Tibor 97
Gilbert, Gordon 22
Gissen, David 17
golem **116**, 117
Gould, Stephen Jay xiii, xiv, 1–4, 12
graviton 96

Hadean epoch 9
hadron 6
Haeckel, Ernst 38
Hansmeyer, Michael 27
Heraclitus 38, 75
Hiorns, Roger 26
Hooke, Robert 141
Hughes, Rolf 165, 168, 170
hygroscopic materials 27, 71, 128, 142, 145
Hylozoic Ground installation 26, 142
hyperbodies 25, 30

Icarus Interstellar 164
Ieropoulos, Ioannis 147, 161
imitation game 57, 77
Intelligent Building (BIQ House) 28, 112

Jarry, Alfred 4, 5
Jedström, Joel 165
Jonkers, Henk 26, 27

Kauffman, Stuart 14
Kelvin, Sir William Thomson and Lord 11
Krueger, Ted 22
Kulper, Perry 22

Lake Vostok 39
Landau, Sigalit 26

Large Hadron Collider (LHC) 96
Latour, Bruno 122
Leduc cells 142
Lefebvre, Henri 30, 57
lepton 6
Lewontin, Richard xvii
Liesegang rings 142
Linnaeus, Carl 7
Lionni, Leo xv
liquid bodies 40
lively matter xiii, 6, 7, 9, 12, 14, **17**, 23, 26, 33, 40, 56, 59, 61, 68, 178
Living Architecture project xviii, 23, 28, 87, **137**, 138
living bricks xvi, xviii, 137, 139, 146–8, 154
living stones 43, 105, 145
living technology xvi
Lovelock, James 38
Luis, Lira 73
Lynn, Greg 25

Maki, Fumihiko 102
manatee 116, 118
mandragola 169
mangroves 116, 173
Marshall Islands 40
Medaka fish 109, 166
medusae 101, 112
Melchiorri, Julian 157
mermaid 118–19
metabolic 'apps' 28, 87
metabolism 11, 13, 16, 25, 26, 38, 62, 68, 71, 82, 85, 87, 93, 97, 113, 116, 123, 138, 142, 154, 165, 171
metabolism first hypothesis 10
microbial fuel cell (MFC) 28, 84, 138, 146, 161
microbiome 47, 86
modern synthesis xiii
MOdulo Sperimentale Eletromeccanica (MOSE) 42, 46, 128, 141, 152, 156, 160
montmorillonite 10, 116
morphological computing 59
Morrisson, Nathan 164
Morton, Timothy 38, 39
mosquito 95, 157, 158
Mother Shipton cave 114, 115

# INDEX

Movile Cave 39, 55
multiverse 4
muon 6
mycorrhiza 28, 55

natural computing 12, 23, 26, 57, **59**, 64, 69, 87, 94, 144, 148
Nebula Sciences 168, 169
necrobiome 46
negentropy 16
neutron 6
New Orleans 126, 127
Newton, Isaac 96
Nostradamus 101, 102

oceanic ontologies 40
origin of life xvi, 6, 8, 55, 97, 185
osmotic structures 62

panspermia 11
paper architecture 29
parallel biology xiii, 16
parallel worlds xv, xvi, xviii, 4, 5, 11, 14, 18, 21, 22, 41, 55, 61, 75, 79, 91, 101, 107, 109, 111, 117, 124, 128, 134, 137, 142, 143, 147, 151, 155, 158, 159, 161
Pasquero, Claudia 26
'Pataphysics 4
Perry, Mike 157
Persephone **163–70**
phantasmagoria 14, 15, 89, 99, 107, 109
plastics 21, 28, 36, 44, 71, 72, 95, 106, 144, 149, 153, 157, 161, 168, 174
Poletti, Marco 26
polystyrene 158
Poveglia 92
Prigogine, Ilya xiii
protocols of life xii, xiii, xiv, 81
proton 6, 138

Qualitative Computing 56
quantum biology 11

Rafler, Stefan 98
Rahm, Philippe 27
Rashid, Hani 22
Ratti, Carlo 26

Raushenberg, Robert 116
Rayleigh–Bénard convection cells 13
replaying the tape of life xiv, **2**, 7, 103, 177
Richet, Charles 99
Rimbu, Gimi 147
*risalta salina* 144
rising waters 42, 127, 132
RNA world hypothesis 10
Robert Rauschenberg Foundation 119–21, 134, 135
*rôti sans pareil* 45
Ruskin, John xvi, 42, 94, 140

Sandberg, Olle 165
Scarpa, Carlo 94, 128
Scarpa, Tiziano 91
Schrödinger, Erwin 5, 37
scrying 89, 101, 102, 114, 165, 166, 167
sea level rise 116, 119, 121, 125, 133
sensible fabric 104
Serres, Michel 31
shipping forecast 130, 132
Simpson, Buster 116
slime mould 57, 59, 63
Smout, Mark 22
Sorkin, Michael 22
Spiller, Neil 22
Stelarc 86
Stromatolites 67
Studio Swine 157
subnatures **17**, 25, 30, 68
supersoils 71
supramolecular chemistry 6
sustainability 125, 140

Tansley, Arthur 38
Temptations of the Non-linear Ladder 109, 165
Terreform ONE (Open Ecology Network) 26
thanatobiome 46, 47
Thesian ship 92
Tiatini, Pietro 156
tornado 12, 60
Traube cell 9, 142
trovant 8
Trumbull, Douglas 102
Turing, Alan 59, 77
Turing machine 57

Utopia **35–7**

Venice xvi, xvii, 31, 32, 41–4, 48, 50, 91–4, 102, 104, 105, 127, 128, 137, 143–5, 148, 150–4, 159, 160
Venice Biennale 142, 147, 158
Venter, J. Craig 3
vitalism 9, 97
Vivaldi, Antonio **104–5**
vivogenesis xiii, **11–13**
Von Bertalanffy, Ludwig 38
Von Leibniz, Gottfried Wilhelm 57, 96

Walcott, Charles Doolittle 11
Wall of Shame, Berlin 160

Webb, Michael 22
Weiss, Glenn 116
wet printing 65
witch bottle **119–21**
witch's ladder 106
Wongtrakoon, Methinee 165
Woods, Lebbeus xv, 22, 43
worlding xv, xvi, xvii, 1, **18–19,** 23, 24, 35, 87, 89, 163, 168, 177
worlding instrument **164–5**

Yshiok, Tokujin 26

Zanzara Island 157
zircon crystals 6

www.ingramcontent.com/pod-product-compliance
Lightning Source LLC
Chambersburg PA
CBHW070316230426
43663CB00011B/2153